WORLDS
WITHIN
WOMEN

WORLDS
WITHIN
WOMEN

MYTH AND MYTHMAKING IN FANTASTIC LITERATURE BY WOMEN

THELMA J. SHINN

CONTRIBUTIONS TO THE STUDY OF
SCIENCE FICTION AND FANTASY,
NUMBER 22

Greenwood Press
NEW YORK • WESTPORT, CONNECTICUT • LONDON

Library of Congress Cataloging-in-Publication Data

Shinn, Thelma J., 1942–
  Worlds within women.

  (Contributions to the study of science fiction and
fantasy, ISSN 0193–6875 ; no. 22)
  Bibliography: p.
  Includes index.
  1. Fantastic fiction, American—Women authors—
History and criticism.   2. Myth in literature.
3. Mythology in literature.   4. Future in literature.
5. Women and literature.   6. Science fiction, American—
Women authors—History and criticism.   I. Title.   II. Series.
PS374.F27S45   1986   813'.0876'099287   86–7592
ISBN 0–313–25101–0 (lib. bdg. : alk. paper)

Library of Congress Catalog Card Number: 86–7592
ISBN: 0–313–25101–0
ISSN: 0193–6875

First published in 1986

Greenwood Press, Inc.
88 Post Road West, Westport, Connecticut 06881

Printed in the United States of America

The paper used in this book complies with the
Permanent Paper Standard issued by the National
Information Standards Organization (Z39.48–1984).

10 9 8 7 6 5 4 3 2 1

Copyright Acknowledgments

Earlier versions of some of this material have appeared in the
following publications:

"The Fiction of Octavia Butler" in the *Fourth Annual Meeting of the
Southwest and Texas Popular Culture Associations with a Topical
Index* (microfilm), Comp. and Ed. Michael K. Schoenecke (Oklahoma
Historical Society, 1984): 163–75. Used with permission.

"The Wise Witches" in *Conjuring: Black Women, Fiction, and Literary
Tradition.* Ed. Marjorie Pryse and Hortense Spillers (Bloomington:
Indiana University Press, 1985): 203–215. Used with permission.

"Worlds of Words and Swords: Suzette Haden Elgin and Joanna Russ
at Work," in *Women Worldwalkers: New Dimensions of Science
Fiction and Fantasy.* Ed. Jane B. Weedman (Lubbock: Texas Tech
Press, 1985): 207–222. Used with permission.

For William Joseph O'Brien
who might have found within
a world worth living in.

Contents

Preface

To discuss myth and mythmaking in contemporary writing is essential; as Wallace W. Douglas asserts in "The Meanings of 'Myth' in Modern Criticism" in John B. Vickery's edition of essays on *Myth and Literature* (1966), "at times 'myth' seems to be the most important and inclusive word in modern criticism" (p. 119). However, what does "myth" mean to the literary critic? Lauri Honko has offered no less than twenty-two definitions—ten from antiquity and twelve from current usage—in "The Problem of Defining Myth" in Alan Dundes's edition of *Sacred Narrative* (1984: 41). It is not surprising, therefore, to discover contradictory uses and judgments of mythic criticism. Specifically in reference to fantastic literature, for example, Casey Fredericks offers a flexible use of the term in his study of *The Future of Eternity* (1982), arguing that in science fiction "creative science and the myth-making faculty" can be "mutually complementary" and that the patterns are "dynamic encounters" rather than "static archetypal images" (p. 41). Less encompassing, on the other hand, is Albert Wendland's definition of mythic science fiction in *Science, Myth, and the Fictional Creation of Alien Worlds* (1985) as "conventional" entertainments: "The comparable activity here is not science but *myth-making*, the establishment of an over-all 'legend of

the future' that provides comfort and promise for those who
are closest to the scenario's products, like space travel and
technological development" (p. 3).

In light of these contradictions, some prefatory definitions
are essential. In this study, I too employ more than one definition of myth. Behind most of the stories I will examine is an
ancient myth, the essential human explanation for observed
or imagined phenomena. This underlying ancient myth is preserved in a written form which I refer to as the cultural myth.
The buried ancient myths associated with the Goddess are uncovered and rediscovered, for instance, by many of the women
writers I will be discussing, often with the help of recent explorations into the origins of cultural myths.

The cultural myths most familiar to the English-speaking
audience and writers of fantastic literature include those from
Greek, Roman, Celtic, African, Semitic, and Eastern mythologies. I hope to show that the contemporary writer not only
draws on these cultural myths in recognizable forms but also
transforms them through the techniques of fantastic literature
in an attempt to rediscover their foundation of ancient myth.
Furthermore, the writer of fantastic literature is also a myth-
maker—a storyteller attempting to explain existence in human
terms. Often, therefore, that writer creates science fiction
myth—a new story which once again embodies the ancient
myth in the language of our time and place.

This study will examine all three—ancient, cultural, and
science-fiction myth—as they influence fantastic literature by
women. The importance of this examination is to find not only
the ancient myth, which has been obscured by intervening
cultural expressions, but also its contemporary expression—
the way in which the myth can be made new. Contemporary
mythmakers in fantastic literature by women can use the
mythmaking possibilities of this genre to recreate the ancient
myth while, at the same time, the surface reality created in
this fiction can suggest alternatives to our present reality—a
reality which, these writers often reveal, is in conflict with the
explanations offered by the rediscovered ancient myth.

Goddess myths are particularly important to these women
writers, as they have been to other women artists and writers

of our time. Estella Lauter convincingly argues in *Women as Mythmakers* (1984), for instance, that "a myth has been taking shape for centuries, its roots in pre-Christian religions covered for centuries except in brief periods when women gained the wherewithal to express their visions" (p. 171). She traces the emergence of this myth in the art of twentieth-century women and points out that it transcends cultural boundaries, becoming "not the product of community life in a particular geographic region so much as the product of women's common 'ground' of experience in patriarchal societies" (pp. 213–14). Nor is it stopped by human boundaries, Lauter argues; rather, she discovers "a story about our relationship with nature that emphasizes not subservience or fear, not husbandry or dominance, but equality arising from acceptance of our similarities to other forms of nature without obliterating our differences from them" (p. 215).

Still, while the visual arts and poetry can confront truths on a personal level, it remains for fiction to realize this vision in action in the social context. The realistic fiction of today, however, is locked into current perceptions of reality—to, if you will, our cultural myths. Fantastic literature, on the other hand, has always been open to alternatives. In her study of *The Novel of the Future* (1968), Anaïs Nin has recognized the need of our fiction to challenge boundaries:

In the future novels I see a greater liberation of the imagination (which had taken refuge in science fiction, having nowhere else to go). I see in it a freedom from boundaries parallel to that claimed by science, a freedom from time, a freedom from geography. The realist has been too much of a map maker, tracing roads already in existence. (pp. 191–92)

Nin isn't alone in predicting the development of the mainstream novel in the direction of fantastic literature; Fredericks has also asserted that "in a few decades, or even years, it will be difficult to distinguish SF as a special genre at all; it is becoming *the* mainstream so quickly" (*The Future*: 177). Meanwhile, however, it is to the mythmaking possibilities of this genre that we must turn when realistic fiction inadequately examines the four major concerns of fiction—the relation of the individual self to itself, to the other, to its society, and to the universe. Fantastic literature is already free from time and geography and capable of encompassing the creative expansiveness of science. Here the storyteller can meld what was and what can be in terms of what is.

It is also important here to acknowledge the subdivisions within fantastic literature. In this study we will be examining works of fantasy as well as those which fulfill Darko Suvin's definition of science fiction (hereafter referred to as SF) as "cognitive estrangement." In his study, *Metamorphoses of Science Fiction* (1979), Suvin acknowledges that estrangement, or the ability to distance ourselves from the familiar so that we can examine it freshly, is found not only in SF but "both as underlying attitude and dominant formal device is found also in the *myth*, a 'timeless' and religious approach looking in its own way beneath (or above) the empiric surface" (p. 7). He argues, however, that whereas "myth claims to explain once and for all the essence of phenomena, SF first posits them as problems and then explores where they lead; it sees the mythical static identity as an illusion, usually as fraud, at best only as a temporary realization of potentially limitless contingencies" (p. 7).

While this study owes much to Suvin's definition of SF as "*a literary genre whose necessary and sufficient conditions are the presence and interaction of estrangement and cognition, and whose main formal device is an imaginative framework alternative to the author's empirical environment*" (pp. 7–8), neither Suvin's definition of fantasy nor his conclusion that SF rejects any "mythical static identity" seems supported by this research. First, the fantasy we will be treating is based on neither the wish-fulfillment Suvin attributes to fairy tales nor the arbitrary mystification he sees in fantasy. It is rather closer to his definition of the "closed collateral world indifferent to cognitive possibilities" that he attributes to the folktale (p. 8). These "closed collateral world[s]" closely resemble our own, but they are not limited by what we consider inescapable realities. Yet, their realities are not without external sources—the authors have chosen the authority of myth rather than science for those sources.

Nor has SF totally rejected myth as a source, as I have tried
to assert with the recognition of SF myth. While those works
identifiable as SF do employ a cognitive approach to define and
explain their imaginative surface, the alternative realities they
offer can be seen to share the "apparently constant motifs" that
myth seeks to identify in known societies (Suvin, *Metamorphoses*: 7). This study will try to provide a better understanding
of the ancient myth underlying more familiar cultural myths
as retold by contemporary women writers, which will in turn
help us identify similar motifs in SF by women which reveal
the mythmaking potential of SF. The dual nature of the worlds
within this SF—as problems to be solved through cognitive
estrangement and as human environments to be understood
through myth—truly fulfills Suvin's description of twentieth-
century SF as "a diagnosis, a warning, a call to understanding
and action, and—most important—a mapping of possible alternatives" (p. 12).

Finally, the literary form of utopian fiction must be considered here. I have no quarrel with Suvin's definition of Utopia
as "the verbal construction of a particular quasi-human community where sociopolitical institutions, norms, and individual
relationships are organized according to a more perfect principle than in the author's community, this construction being
based on estrangement arising out of an alternative historical
hypothesis" (*Metamorphoses*: 49). However, his subsequent
qualifications that this "verbal construction" does not offer human characters so much as embodied discourse and that the
system proposed must necessarily be hierarchical (pp. 49–50)
would exclude many of the worlds within women we will
discuss.

Some of these works have, however, been called feminist
utopias in utopian criticism collected by Ruby Rohrlich and
Elaine Hoffman Baruch in *Women in Search of Utopia* (1984).
For Lee Cullen Khanna in "Change and Art in Women's
Worlds," for instance, utopia "is not, finally, any one place or
time, but the capacity to see afresh—an enlarged, even transformed vision" (p. 273).

Rather than challenge these various definitions, I do not
intend to differentiate between utopian fiction and the works

I refer to as SF myth. Both belong to fantastic literature, to what Suvin calls the literature of estrangement, and both offer alternatives to "the author's community" which can challenge the reader to "see afresh."

Perhaps it is the foundation of myth which carries these works beyond the "anatomy" tradition in which Suvin would place utopian fiction to the literary realization of human communities, enabling them to realize fully the possibilities inherent in SF—the science of its surface reality and the fiction of its human interaction. Certainly it is the nature of that myth defining these worlds within women—a nondualistic, cyclical affirmation of life and love—to offer a dynamic, flexible surface reality open to individual expressions and resistant to hierarchical organization. As a verbal construction, SF myth is as fixed as any earlier cultural myth, but when that construction is read metaphorically its possibilities become apparent, and the reader can see *through* the words to the archetypal patterns of ancient myth, can know that as this surface offers a shift from the world we live in, it too can shift. "The good society," Khanna argues, "is thus viable only so long as it is constantly re-evaluated, revised, responsive to individual and communal growth" (p. 271).

Acknowledgments

I would like to thank Marshall Tymn for recommending my study for this series. For assistance of various sorts—a sabbatical leave, a summer grant, and ongoing secretarial and photocopying support—I am indebted to Arizona State University in general and the English Department and Hayden Library in particular. I would also like to thank my Women & Myth and Women SF Writers classes at ASU for the insights they have given me, and my family and friends for their patience, support and understanding.

WORLDS
WITHIN
WOMEN

Introduction

What have women writers done to SF? The rapidly increasing number of women writing in this genre in the past thirty years has led many critics to analyze the effect of a female perspective on what, according to Sam Lundwall, "is really not so much a literary genre as a point of view" itself.[1] The prospect of change defines SF, Lundwall asserts, and he reaffirms Frederick Pohl's belief that "it isn't really science fiction's business to describe what science is going to find" so much as "to try to say what the human race will make of it all."[2]

Within the wide definition of the genre as given by Lundwall and Pohl, the "hard tech" aspects of science fiction seem to be only a taking-off point for the "real" business of social definition, of "what the human race will make of it all." Certainly this is inherent in the purpose of fiction in general, the literary form designed to examine relationships within the self—already an amalgam of social, biological, and spiritual forces—and between that self and the other, the society, and the universe.

Yet SF has been accused of dehumanization—of its women characters particularly. As Beverly Friend and others have pointed out,[3] women have been almost indistinguishable from the other gadgets cluttering up the common "hard SF" story. Concentrating on creating and/or cleverly employing such scientific and technological clutter, these stories make up much of the popular SF market, but they have usually been identified as space opera or adventure rather than as literature.

This is less true of SF by women, however. "Women's science fiction is marked by greater emphasis on characterization than is men's," argues Elaine Hoffman Baruch in her introduction to *Women in Search of Utopia*.[4] In fact, much of recent SF has earned critical attention by extending its concerns to human interrelationships and demanding of its writers the artistic control of character and plot as well as expression of ideas. Such critical attention has often focussed on defining the genre— differentiating it on the one hand from other forms of fantastic literature and on the other from so-called "mainstream" or realistic fiction. The latter has become increasingly difficult as these mainstream authors experiment with imaginative forms ranging from surrealism to magic realism. "To create works that reflect the reality of his age," Sharon Spencer argues in *Space, Time and Structure in the Modern Novel*, the serious novelist must "search for ways of attaining a fusion of time and space."[5]

In making such an assertion, Spencer recognizes a movement away from what Darko Suvin has defined as "naturalistic fiction" toward what he refers to as "estranged fiction" in his study, *Metamorphoses of Science Fiction*.[6] Suvin divides fiction "according to the manner in which men's relationships to other men and their surroundings are illuminated," considering detailed copies of "empirical textures and surfaces vouched for by human senses and common sense" as naturalistic fiction, while an attempt "to illuminate such relations by creating a radically or significantly different formal framework—a different space/time location or central figures for the fable, unverifiable by common sense" defines for him estranged fiction. SF, he argues, belongs to the latter category.[7]

In this category, which I call fantastic literature, empirical truth gives way to the truth of myth. Storytelling has always been a way of knowing—and a way of communicating—what goes beyond the definable and demonstrable realities. Myths, legends, folk tales and fairy tales—as Sigmund Freud and Carl Jung remind us—plug in to our unconscious; beneath their seemingly solid surfaces are found universal undercurrents. After these oral and cultural forms of fantastic literature follow individual—hence artistically controlled—forms, from the parables of Plato's philosophizing and Christ's preaching through fables, allegories, satires, symbolic romances, to the roots of SF itself in Mary Shelley's classic *Frankenstein* in 1818. Suvin recognizes this mythic ancestry of SF, although he argues that SF is finally unlike its ancestor because "myth is oriented toward constants and SF toward variables,"[8] an assumption we will examine more closely later.

As Nathaniel Hawthorne has explained of the romance, fantastic literature takes place in a shifting surface, "a neutral territory, somewhere between the real world and fairyland, where the Actual and the Imaginary may meet, and each imbue itself with the nature of the other."[9] Here the writer strives to explore "the truth of the human heart."[10] For SF, isn't that truth "what the human race will make of" the changes that will come its way? In her description of SF as the contemporary form of myth, Patricia Warrick also acknowledges the direct line of descent from myth to SF.[11]

Warrick is careful, however, to differentiate between earlier myth and SF myth. As the unique characteristics of the latter Warrick has listed its placement in the future (rather than "outside time"), its acceptance as present fiction but possible future truth (as opposed to the accepted truth of earlier myths by their audience), and its ambiguity concerning the concepts of good and evil (clearly defined in earlier myth).[12]

Yet are these significant or only surface differences? That SF is always set in the "future" ignores scientific theories on the nature of time itself as a dimension through which one might pass. Time and space, seen from a fresh perspective, are merely elements of that surface which shifts in SF, elements merging even in the modern novel Spencer envisions. Indeed, as Carol S. Pearson points out, in contemporary feminist science fiction, "when past, present and future are not imagined as simultaneous, they are circular or spiral."[13] Much of Doris Lessing's *Re: Colonized Planet Five: Shikasta* (hereafter referred to as *Shikasta*) takes place in our past, for instance, but what is that from a Canopean perspective? SF is just as capable of a speculative timelessness as is myth, and its place is still "where the Actual and the Imaginary may meet" whether the surface is designated as our world in 2110 or in the Pliocene era (the movement in time encompassed in Julian May's *The Many-Colored Land*) or as the distant planet Destiny in Sydney J. Van Scyoc's *Sunwaifs*. That it gives the coordinates and textures of the time and place it fabulates more completely than did earlier forms of fantastic literature merely reflects the techniques it has learned from the developments of realistic fiction.

Nor is the SF myth less "true" than the earlier myth. Certainly not every story told as SF can be considered myth any more than every story told by our ancestors was considered myth at that time. But when fantastic literature recreates for us Hawthorne's "neutral territory," we still recognize in it "the truth of the human heart." When that happens, in fact, the literal-minded reader even accepts the surface reality, as SF fans might try to recreate the literary surface of their favorite authors through costumes, structures, even "religions." Such attitudes of devotees led Lessing in her preface to *The Sirian Experiments* to assure her readers that "if I have created a cosmology, then it is only for literary purposes!"[14]

Here we should pause to differentiate between ancient myth and cultural myth. The oral tradition of ancient myth was always fresh, always being retold with the particular embellishments of each storyteller, open to the perspective of the present moment. The myth as it comes down in written form to us, however, is cultural—locked into the telling of its time and place. The internal tension of the cultural myth is between the story and its teller, between the ancient myth and the contemporary interpretation and expression of its meaning. It is to this static quality of cultural myth that Suvin refers when he argues that "myth is diametrically opposed to the cognitive approach [which he considers central to SF] since it conceives human relations as fixed and supernaturally determined."[15] At this surface level, SF seems much more "truthful" in considering the "mythical static identity" as only one possible solution to the problems posed by phenomena and recognizing, as does Baruch, that "what literary utopias reveal as much as future possibilities are the problems in the societies which conceive them."[16] If their "solutions" to the problems posed in the fiction garner them followers, is that very different from the followers of earlier recorded myths? Lessing has commented that the reason "readers yearn to 'believe' cosmologies and tidy systems of thought is that we live in dreadful and marvellous times where the certainties of yesterday dissolve as we live."[17] What are those dissolving certainties but the cultural myths in which we no longer believe?

At the same time, SF can offer new tellings that embody the ancient myths because it too is in the poetic tradition defined by Northrop Frye, who himself refers to Paul Valéry's definition of "cosmology as one of the oldest of literary arts."[18] Frye notes the poetic rather than the historic truth of what the poet conveys:

The poet has no external model for his imitation, and is judged by the integrity or consistency of his verbal structure. The reason is that he imitates the universal, not the particular; he is concerned not with what happened but with what happens. His subject-matter is the kind of thing that does happen, in other words the typical and recurring element in action. . . . The verbal imitation of ritual is myth, and the typical action of poetry is the plot, or what Aristotle calls *mythos*, so that for the literary critic the Aristotelian term *mythos* and the English word myth are much the same thing.[19]

In this sense, SF myth is "true" beyond any validation of the reality—or lack of it—of its surface cosmology. This is its myth-making potential, its contribution to understanding "the truth of the human heart." It also has value as a literary genre which can offer a surface of alternate possibilities subject to validation, however. Its Janus-faced relationship to the science of its surface and the fiction of its message can be seen in Frye's further discussion of literature as "an area of verbal imitation midway between events and ideas": "Poetry faces, in one direction, the world of *praxis* or action, a world of events occurring in time. In the opposite direction, it faces the world of *theoria*, of images and ideas, the conceptual or visualizable world spread out in space, or mental space."[20]

Firmly rooted in this poetic and mythic tradition, SF offers a surface of actions which in themselves embody myriad perceptions of time and space and an undercurrent of ancient myth which forms and informs that surface with its "truth of the human heart." "The poet seeks the new expression, not the new content," Frye reminds us,[21] and true to this purpose SF myth offers a contemporary cultural myth to replace those of yesterday and to imagine the unity of historical and mythic truth in a possible tomorrow. Realism at best can only reflect opposition to the way things are, caught as it is in the historic surface; and as Ursula K. LeGuin's androgynous protagonist Estravan says in *The Left Hand of Darkness*, "to oppose something is to maintain it.... You must go somewhere else; you must have another goal; then you walk a different road."[22] Echoing Lessing's observation on the "dreadful and marvellous times" in which we live and which impel us to search for new expressions of the ancient myth, Estravan offers a method if not a solution: "to learn which questions are unanswerable, and *not to answer them*: this skill is most needful in times of stress and darkness" (p. 110). The twentieth century could well be described as such a time. Realism has proved inadequate for many writers to answer the questions posed by today's world: what future can a historic perspective promise us?

The fantastic literature we will be examining does not seek to escape from these questions into comfortable fantasies where the answers are simple and magical. Rather, it seeks to rediscover truth through a "conceptual or visualizable world" which "is concerned not with what happened but with what happens." If realistic fiction has moved closer to these speculative forms, it is because fantastic literature allows the surfaces to shift to reveal the ancient myth once again. As Lessing complains,

Once upon a time, when I was young, I believed things easily, both religious and political; now I believe less and less. But I wonder about more ... I think it is likely that our view of ourselves as a species on this planet now is inaccurate, and will strike those who come after us as inadequate as the world view of, let's say, the inhabitants of

New Guinea seems to us. That our current view of ourselves as a
species is wrong. That we know very little about what is going on.[23]

Fantastic literature walks different roads to offer us new
perspectives from which to view ourselves, visualizing new surfaces. It can itself achieve the level of SF myth when these
surfaces convey old—and perhaps forgotten—answers and suggest ways to balance these answers with the unanswerable
questions that will continue to plague our human and finite
search for truth, because its shifting surface frees it from the
nightmare of contemporary reality. As Lessing has written
elsewhere, "the artists have been so busy with the nightmare
that they have had no time to rewrite the old utopias."[24] SF
myth expands time to accomplish this—finds time, as T. S. Eliot
had sought for Prufrock, for "visions and revisions."

For it is the "old utopia" that is rediscovered in SF myth by
women, the ancient myth realized through new surface possibilities. I hope to show in this study that both the truths
uncovered and the surfaces suggested in SF myths by women
attempt to offer a future rooted in ancient myth, rejecting the
cultural myths of patriarchy. "Women's utopian quest," Baruch
has argued, "is often an attempt to recover a real past. What
we now call utopia was once our reality. In many ways, the
contemporary dream of equality existed in pre-state egalitarian
societies."[25]

Consideration of the ancient myth also helps us answer Warrick's final argument that SF myth offers ambiguity where
earlier myths offer clarity concerning the concepts of good and
evil. The clarity Warrick attributes to myth is defined in the
recorded cultural myths and represents what that culture has
identified as good and evil. In Western society, our dualistic
heritage divides everything between God and the Devil. In
ancient myth, however, such dualistic attitudes are not present. Rather, as Robert Graves has cogently argued in *The White
Goddess*, the ninefold Goddess has both Her dark and light
aspects;[26] as "Tormer's Lay" reminds Genly Ai in LeGuin's
novel, *"Light is the left hand of darkness"* (p. 168). In its rejection of patriarchal cultural myths and its return to ancient
myth, fantastic literature by women also rejects such duality.

The unanswerable questions of absolute good and evil remain unanswered, while the archetypal patterns of ancient myth find their contemporary expression in SF myth by women in surface realities capable of maintaining a balance which supports the preservation and improvement of community, communication and ecology. Concerning the necessity of maintaining such a balance, SF myth by women is entirely unambiguous. This allows women to envision dynamic rather than static surfaces, as Ruby Rohrlich has observed: "Unlike the planned, rigidly controlled, and static utopias, real and fictional, generally devised by men, these societies are subject to transformation as the world within and around them changes."[27]

It is this dynamic surface and adherence to ancient myth that leads me to identify certain works of SF by women as SF myth. The very flexibility of the metaphorical surface saves these works from being what Suvin would call "private pseudomyths" which, he argues, result from "all attempts to transplant the metaphysical orientation of mythology and religion into SF."[28] The ideological constants which Suvin sees as definitive of myth and opposed to the flexible variables of SF are, I would argue, characteristics of cultural myth, which solidifies and stereotypes the ancient myth within. Archetypes, on the other hand, are flexible patterns; and ancient myth, as we shall see, leaves the "unanswerable questions" unanswered while offering archetypal patterns of human action which emerge once again in the metaphorical surfaces of SF myth.

Several studies have already examined the values common to fantastic literature by women. The Spring 1982 issue of *Extrapolation*, for example, offered Phyllis J. Day's "Earthmother/Witchmother: Feminism and Ecology Renewed," which asserts that "wholeness of women within the context of nature completes the new pattern we see emerging in science fiction" and concludes that "whether witchmothers, Earthmothers, or both, this pattern of science fiction is beginning to show women in the new light of creative power, and it is dealing with their innate connection to the creative forces of nature."[29] Even more extensive is Natalie M. Rosinsky's study of *Feminist Futures*, in which she concludes that in fantastic literature by women the "fluid reconfiguration of perceived physical reality, validating temporal simultaneity and spatial relativity, is redolent of the 'feminist consciousness' deliberately articulated by such earlier twentieth century women writers as Virginia Woolf, Dorothy Richardson, and Rosamund Lehmann."[30] It is in this area, of placing fantastic literature by women in the context of the rediscovery and/or reassertion of "feminist consciousness" in twentieth-century women's art, that I have chosen to concentrate this study.

Worlds within women—archetypes drawn from ancient myth as it was shared orally in pre-patriarchal cultures, a reality which still survives in the female unconscious—began to emerge through earlier women's fiction as well. Although the continued acceptance of the patriarchal cultural myths in her time offered her an imperfect (at best) vocabulary for her insight, for instance, Charlotte Brontë is surely invoking the Goddess when the title character of her novel *Shirley* describes Eve as the mother of Titans and later of the Messiah:

The first woman's breast that heaved with life on this world yielded the daring which could contend with Omnipotence; the strength which could bear a thousand years of bondage—the vitality which could feed that vulture death through uncounted ages—the unexhausted life and uncorrupted excellence, sisters to immortality, which, after milleniums of crimes, struggles, and woes, would conceive and bring forth a Messiah.[31]

"I will stay out here with my mother Eve, in these days called Nature," Shirley tells Caroline after rejecting Milton's interpretation of Eve ("Milton was great; but was he good? His brain was right, how was his heart?").[32] Brontë too had discovered a "truth of the human heart" which helped her penetrate the cultural myth to rediscover ancient myth.

In the twentieth century, faith in patriarchy and its myths has been seriously undermined. While those in power are inevitably threatened by any breakdown in cultural values, the oppressed members of society—women and minorities in the United States in particular—might find such a breakdown to their advantage as they see the stereotypes which have predefined their characters and their society disintegrating. The importance of women and minority writers in post–World War II American fiction has been well documented.[33] I would posit that it is this very loss of faith in patriarchy that has opened the social possibilities of fiction to reinterpretation from their perspectives.

Which brings us to the real question of this introduction: not what have women writers done to SF but what has SF done for women writers? The possibilities inherent in this genre of shifting surfaces—the possibilities of social and cultural as well as individual change—free women from the limits that define them in patriarchal society. Octavia Butler, for instance, asserts that by writing SF, "I was free to imagine new ways of thinking about people and power, free to maneuver my characters into situations that don't exist. For example, where is there a society in which men and women are honestly equal? Where do people not despise each other because of race or religion, class or ethnic origin?"[34]

Where indeed? In her study of *Archetypal Patterns in Women's Fiction*, Annis Pratt has argued that women's fiction reflects an "ancient, unresolved tension between feminine power and feminine powerlessness in the history of human culture."[35] When fantastic literature by women is examined as a subgenre of women's fiction, this child is no misbegotten Frankenstein's monster. Rather, it is the butterfly releasing the beauty and power only dreamed of in the caterpillar (which, however, was still only itself trapped in the cocoon of patriarchal expressions and limitations). Rosinsky has examined effectively those works by women which use "narrative techniques that engage active reader involvement in the de/construction of textual meaning" in order to overcome the difficulty of expressing new perceptions of Western society's contemporary reality in old forms and words.[36] This female perspective is difficult to express, Rosinsky argues, because "it is conceptually antithetical to the West's classically logical, 'either-or' mentality," because "language, a symbolic system, is necessarily at odds with such non-dualistic lived experience" and because "any understanding or model of a system implicitly involves giving up some other ways of conceiving of it."[37] The writers she discusses often develop radical new techniques to overcome these problems.

Another way to overcome such difficulties, however, lies with the reader, who can learn to see *through* the words just as we see through the surfaces in fantastic literature to discover simultaneous meanings. A word too is a surface (an abstraction of reality) and a poem (an image of that reality). Since language is symbolic, it can be read metaphorically. The language of metaphor is the language of myth; as Frye further observes, "The 'ideas' the poets use, therefore, are not actual propositions, but thought-forms or conceptual myths, usually dealing with images rather than abstractions, and hence normally unified by metaphor, or image-phrasing, rather than by logic."[38]

Reading fantastic literature metaphorically also allows us to escape the "logical, 'either-or' mentality" as these women writers describe their worlds within while presenting, through images, new conceptions of surface reality. As H. Lee Gershuny has argued, "Feminists are wrenching familiar terms from dualistic contexts and charging them with new meaning." The words may not be new, but we see them freshly. "In feminist contexts," Gershuny continues, "the metaphors are not only ameliorated, but connected in images of spiralling processes."[39] Gershuny particularly mentions terms that have been used negatively by men but which are identified with women or nature. These words need to be reconsidered, not dismissed. For instance, as negative as the word *witch* is thought to be in our society, it might be related to the Old English *witan*, "to know," or to the Old High German *wih*, "holy," which is given among its roots in *Webster's New Collegiate Dictionary* (1977).

Women's fiction, as Pratt has effectively shown, has always offered more than the patriarchal surface—could be read as well as "a mutually illuminative or interrelated field of texts reflecting a preliterary repository of feminine archetypes."[40] These writers, she posits, have not lost sight of pre-patriarchal values even while necessarily expressing themselves through borrowed language and cultural myths which obscured the ancient myth. Pratt finds in this fiction and Lauter has found in women's art and poetry the shared experience of women in patriarchal societies, which has been communicated despite those patriarchal surfaces.

Three centuries of women writers, Pratt would argue, have

penetrated that patriarchal surface and "dug the goddess out
of the ruins and cleansed the debris from her face, casting aside
the gynophobic masks that have obscured her beauty, her
power, and her beneficence."[41] Still, it remains for contemporary women writers of fantastic literature to envision a surface
designed to enhance rather than obscure what they have uncovered, to offer cultural alternatives. Unlike realistic fiction,
fantastic literature can leave behind the nightmare of our contemporary reality to rediscover the dreams of our egalitarian
ancestors.

Fantastic literature by women redefines our past so that we
may perceive other possible futures than the one which seems
to be carrying us to our destruction. These futures embodied
in SF myth offer the symbiotic powers of community, communication, and ecological balance to reaffirm the cycle of life
as they dissolve dualistic and linear limitations on our ability
to perceive change which is not merely an extension of the
present moment. "We can only know what we can truly imagine," Luciente reminds Connie in Marge Piercy's *Woman on
the Edge of Time*. "Finally what we see comes from ourselves."[42]
Yet Piercy finds in this middle-aged, Mexican-American female
protagonist the ability to imagine a future which her conscious
mind wars against, even though in it she recognizes her fam-
ilial roots. "What we observe is not nature itself, but nature
exposed to our method of questioning," asserts W. Heisenberg
in *Physics and Philosophy*.[43] Rooted in the unconscious, fantastic literature can raise questions about nature and ourselves
that the conscious mind may be blocked from considering by
the "method of questioning" it has been taught.

A metaphorical reading of fantastic literature by women uncovers its mythmaking process. "Unless physical action reflects
psychic action," LeGuin says in her introduction to "Vaster
than Empires and More Slow," "unless the deeds express the
person, I get very bored with adventure stories."[44] The fantastic
literature by women discussed in this study presents such a
surface of representative physical action and deeds. This surface in itself is a statement about the potentialities of our society, as "what we see comes from ourselves," while the *mythos*

or plot reveals "what the human race will make of" the changes incorporated into that surface. An exploration of the patterns and images that constitute the surface will help define the worlds within: "The great fantasies, myths, and tales," LeGuin asserts in *The Language of the Night*, "speak from the unconscious to the unconscious, in the language of the unconscious—symbol and archetype."[45] We will use the archetypes identified by Pratt as common to women's fiction and the symbols of ancient myth to "read" the message embodied in the landscape of fantasy, "because when fantasy is the real thing, nothing, after all, is realer."[46]

To defamiliarize us with what we have come to expect and to refamiliarize us with the repository of ancient myth and archetypes, the first chapter of this study will discuss works of fantasy by women who consciously redefine patriarchal myth from a female perspective or who reexamine origins to posit how those myths began and what they really mean. Uncovering the face of the Goddess is essential because she wears such unrecognizable faces in these cultural myths. "Perhaps because, as we know them, most have been defined and celebrated by males," Marta Weigle comments on the women in these myths in her study *Spiders and Spinsters*, "they appear more often as monstrous and dangerous than as primary creators and gift-bearing culture heroines."[47] Since the cultural source for most English and American fantastic literature is Western Europe, we will begin by considering Evangeline Walton's tetralogy retelling the Welsh *Mabinogion* and Marion Zimmer Bradley's retelling of Arthurian legend in *The Mists of Avalon*. That same heritage is treated from an earlier vantage point in Moyra Caldecott's Sacred Stones trilogy and Julian May's tetralogy of the Pliocene era. These are chosen rather than such other fine treatments of Celtic material as those by Joy Chant because they focus more directly on retracing the ancient myth underlying the cultural material.

Myth is being made in the primitive world of Jean Auel's Earth's Children saga, which we will examine next; it is being examined from a Canopean perspective in the cosmology of Lessing's *Shikasta*; it is being lived again by the male and female embodiments of the sun in the African and pre–Civil War America settings of *Wild Seed*, which is chronologically the first installment of Octavia E. Butler's Patternist series.

Chapter 2 leaves the world we know to rediscover it metaphorically in the future, on parallel worlds, or on other planets where the processes of the past begin again and myths are inevitably recreated. Discussed in this chapter are Andre Norton's Witch World series, Sydney J. Van Scyoc's *Sunwaifs*, Susan Coon's Living Planet series, and Joan Vinge's *The Snow Queen*—all of which consciously incorporate myth in attempts to uncover the truth of ancient myth. A second group examined in this chapter presents worlds ruled by—or even solely populated by—women. This group includes Bradley's *The Ruins of Isis*, Jayge Carr's *Leviathan's Deep*, C. J. Cherryh's Faded Sun trilogy, Whileaway in Joanna Russ's *The Female Man*, Suzy McKee Charnas's *Motherlines*, Sally Miller Gearhart's *The Wanderground: Stories of the Hill Women*, and Suzette Haden Elgin's Ozark trilogy and *Native Tongue*.

Chapter 3 offers SF mythmaking in process. The surface and the myth unite in Lessing's *The Marriages Between Zones Three, Four, and Five*, LeGuin's *The Left Hand of Darkness*, Van Scyoc's Daughters of the Sunstone trilogy, Pamela Sargent's *Watchstar*, Elgin's *Star-Anchored, Star-Angered*, Russ's *And Chaos Died*, Butler's *Mind of My Mind*, and Piercy's *Woman on the Edge of Time*.

Chapter 4 discusses the transformation of female archetypes in fantastic literature, including Tanith Lee's *Birthgrave* and *The Silver Metal Lover*, Bradley's *The Shattered Chain, Thendara House* and *City of Sorcery*, Russ's *Extra(Ordinary) People* and *The Two of Them*, Butler's *Survivor* and *Patternmaster*, Lessing's *The Making of the Representative for Planet Eight* and Kate Wilhelm's *Juniper Time*.

Chapter 5 summarizes by discussing the conscious and unconscious patterns of myth which undergird women's art in general and which emerge consciously and transformed in fantastic literature by women, transformed because its metaphorical possibilities enable these women writers to reunite the mythic and historical levels of discourse—to make the myth the reality in the worlds they offer us.

NOTES

1. Sam J. Lundwall, *Science Fiction: What It's All About* (New York: Ace, 1971): 24.

2. Quoted by Lundwall in *Science Fiction*: 25.

3. Beverly Friend, "Virgin Territory: The Bonds and Boundaries of Women in Science Fiction," in *Many Futures, Many Worlds: Theme and Form in Science Fiction*, ed. Thomas D. Clareson (Kent, Ohio: Kent State University Press, 1977), on "The Bonds: Women as Gadgets (or Gadgets as Women)": 141–43. See also a more recent argument that SF by men writers "displays women providing services—all of the traditional ones—to men" in Jan Zimmerman, "Utopia in Question: Programming Women's Needs into the Technology of Tomorrow," in *Women in Search of Utopia*, ed. Ruby Rohrlich and Elaine Hoffman Baruch (New York: Schocken Books, 1984): 168.

4. Elaine Hoffman Baruch, Introduction in Rohrlich and Baruch (eds.), *Women in Search*: xiii.

5. Sharon Spencer, *Space, Time and Structure in the Modern Novel* (Chicago: Swallow Press, 1971): xix.

6. Darko Suvin, *Metamorphoses of Science Fiction* (New Haven: Yale University Press, 1979): 18.

7. Ibid.

8. Ibid.: 27.

9. Nathaniel Hawthorne, "The Custom House," Introduction to *The Scarlet Letter*, 2nd ed. (New York: W. W. Norton, 1978): 31.

10. Nathaniel Hawthorne, Preface to *The House of the Seven Gables* (New York: Scholastic Book Services, 1965): vii.

11. Patricia Warrick, "Science Fiction Myths and Their Ambiguity," in *Science Fiction: Contemporary Mythology*, ed. Patricia Warrick, Martin Harry Greenberg and Joseph Olander (New York: Harper & Row, 1978): 6–7.

12. Ibid.

13. Carol S. Pearson, "Of Time and Revolution: Theories of Social Change in Contemporary Feminist Science Fiction," in Rohrlich and Baruch (eds.), *Women in Search*: 262.

14. Doris Lessing, Preface to *The Sirian Experiments* (New York: Alfred A. Knopf, 1980): vii.

15. Suvin, *Metamorphoses*: 7.

16. Baruch, Introduction: xiii.

17. Lessing, Preface: vii.

18. Northrop Frye, "New Directions from Old," in *Myth and Myth-making*, ed. Henry A. Murray (Boston: Beacon Press, 1960): 115.

16 Introduction

19. Ibid.: 116–17.
20. Ibid.: 119.
21. Ibid.: 120.
22. Ursula K. LeGuin, *The Left Hand of Darkness* (New York: Walker, 1969): 110. Subsequent references are to this edition and will be given parenthetically in the text.
23. Lessing, Preface: vii.
24. Doris Lessing, "The Small Personal Voice," in *A Small Personal Voice: Essays, Reviews, Interviews*, ed. Paul Schlueter (New York: Alfred A. Knopf, 1974): 9.
25. Baruch, Introduction: xiii.
26. Robert Graves, *The White Goddess*, amended and enlarged edition (New York: Farrar, Straus & Giroux, 1948); see particularly Chapter 22, "The Triple Muse": 383–408.
27. Ruby Rohrlich, Introduction II in Rohrlich and Baruch (eds.), *Women in Search*: 3.
28. Suvin, *Metamorphoses*: 27.
29. Phyllis J. Day, "Earthmother/Witchmother: Feminism and Ecology Renewed," *Extrapolation* 23:1 (Spring 1982): 20.
30. Natalie M. Rosinsky, *Feminist Futures: Contemporary Women's Speculative Fiction* (Ann Arbor: University of Michigan Research Press, 1984): 106.
31. Charlotte Brontë, *Shirley* by Currer Bell (New York: Derby & Jackson, 1859): 285–86.
32. Ibid.: 285.
33. See my Introduction to *Radiant Daughters: Fictional American Women* (Westport, Conn.: Greenwood Press, 1986) for an extended discussion of this.
34. Quoted by Veronica Mixon in "Futurist Woman: Octavia Butler," *Essence* 15 (April 1979): 13.
35. Annis Pratt with Barbara White, Andrea Loewenstein and Mary Wyer, *Archetypal Patterns in Women's Fiction* (Bloomington: Indiana University Press, 1981): 167.
36. Rosinsky, *Feminist Futures*: 107.
37. Ibid.: 106.
38. Frye, "New Directions from Old": 120.
39. H. Lee Gershuny, "The Linguistic Transformation of Womanhood," in Rohrlich and Baruch (eds.), *Women in Search*: 196.
40. Pratt, *Archetypal Patterns*: 170.
41. Ibid.: 178.
42. Marge Piercy, *Woman on the Edge of Time* (New York: Fawcett, 1976): 328.

43. Quoted by Rosinsky in *Feminist Futures*: 106.

44. Ursula K. LeGuin, *The Wind's Twelve Quarters* (New York: Harper & Row, 1975): 148.

45. Ursula K. LeGuin, *The Language of the Night: Essays on Fantasy and Science Fiction*, ed. Susan Wood (New York: G. P. Putnam's Sons, 1979): 62.

46. Ibid.: 95.

47. Marta Weigle, *Spiders and Spinsters: Women and Mythology* (Albuquerque: University of New Mexico Press, 1982): viii.

1

The Beginnings:
Traditional Myths Retold

While myth has become synonymous with an untruth in much of contemporary usage, Mircea Eliade has reminded us that it can also mean "the *absolute truth*, because it narrates a *sacred history*; that is, a transhuman revelation which took place at the dawn of the Great Time, in the holy time of the beginnings (*in illo tempore*)."[1] Societies which accept myth as such turn to these stories, Eliade continues, for "patterns for human behaviour. In *imitating* the exemplary acts of a god or of a mythic hero, or simply by recounting their adventures, the man of an archaic society detaches himself from profane time and magically re-enters the Great Time, the sacred time."[2]

Eliade is right to use the male pronoun here, because, as Marta Weigle reminds us, when woman looks to our patriarchal myths for a model to imitate she is likely to be disappointed.[3] Classical myths especially, usually the only ones considered when mythology is discussed, depict women as negative or passive models. Hera is a jealous wife, Aphrodite a faithless flirt, and Hecate a witch. Among the mortals, women fare no better—Clytemnestra's murder of her husband condemned all women, if *The Odyssey* is to be believed, while Penelope's patience wins her praise but cannot even protect her handmaidens from condemnation.

Where are women to turn for their mythic models? Some have chosen to identify with male figures when no better mythic model is offered. Such is the case, as Robin Roberts would argue, in what has often been hailed as the first SF novel, Mary Shelley's classic *Frankenstein, or the Modern Prometheus*. The subtitle immediately alerts us to Shelley's mythic concerns; indeed, Paul A. Cantor argues that "*Frankenstein* has as much claim to mythic status as any story ever invented by a single author."[4] Yet both the protagonist, Victor Frankenstein, and the monster he creates are male, as is the mythic Prometheus of the subtitle. Roberts considers this a "codedly female novel," referring "to the process by which an author, forced by cultural, literary, or personal constraints, uses a male character as a cover for a singularly female dilemma. Refocusing their lenses on male characters," she adds, "enables feminist critics to reread texts with a sharper eye for their feminist import."[5]

While these insights are helpful and, I believe, accurate, Roberts is not convincing in her identification of the wintry setting of *Frankenstein* with the Demeter myth: "Like Demeter's," she argues, "Frankenstein's anguish at being separated from his creation and the creation's sorrow are reflected in the winter landscape which pervades the book."[6] Yet even a cursory reading of the text reveals that Victor has abandoned the monster and only suffers anguish at the thought of confronting his creation for any other purpose than its destruction. The image of Demeter weeping for the kidnapped Persephone who has been carried off by Hades seems foreign to the novel.

On the other hand, Shelley's references to myth do help connect her work with "a singularly female dilemma." One cannot ignore the birth imagery so effectively traced by Ellen Moers in *Literary Women*. *Frankenstein* is "most feminine," she argues, "in the motif of revulsion against newborn life, and the drama of guilt, dread, and flight surrounding birth and its consequences":

Most of the novel, roughly two of its three volumes, can be said to deal with the retribution visited upon the monster and creator for deficient infant care. *Frankenstein* seems to be distinctly a *woman's* mythmaking on the subject of birth precisely because its emphasis is not upon what precedes birth, not upon birth itself, but upon what follows birth: the trauma of the afterbirth.[7]

"More deeply rooted in our cultural mythology, and certainly in our literature," Moers has pointed out, "are the happy maternal reactions."[8] These myths would truly seem to be lies to Shelley, who was "pregnant at sixteen, and almost constantly pregnant throughout the following five years; yet not a secure mother, for she lost most of her babies soon after they were born; and not a lawful mother, for she was not married—not at least when, at the age of eighteen, Mary Godwin began to write *Frankenstein*."[9]

Shelley's experiences with motherhood were atypical, but it took an atypical woman to oppose the firmly entrenched patriarchal myths of the nineteenth century. If mothers were responsible for any flaws in their creations, the myths told her that male creators felt no such guilt. The original Prometheus, assigned the task of creating men after most strengths had already been distributed among the other creations, has only "a nobler shape" to offer them.[10] Later, however, he steals fire from the gods for them. Certainly fire can be seen as symbolic of the help given by science and technology and whatever else one is able to steal from the gods—including the ability to create the spark of life itself. Victor succeeds in giving this spark to his creation, but despite his Promethean efforts toward providing a godlike appearance, the monster is unforgivably ugly. It is this ugliness which causes Frankenstein to reject his flawed creation: "Unable to endure the aspect of the being I had created, I rushed out of the room."[11]

The creator in the other myth Shelley alludes to in the novel also rejects his creation, punishing it rather than claiming any responsibility for its imperfections. The epigraph from Milton's *Paradise Lost* which Shelley offers has already alerted us that the Biblical myth of creation lurks behind the surface science of the "artificial man." Frankenstein is now God himself, rejecting the monster as God had rejected Adam and Lucifer: "I ought to be thy Adam," the monster reproaches him, "but I am rather the fallen angel whom thou drivest from joy for no misdeed" (p. 113).

If these mythic models both turn their backs on the imperfect creation, however, the Goddess does not. Despite the preponderance of wintry settings in the novel, the monster assures us that Nature has not abandoned her unnatural child. In a forest he first appreciates the "radiant form" of the sun which "enlightened my path" and the "various scents" which "saluted me"; here he also "saw plainly the clear stream that supplied me with drink and the trees that shaded me with their foliage" (p. 117). He even finds refuge in "the caves of ice, which I only do not fear" which "are a dwelling to me, and the only one which man does not grudge. These bleak skies I hail, for they are kinder to me than your fellow beings" (pp. 113–14).

The monster, accepted by the Goddess and rejected by the father figure and the rest of society, is experiencing a "singularly female dilemma" in this novel, one with which Shelley's mother, Mary Wollstonecraft, was well acquainted, as is apparent from her study *A Vindication of the Rights of Women*. If Frankenstein is a metaphorical mother, he is also a father, representing patriarchal values. As such, he expresses the social rejection of the "other," the "alien." In patriarchal society, the alien is woman, as Ursula K. LeGuin has argued, for instance, in "American SF and the Other."[12] With this in mind, *Frankenstein* could be read as a "codedly female novel" initiating the SF pattern of alien encounter. Thus, Frankenstein himself can be seen as conveying the female dilemma of unwelcome or unsuccessful motherhood, while the monster experiences the rejection women feel in a "man's world" ameliorated only by the unquestioning acceptance of the Goddess, who has more "fire"—more warmth to offer him—in her wintry aspect than does the sunniest member of society.

But it is a human identity that the monster craves, and his creator refuses him that—never even gives him a name. Perhaps a mythic parallel can be seen here as well in the namelessness of the Goddess in our society. "Mythographers use three tactics to restrict information about goddesses," Patricia Monaghan asserts in *The Book of Goddesses and Heroines*. These tactics include ignoring them completely, failing to give them names, and designating them only by their relationship to a male.[13] So too in Shelley's novel, Victor tries to ignore the monster by abandoning him, never gives him a name other than the general appellations of "monster" or related terms, and refers to him as his creation. Finally, the monster is rejected because of his appearance, and their female appearance rather than individual characteristics defines and limits women in patriarchal society. Thus in male characters and through male mythic figures Shelley still examines the female experience in her "codedly female" novel.

Charlotte Brontë, on the other hand, chose to work through the mythic character of Eve in *Shirley*, but to do so she had to completely retell the myth, rejecting Milton's interpretation in the process, to rediscover the Goddess obscured by the Biblical version of Eve. Still, her adherence to women in myth is the approach common to most women artists of the twentieth century who are seeking mythic roots. As the cultural myths of patriarchy are questioned, researchers and creative writers alike begin to reread the myths and to reexamine old and new discoveries in their efforts to uncover the ancient myth behind the surface stories. Such studies as those of Merlin Stone and Patricia Monaghan work at "renaming the Goddess and thereby restoring a lost world."[14] For Greek myth, Charlene Spretnak recreates the pre-Hellenic stories of eleven goddesses, arguing that her aim is "not the reinstatement of prehistoric cultural structures, but rather the transmission of *possibilities*."[15]

It is in this tradition that Evangeline Walton offers her retelling of the four branches of the Welsh *Mabinogion*. Walton's first contribution in 1936, then titled *The Virgin and the Swine*, was apparently so ahead of its time that republication of the volume, under the new title of *The Island of the Mighty*, had to wait until 1970. Its success then, however, led to the rapid publication of the other three volumes, *The Children of Llyr* (1971), *The Song of Rhiannon* (1972), and *Prince of Annwn* (1974). Bob Collins attributes this new interest in Welsh myth to "the Tolkien-generated taste for fantasy . . . in the 70s," but the same decade hailed extensive publications of other women scholars which owed nothing to Tolkien but did share with

Walton an interest in reexamining women in myth. Although Collins hesitates short of calling Walton a feminist, he does acknowledge that her vision "was startlingly modern in 1936, and still in the forefront by 1970."[16] If one doubts the feminist consciousness of her retelling of cultural myth from the point of view of the women, however, Walton's subsequent publication of *The Sword Is Forged* with its focus on the Amazon Antiope's influence on the Greek Theseus reconfirms it. That her retelling of these myths serves a similar purpose of expanding possibilities as did Spretnak's versions of the pre-Hellenic tales is implicit in Walton's remark that "in the *Mabinogion* tetralogy I tried to picture the waning of the power of women, something which, in these stories, seems to be identical with the waning of magic."[17]

The magic that wanes with the loss of female power, the magic of ancient myth, becomes apparent as Walton not only retells but reinterprets the Welsh cultural myths. Had these myths been more available to Mary Shelley she might not have turned to male figures to challenge the motherhood myth of the Romantics. However, even Lady Charlotte Guest's earlier translation of the Welsh tales was not published until 1849, so Shelley was not familiar with Arianrhod and her rejection of motherhood in the fourth branch of the *Mabinogion*, which Walton retells in *The Island of the Mighty*. The story shares other themes with Shelley's *Frankenstein* as well, including an artificial creation and male "motherhood."

In Walton's retelling, Arianrhod is caught in the shift from matrilineal to patrilineal culture, which is symbolized by her rejection of motherhood and her brother Gwydion's assumption of it. Arianrhod initially refuses to have a child because she wants the mystery and reverence associated with the "virgin" by the New Tribes—and, for her, the only apparent difference between virgins and other women is that virgins have no children. But appearances are deceiving, as a test for virginity reveals, and Arianrhod unwillingly gives premature birth to two sons by different fathers.

The second son, fathered by Gwydion, is "mothered" by him as well, as the fetus is kept in a magical box at the foot of his bed until ready to be born. Gwydion's druidic powers associate him with science; as Charles Squire asserts, the druids "were at once the priests, the physicians, the wizards, the diviners, the theologians, the scientists, and the historians of their tribes."[18]

In Walton's presentation of Arianrhod, the motherhood myth that haunts Shelley's novel is laid to rest as a cultural rather than universal definition applied to women. Arianrhod feels "intolerably disgraced in her own mind because she had given birth" because she can no longer claim the desired virginity.[19] Furthermore, she realizes that "she had been used as a tool to bring forth a child she did not want, and whose existence was the gravest menace her reputation had yet known" (IM:196), which might be considered a foreshadowing of woman's role in patriarchy as a "tool" by which men have children. On the other hand, "doing that which made it possible for her to give birth never caused her one slightest twinge of guilt" (IM:158), which shows that Arianrhod's values do not limit women's sexual freedom.

Furthermore, even though Walton presents Gwydion's desire for active and acknowledged fatherhood as rooted in love, she clearly shows that the changes it heralds were not all intended by him. "My wish for a son has riveted the custom of marriage upon Gwynedd," he comes to realize. "Marriage, that I have never wanted, is the end that all my plans and doings shape to" (IM:242). And marriage is the end to the "Ancient Harmonies," Walton suggests, as women become trapped in its inequities. Women "are ill property, but sweet comrades. And guile is always their answer to force. You, who lay bonds on them that you do not lay on yourselves, will never get from them the honesty that we of the old time knew" (IM:350). So speaks Mâth, the ancient king of Gwynedd, as he realizes that the treachery of the women Arianrhod and Blodeuwedd results from the changes that are coming on his world, coming perhaps too early because of Gwydion's desire for a son and heir to his throne.

While Arianrhod and her other child, Dylan, will provide the mythic underpinnings for another, more recent, SF myth—Joan Vinge's *The Snow Queen* (1980)—most of the stories in the *Mabinogion* focus on men. Through their stories, however,

Walton continues to examine evidences of the shift from the Goddess beliefs of the Old Tribes to the patriarchal beliefs ushered in by the New Tribes. "The first thing that strikes one in reading the *Mabinogion*," Matthew Arnold has noted in his *Study of Celtic Literature*, "is how evidently the mediaeval story-teller is pillaging an antiquity of which he does not fully possess the secret."[20] With the advantage of perspective and further research, Walton can more completely appreciate and try to recreate that antiquity than could the earlier storyteller. At least her retelling of the stories is not distorted by the Christian references and interpolations, she assures us in her notes to *The Island of the Mighty* (IM:367).

What emerges most strongly in Walton's version is a world in the throes of cultural change, and even Mâth—especially Mâth with the unique perspective of an almost endless human life—knows that change is inevitable. "But remember if you can," he tells his nephew Gwydion, "to look back upon what was good in the past; or the future that you build may fall in worse ruin.... Woman's power wanes, but nothing ever passes except to wax again" (IM:203). Walton follows this advice in her own retelling of the tales, and her heroes are both agents of change and perservers of the "Ancient Harmonies."

As Walton's characters find themselves in the twilight of one age suffering from the birth-pangs of the next, their own human dilemmas reflect the influence of both cultures. From her female perspective and careful research, Walton ignores earlier interpretations such as Squire's 1905 study which would apply Western dualism to the characters. Squire pits the two families or tribes of the *Mabinogion*—the Children of Llyr and the Children of Dôn—against each other, and argues that "their struggles seem to symbolize in British myth that same conflict between the powers of heaven, light and life and of the sea, darkness, and death which are shadowed in Gaelic mythology in the battles between the Tuatha De Danaan and the Fomors."[21] Following this dualistic logic, he identifies the two sons of Arianrhod, Dylan and Llew Llaw Gyffes, as "representing the twin powers of darkness and light."[22] Yet the only "dark" actions Squire can attribute to Dylan are his immediate plunge into the sea after birth and his treacherous death at the hands of his uncle Govannon, neither of which reveals any evil in his character. Even Squire admits that "beautiful legends grew up around his death."[23]

Walton, on the other hand, chooses to present both the Children of Llyr and the Children of Dôn as potential heroes with strengths and weaknesses. The world she depicts is indeed one of possibilities. Even her retelling of the first branch of the *Mabinogion* in *Prince of Annwn*, which is set in Death's kingdom of Annwn, does not present us an underworld of evil as we would find in Satan's Hell. Rather Arawn, the Grey Man, is a servant of the Mothers, providing death as the cure for suffering and age which prepares the soul for its next life on the route to perfection. Even in the villain Eurosswydd, who betrays Llyr, Arawn "yet saved the little that was good enough to be used again."[24]

Annwn is not the only other world; the beautiful Rhiannon comes from the immortal Bright World to accept mortality in order to become the wife of the human Pwyll. As with most cultures who worship the Goddess in some form, the worshippers of The Mothers in Walton's retelling accept that most things are grey (note that death is the Grey Man) rather than black and white. A hero like Bran in *The Children of Llyr* can be selfish one minute (as in his ambition to make his son Caradoc the next king even though the matrilineal traditions of his tribe would be broken by the action) and selfless the next (as when he magnanimously offers the kingship of Ireland to his sister Branwen's son and looks "upon everybody with eyes of love. He thought, *It is better this way. Better not to hold a nation prisoner until I die*"—CL:145). As with the ambiguity Patricia Warrick attributes to SF myth, this is the ambiguity of a dynamic world. The myths of the Mothers, Walton's reading of the *Mabinogion* seems to suggest, did not assert absolutes of good and evil so much as they presented dynamics of human interaction. "Utopia is process," Elaine Hoffman Baruch argues in *Women in Search of Utopia*. "The fixed divisions between ideal and real, reason and madness, before and after, inside and outside, dissolve. Definitions become fluid. Either/or polarities disappear."[25]

That the darkness is not always evil is also implicit in Wal-

ton's description in the *Prince of Annwn* when Pwyll confronts
the white dogs of Arawn (a description important to remember
when he later confronts Havgan—Summer-white): "Blackness
terrifies; it is sightlessness, it blinds a man and hides his enemies; yet the darkness within the earth is warm and life giving,
the womb of the Mother, the source of all growth. But in snow
or in white-hot flame nothing can grow. Whiteness means an-
nihilation, that end from which can come no beginning."[26]

Significantly, Death in the culture ruled by the Mothers is
grey, already embodying ambivalence. A "universal characteristic of mother worship," James J. Preston confirms in his
compilation of studies on the topic, "is ambivalence. Female
deities are fraught with paradox, combining such opposites as
love and anger, trust and terror, forgiveness and vengeance."[27]
Preston does not end with this dualistic description which
seems only to intensify "good and evil" definitions even here;
rather, he concludes that "mother goddesses are symbols of
transformation, whatever shape they may take. Rebirth is the
key theme of the religious life, and mother deities are profound
reminders to us all of the primacy of the mother/infant bond—
a source both of stability and of change."[28]

So too are Walton's characters part of a world of the Mothers,
a world "both of stability and of change." In each branch of the
Mabinogion she examines the ability to survive change, for
change is the condition of this world trapped in time and space
(as the other worlds mentioned in the *Mabinogion* are not). As
Manawyddan, a character who survives many changes, asserts
in *The Song of Rhiannon*, "that is what men are sent to earth
for: to learn and to try."[29]

In contrast to the values of the Mothers are the ideas that
are entering this society with the New Tribes—values coming
from the East, the flood of patriarchal invasions that threatened to obliterate the Old Tribes and their beliefs. In *Prince of
Annwn*, Havgan embodies those Eastern values. He is presented as a new concept of death, ready to take Arawn's place.
Havgan means summer-white, recalling for us Walton's identification of whiteness with "the end from which can come no
beginning." The beautiful Havgan is announced by his herald
as Nergal, "he that of old dragged Ereshkigal, Queen of the

Eastern Dead, from her ancient throne by the hair of her terrible head." Now he is ready to take on the Mothers: "Even so will he deal with your Brenhines-y-nef, with your Modron, the Mother.... She shall learn Her place, the woman's place!" (PA:79). Ereshkigal is described by Barbara G. Walker in *The Woman's Encyclopedia of Myths and Secrets* as the "underworld counterpart of the Babylonian Goddess Ishtar," and Nergal as her consort who was "later transformed by Christian mythographers into a demonic official of hell."[30] Walton has added these names to the original version of the *Mabinogion* to clarify the conflict she has detected beneath the surface of the recorded cultural myth.

Walton again underlines the conflict of ancient and cultural myth as Taliesin sees an Eastern contrast to the power of Mâth, the Mothers' chosen King, in *The Song of Rhiannon*:

In the Eastern World there is a God men say, who loathed change and its evils as Mâth does, and wished to keep His people at peace and in the Golden Age. So He forbade them to eat of the fruit of the Tree of Knowledge, and was disobeyed. But Mâth is a wiser god than that; He will not forbid his people to do what, soon or late, they are bound to do, and so lay upon them the sin of disobedience. (SR:10)

"That is because Mâth still wears a human body," he is answered by Manawyddan, "and can speak for Himself, instead of through the mouths of priests who cannot fully understand His word" (SR:10). The god speaking for himself is central to the value of oral myth as well. If the myth is "absolute truth" then it is always "what happens" and can be seen in the present moment and in the person presently, as Eliade has said, "*imitating* the exemplary acts."[31] Clearly, then, the "absolute truth" of myth is the truth of the archetypal pattern of action—the plot or *mythos*—that it offers us.

Surfaces, consequently, can shift in the telling of the myth without altering its "absolute truth." Thus Walton can present Mâth as a living king and at the same time as the god Taliesin names him. The reader who can see *through* the surface image will not be limited as is Pryderi of the New Tribes when he argues in his need to resolve ambiguities that "Mâth is a man. A man of Illusion and Glamour, but human" (SR:10).

On the other hand, the cultural myth has come "through the mouths of priests" and is therefore not as trustworthy as the oral myth. It records "what happened" instead of "what happens"—freezes the pattern into an inflexible expression of the cultural time and place. When metaphorical surface becomes ritual, the god no longer "wears a human body" and "speak[s] for Himself." This can be seen in the perversion of the mythical white mare which Walton discusses in *Prince of Annwn*, for instance. Although Rhiannon is worshipped in the living form of the White Mare, she repudiates the ritual that would force Pwyll to have sex with a real mare to ensure the fertility of the kingship. "The mare would have been as defiled as you," Rhiannon explains. "I would take no shame in putting on her flesh to meet any stallion in your fields, for all that lives and breathes in Dyved is part of Me. But man and mare—hah!" (PA:38). She recognizes in this ritual the deterioration of the druidic line as the culture is changing: "Only your druids of the New Tribes could have devised such sacrilege, they who reject the Ancient Harmonies" (PA:39). Yet she doesn't blame the new druids only: "Even among the true druids, those of the Old Tribes, wise men grow few" (PA:39). Change is inevitable.

Finally, however, change will reinstate the values of ancient myth as well, Walton reminds us, and the pain and process of change will have taught humanity much. The Mothers provided a world in tune with nature, accepting the ambiguities of life, maintaining a community of all living things. "It is only in man that consciousness burns," Gwydion tells his son (IM:212). And it is through that consciousness that Gwydion sees the evolution of man finally returning to what the Mothers have always taught, but with a new awareness: "But before we were conscious only of our own species; that was all we could grasp of the Whole. And when we recover that wider consciousness it too will have widened; and we shall be one with all species, and know all creatures alike for our fellow beings" (IM:212).

Retelling these tales of the past, Walton has found in them a metaphor for present consciousness of a culture in transition and the promise of a future consciousness which builds on the values of ancient myth to achieve a unity of all life. Perhaps the twilight of one age is speaking to the twilight of another, reminding us of old values which are about to be reinstated. "Why this new interest in mother worship, both at the popular level and among scholars?" Preston has asked. "Could it be that we have come to realize the limits of Western science, particularly when it comes to understanding the human imagination? A profound exercise of the imagination is at the root of the mother goddess phenomenon, creating a multitude of forms to express something mysterious at the heart of human experience."[32]

For Walton, making the old stories new is the way to that mysterious "truth of the human heart." "Doubtless mediaeval audiences and readers already knew what was coming, and cared only for the way in which the old tale was retold," Walton reminds us (PA:178). Fortunately for us, the storyteller has not been lost: as Manawyddan sang to Caswallon in *The Song of Rhiannon* and Gwydion sang to Arianrhod in *The Island of the Mighty*, so Walton sings to us the songs that are always being made new.

As Walton has retold the stories of the *Mabinogion* from a female perspective—from within a world where woman's power, although waning, still held its own—Marion Zimmer Bradley has added to that perspective a focus on the women characters in the later legends of King Arthur and Camelot in *The Mists of Avalon*. Thus, while Arthur and Lancelet are still followed from birth to death, this is the story of Arthur's sister Morgaine; and when in Camelot and elsewhere, we sit and travel with the women—which would mean, in earlier versions of these tales, that we would miss the "important action" of battle and quest. While we do learn "what happened" in the realm of male action, Bradley's story clearly gives this secondary importance.

Center stage in *The Mists of Avalon* instead is the struggle between the followers of the Goddess, whose priestesses inhabit the misty and mystical Avalon, and the followers of the Christianity represented by the Bishop Patricius—who happens to be the same St. Patrick who drove the snakes out of Ireland. Those snakes turn out to be symbolic of the Druids, known as the "serpents of wisdom" to their followers.

As a backdrop to this metaphorical action Bradley has carefully preserved the ties between the Arthur of legend—and perhaps history as well—and the Arthur who is a descendant of the myths that predate Christianity. Arthur is originally named Gwydion, as is his son Mordred, and the patterns of that tale which are repeated in this later version are carefully traced for us, echoing not only the Welsh tale we find in Walton but also the Gaelic version that is central to Irish myth. Indeed, Bradley's Arthur is given the round table "Tara" by Gwynwhyfar's father, who had gained it himself from the battles he fought in Ireland.[33] Furthermore, his Knights of the Round Table—called his Companions by Bradley—seem to come from the legends of Finn's Fenians in the third Gaelic cycle of myth, as Squire points out while noting further parallels between the stories of Arthur, Gwynhwyfar, and Mordred and those of Finn, Grainne and Diarmit.[34] As if to remind the reader of these parallels, Bradley not only names Arthur's mother Igraine but even gives her the nickname of Grainné.

Still, the parallels to the Welsh Gwydion are more definitive of the mythological significance of Bradley's Arthur, a judgment with which Squire agrees, pointing out that the tales of Gwydion and Arianrhod are adapted to Arthur, showing "an almost exact correspondence in everything but name."[35] As this earlier brother and sister produce the twins of light and darkness, Squire argues further, so too do we find a new Llew Llaw Gyffes called "Gwalchmei, that is, the 'Falcon of May,' " and "the new Dylan is Medrawt, at once Arthur's son and Gwalchmei's brother, and the bitterest enemy of both."[36] Although Squire originally identifies Gwalchmei with Sir Gawaine, he also shows that Sir Galahad fills this role.[37] Bradley offers both figures, with Gawaine the foster-brother of Mordred and Galahad the son of Elaine and Lancelet who is "adopted" by Arthur as heir to the throne and thus brother and competitor of Mordred. That Galahad embodies the forces of light is clear in his—and only his—successful quest for the Holy Grail.

Again, however, this reexamination of myth from the female perspective doesn't allow us to pit forces of light so simply against forces of darkness. *The Mists of Avalon* portrays the amalgamation of old and new religions rather than the triumph of Christian light over pagan darkness. Morgaine must learn that, while the historical moment denies the existence of Avalon and constructs the abbey of Glastonbury on the very same spot, and while this denial pushes Avalon into the mists—into an existence on another plane only, yet the Goddess herself remains in the world. Her Holy Regalia of the sword, the cup, and the dish serve Arthur in his role as the first Christian king of Britain even though they were given to him originally in his role as King Stag as a reaffirmation of the old religion. The surface reality can shift without displacing the Goddess: the cup now becomes the Holy Grail, the symbol of spiritual quest for the British people. The miracle in which these sacred items reveal themselves is still a manifestation of the Goddess and Her Holy Cauldron to most of the people; only afterward is it defined by the bishop as the Holy Grail from Christ's Last Supper. The form is unimportant: "Galahad was white, overawed. Did he see it as the cup of life or as the holy chalice of Christ? Did it matter?" (p. 771).

This is not to say that, since all gods are one God, the religious form that faith takes is irrelevant. Both Taliesin and Kevin the Harper, as the latter succeeds the former in the position of High Druid or Merlin, realize that the changes wrought by Christianity are far-reaching. As the Merlin Taliesin explains to Igraine, Christianity demands its followers to reject any other belief as of the devil, "And as men believe, so their world goes. And so the worlds which once were one are drifting apart" (p. 13).

This inability to coexist with other faiths has been a characteristic of the patriarchal monotheistic Christian, Jewish and Moslem faiths, all of which share the same beginnings. That rejection has, as Bradley suggests, changed our perception of the world. Linguistically, for instance, as Stone has explained,

Though heathen literally means from the heath, as pagan is derived from the Latin *paganus*, a country person—both heathen and pagan are defined by Webster as *other* than Christian, Jew, or Mohammedan. It is in this way that the distinction between how we are to perceive the religious beliefs of those whose sacred accounts are classified as mythology, and those whose are to be considered as religious truth, is semantically structured.[38]

Affording myth the same respect we give religious truth helps us avoid this bias and expand our perception.

Since the Merlin must function in the world of history while the priestesses of Avalon can slip in and out of time and space, it is Taliesin and Kevin who first recognize and accept the changes that are coming. These males that serve the Goddess illustrate that the ancient myths were not exclusive or hierarchical; the role of the druid may be different but is at least as important as that of the priestess. If the priestess embodies the Goddess and with the help of Her "Sight" communicates Her wisdom, the Merlin acts upon that wisdom in the world. Viviane, the Lady of the Lake, and her chosen successor Morgaine resist what they see as the desecration of the symbols of Goddess worship, but the Merlin knows that to keep them in the world even as part of the Christian ritual will preserve a link between the drifting worlds for the people—those pagans and heathens whose faith can survive the shifting surface of religions.

To this goal Kevin is willing to risk his life by "betraying" the priestesses. He gives the Holy Regalia to the bishop, and Morgaine has him put to death for the sacrilege. Even a priestess is human; her gift of "Sight" can not answer the unanswerable questions of divine purpose. In an attempt to explain his motives, Kevin tells Morgaine that "even if Avalon must perish, I felt it right that the holy things should be sent forth into the world in the service of the Divine, by whatever name God or the Gods may be called" (p. 800).

Yet Kevin's vision too is human and thus limited. Avalon will not perish. Its reality will not be our reality, but those who seek it will perceive it, as does Sir Galahad when he reaches between the worlds to grasp the Holy Grail. His vision frees him from this life; his goodness carries him into worlds beyond time and space as we know it. If our perceptions could be freed from the narrowness of priests and the contemporary rejection of other truths, Bradley seems to suggest, we too could see through the mists that separate us from the wisdom of Avalon.

Bradley attributes continuing existence not only to Avalon but also to other earlier inhabitants of Britain within the scope of her tale. All are accessible to those who are themselves open to possibility, as contemporary feminists like Carol Pearson would agree. "We each have the potential to 'step off the edge' and fall into ourselves and into an alternative utopian world by moving outside of concepts of linear time and causality into the elliptical present of infinite potentiality," Pearson asserts.[39] In *The Mists of Avalon*, the queen of the fairies tells Morgaine that "my kind know neither Gods nor Goddesses, but only the breast of our mother who is beneath our feet and above our heads, from whom we come and to whom we go when our time is ended" (p. 225). Morgaine herself tells Nimue about the Old People, who haunt the hills and forests, avoiding villages and farms because they "cannot bear to see the earth, who is their mother, raped by the plow and forced to bear" (p. 631). For the fairies and the Old People, the realities of Arthur's time are not theirs; yet some of the country folk of Arthur's time accept them as real, setting food out for them and remembering the rituals that can protect one from being carried to the plane of the fairies. The old religions comfortably coexist; only the new religion that comes to power with Arthur's reign will relegate all other concepts of reality to nothingness or condemn them as manifestations of the works of the Devil.

In the historic moment of Camelot, Tribesman and Christian clash in the throes of cultural change. The influence of the Celts, the Saxons, the Romans, and the intolerant Christianity of the Bishop Patricius must come together to offer a pattern for Britain's future. It is Arthur—or the king as servant of his people that Arthur represents—who embodies their beliefs and their need for rebirth. It is he who must resolve the internal and external conflicts of his people on a human and individual level. In her vision of an earlier life on Atlantis, Igraine recognizes and accepts her role as mother of this returning hero (p. 59), and the legend that Arthur too will return finds its echo for her in the story of Christ's birth, death, and resurrection.

Bradley has chosen, as did the early Welsh tales, to examine the internal rather than the external struggles of Arthur. "Conqueror he is, but his conquests are not in any land known to geographers," Squire says of the Arthur in these twelfth-century tales, in which the storyteller already "seems to be stretching out his hands to gather in the dying traditions of a very remote past."[40] Bradley too seeks that past, and in the process she helps us see through the intervening cultural layers which obscure it. In the human struggle she emphasizes the Welsh parallels of Morgaine to Arianrhod, of Gwynhwyfar to Blodeuwedd, of Arthur to Gwydion, of Mordred and Galahad to Dylan and Llew Llaw Gyffes, and of Drustan and Isotta to Grainne and Diarmid. Behind Arthur stands "Llyr and the children of Da'ana" (p. 758); behind Morgaine stands Rhiannon as the goddess accepting the limitations of humanity out of love for a mortal.[41] Morgaine, like Merlin, is really a title— "not a name, but the title of a priestess, meaning no more than 'woman come from the sea,' in a religion even the Merlin of Britain would have found a legend and the shadow of a legend" (p. 56).

Morgaine parallels Rhiannon by acting out her legend with Arthur, a pattern which her mother and Uther Pendragon before her and Nimue and Kevin after her also act out. The legend is revealed to Igraine in her vision of Atlantis, in which the priest of the serpents and the priestess of the Old Temple commit themselves to human rebirth for love of each other and of the land of Britain, upon which they had established a new temple of a ring of stones after the destruction of Atlantis (p. 59). In that earlier religion that Bradley recreates can be found the prototypes for Arianrhod and for Arthur as well. Arianrhod is her heavenly self, the constellation in the north of the "Wheel of Birth and Death and Rebirth" (p. 59); while the other constellation of Orion, the "Greater-than-Gods" (p. 57) who "strode across the sky, the sword hanging from his belt" (p. 59), is the hero who will be Arthur in Morgaine's time, in this reincarnation.[42] Mother, sister, and lover to him, Morgaine will be his manifestation of the Goddess.

Morgaine is also the Goddess as maiden, mother, and death crone/wise woman as her story unfolds in Bradley's version. "*I have called on the Goddess and found her within myself*" (p. 803), she realizes. The Goddess can also be seen in the "trinity" of Igraine, Morgaine, and Viviane (p. 23). Morgaine does not recognize, however, that the wise maiden mother of Christ will be yet another face of the Goddess.

Bradley even incorporates Greek myths to suggest the "absolute truth" that can be found when we find the pattern of "what happens" in these tales. Thus Morgaine is brought back to life like Eurydice when Kevin sings to her of Orfeo after she has given up (p. 755). Earlier, Orion in Igraine's vision is also recognized as Prometheus, who had given humanity a mixed blessing as the bringer of the light; "Great good came of that gift of fire, but great evil too, for man learned misuse and wickedness..." (p. 57). That the light of Christianity which Arthur will win for Britain can also be misused is clear when Morgaine realizes that "my quarrel was never with the Christ, but with his foolish and narrow priests who mistook their own narrowness for his" (p. 758). Again we are warned against the cultural myth which is spread by priests when the god no longer "wears a human body." The ancient myth is locked into the narrowness of time and place, and the archetypal pattern of ancient myth can be perverted, obscured, or even obliterated in the straitjacket of an inflexible retelling of the myth.

Being human, Morgaine must come to recognize her own narrowness and see the Goddess embodied in the Virgin Mary for the Christians who seek Her. As the symbols of the Goddess are preserved in the cup or cauldron now sought as the Holy Grail, so too does Morgaine feel the power emanating from the statue of Brigid, an Irish form of the Goddess who has now been designated a Christian saint.

Uncovering legend within legend, ancient myth within cultural myth, Bradley retells the Arthurian story to let the face of the Goddess be seen again and to return women to their equally important role in human life despite the denigration of that role historically and spiritually in the centuries since Arthur. Morgaine is Queen of North Wales and Cornwall as well as priestess of Avalon, and under the old religion women as well as men concerned themselves with both historical and spiritual reality.

Arthur offers similar power to his queen Gwynhwyfar, but this "unnatural woman" is a product of the convent and the guidance of Christian priests. She rejects his offer with as much fear as she rejects the world of nature, seeking always to have thick, protective walls around her. It is in this Christian woman, incidentally, that we again encounter that loyalty to appearances—to the surface reality—that denies what lies below. Thus she can love Lancelet throughout her married life with Arthur as long as the appearance of marital fidelity is maintained. Only when the facade is torn away by Mordred does she confront her own duplicity, and even then she chooses to maintain the lie. Maintaining the appearance of false accusation, she commits herself to a convent for the rest of her life. Another indication of her shallowness is her rejection of Kevin the Harper on the basis of his deformity. She even accuses him of causing her miscarriage by frightening her, and suggests to Nimue that God's own perfection means that anything ugly must come from the Devil (p. 782).

Tied to the world of appearances, Christianity seems inevitably to be tied as well to hypocrisy and artificiality. Like Blodeuwedd in the *Mabinogion*, Gwynhwyfar is told whom to love and is considered sinful if she should love anyone else. In the world of the older religion women chose their lovers and descent was matrilineal; patriarchy demands sexual confinement of potential mothers to insure patrilineal descent. In Walton's works, Arianrhod felt no guilt even about her incestuous love for Gwydion, but already the New Tribes were introducing the concepts of fatherhood and marriage. By the time of Camelot, Morgaine and Arthur both feel the social condemnation of their incest, reflecting in their own attitudes that the wave of change is inevitable. Actually, the protected, devious, and beautiful Gwynhwyfar shows what women must become to survive in the new age.

While some women may be blessed with beauty, all humans are imperfect in some way, as each of the characters must learn in *The Mists of Avalon*. The older religion accepts human limitations even in its druids and priestesses, who only take on the "Glamour" and the "Sight" of the Goddess when She grants them and who could turn out to be as destructive as do Mordred and Morgause. "Everywhere sacred mother figures are associated with the advent and resolution of human problems," Preston explains;[43] in this religion the Goddess still "wears a human body" and commits Herself through love to the limitations of human life in time and space.

The ancient myth—the truth of "what happens"—seems closer to the surface in the older religion, and even if it has been obscured, these writers are renewing our awareness that it cannot be destroyed as can the history of "what has happened." "History does not exist," Pearson asserts; "there are only people, and people can always choose to change."[44] When Mordred tells Niniane that both Arthur and the Goddess will be eliminated by "time and change" (p. 65), he is only half right. "Mother worship remains vital today as a form of religious experience, even in highly secularized societies," Preston assures us. "We know that the most popular pilgrimage shrines in Christianity are those devoted to Mary, and numerous Marian shrines have been established throughout the world in recent years."[45] "Sometimes when you are alone with the Holy Mother, She can make things clear to you," a young novice at Glastonbury tells Morgaine, speaking of the chapel of the Virgin (p. 276); and Morgaine finds her Goddess there as well, ready to "make things clear."

Using the same heritage of pre-Christian and Celtic myth in their fantastic literature, Moyra Caldecott and Julian May expand both time and space to retell the old stories with new insights. Setting her Sacred Stones trilogy perhaps on the very ring of stones that will later emerge as the temple of the druids in *The Mists of Avalon*, Caldecott traces a path through pre-Roman Britain on the surface and "beyond the image to the Reality" in the metaphorical possibilities of her Britain.[46]

In quite another fashion, Julian May's tetralogy, especially the first two volumes—*The Many-Colored Land* and *The Golden Torc*—finds in our future a route even further back to the Rhône Valley of France in the Pleistocene era, where she uncovers the roots of Celtic myth in an intermingling of space and time travelers. May explains myth as early history—on an intergalactic scale spanning millions of years. Her treatment of "mythic situations as historical material" fits Darko Suvin's discussion of the employment of SF for demystification: "extracted from a mythological paradigm and fitted into an SF one, what results is perfectly legitimate, often first-class SF."[47]

Yet why would we want to "demystify" myth? The simultaneous reality of history and myth is the basis of all Mysteries, such as transubstantiation, for instance. Caldecott offers a spiritual quest which seeks the inner truths of druidic tradition, while May provides an imaginative explosion of possibilities to explain surface reality preserved in Celtic myth. Unfortunately, instead of uniting the realities of myth and history as do our other writers, each sacrifices one for the other, letting the worlds drift even further apart.

In her Sacred Stones trilogy, Caldecott offers only the bare stones of pre-Roman civilization in Britain, with the people living in separate and often disparate villages and subject to violent incursions from hostile strangers. Many villages are united by sharing a common faith, with a druid serving each in its circle of sacred stones and with a remote Temple of the Sun training, supplying, and connecting the priests. Much less attention is spent making this surface convincing than is concerned with other levels of reality. Yet those levels are sought by Kyla, who is destined for the priesthood, and by a handful of other sensitive individuals outside the priesthood precisely because they believe that "there should not be one life for the priest and another for the ordinary person" (TS:131).

At fourteen, Kyla begins recognizing her telepathic and "spirit-travelling" powers when their village druid Maal seeks her help. In *The Tall Stones* she and her brother Karne gain knowledge of other worlds of awareness as they help Maal prepare for his death and struggle against the false priest Wardyke who wants to take over the village and change its peaceful patterns of life. In *The Temple of the Sun* Karne and his pregnant wife Fern accompany Kyla to the Temple, where she will receive the training of a supreme priest—a Lord of the Sun— and will meet and marry Lord Khu-ren, who already holds that rank. The final volume of the trilogy, *Shadow on the Stones*, finds Kyla and Khu-ren helping Karne and his son Isar stop the invasion and violent religious domination of the followers of the dark god Groth.

Caldecott's series would have benefited as fiction from character, setting, and plot development. In a thinly disguised discussion of spiritual quest, she does try to offer historical

evidence of druidic worship to tie together much of the symbolism of the series, however. The holy circle of stones in which
early Britons worshipped and its relationship to cosmic align-
ments provide the setting for religious explorations. Furthermore, in Fern can be seen one more face of the Goddess. Attuned
to living things, Fern counsels her son Isar to reach her through
the rowan-tree, which will protect and strengthen him. Graves
has noted that this tree, whose other name of "Quickbeam"
means the "tree of life," had oracular uses and was often
planted "in the neighborhood of ancient stone circles."[48] Even
Fern's name, besides its natural connotations in current usage,
echoes the Gaelic *faern* or alder, which is "the tree of fire" whose
"buds are set in a spiral."[49] In *The Tall Stones* Wardyke sets
the woods and home of Fern on fire, and throughout the series
the symbol of the spiral (which, Robert Graves tells us, is "ante-
diluvian: the earliest Sumerian shrines are 'ghost-houses,' like
those used in Uganda, and are flanked by spiral posts"[50]) is as
central as that of the concentric circles symbolizing the cycles
of birth and death and rebirth. The spiral adds the gradual
progress of the inner or Real self toward enlightenment
through its human reincarnations.

Caldecott's priests fit the description of druids by Thomas
Bulfinch as moral teachers who made no images but taught

the existence of one god, to whom they gave the name "Be'al," which
Celtic antiquaries tell us means "the life of everything" or "the source
of all beings," and which seems to have affinity with the Phoenician
Baal. What renders this affinity more striking is that the Druids as
well as the Phoenicians identified this, their supreme deity, with the
Sun.[51]

Bulfinch suggests as well that the relationship between the
priest and the people of the tribes was "closely analogous to
that in which the Brahmans of India, the Magi of Persia, and
the priests of the Egyptians stood to the people respectively by
whom they were revered."[52] Caldecott renders these connections on a spiritual plane; in her trilogy, the Lords of the Sun
come from India, from Egypt, from throughout the world in
their spiritual essences when needed by other priests. To save

her village from Wardyke, Kyra has to call them together even before she is trained as a priest, and later she becomes one of them. The essence of Caldecott's trilogy, therefore, is an examination of the relationship between the individual and "the source of all beings." "We are parts of a Whole and nothing is separate," Maal tells Kyra (TS:114). Yet he further assures her that the individual has free will:

Our ability to choose, to make decisions, is crucial to our development in all the different levels of existence through which we are journeying. When we reach the Source of Light and Consciousness, we will no longer see bits and pieces among which we have to choose, but will see the whole of a magnificent pattern in which everything fits together in harmony. (TS:141)

It is a harmony with the stones that allows the priest to draw on their power in the sacred circle, a harmony with plants that makes Fern an excellent gardener. In the human community, too, a harmony is developed within each village as newcomers are accepted and even as the priest designates the piece of land on which they should live to maintain the balance.of the community. Wardyke and the Strangers who follow him disrupt this harmony in *The Tall Stones*; the fear and despair engendered by the followers of Groth destroy it in *The Shadow of the Stones*. While the priests are taught to explore the realities within their inner levels of consciousness and then within the unities of the universe, the village priests are expected also to maintain the unities within their communities.

The power generated by existence itself is not dualistic: "nothing is good or evil in itself," Maal assures Kyra. "It is the way it is used that makes it good or evil.... It is in *us*, in the inner drive we call the *will*, in the key to action we call *motive*" (TS:130–31). Nor does he pit the body against the spirit, because "spirit and matter are part of the same Whole: different manifestations of the same God. The same Source. Each develops because of the other, not in spite of the other" (TS:69).

Not only do Caldecott's priests explore themselves and their universe, expanding through inner and outer space to encompass the Whole; they also expand through time, as they recall past lives and plan for future ones. Thus Maal is concerned that his burial mound will be in alignment with the lines of power in the earth and from the stones of the sacred circle so that he can best be prepared to influence his next reincarnation. Thus, in *The Temple of the Sun*, Kyra and Karne must learn that their children Isar and Deva have met in previous lives and have relationships and problems still to be resolved. Here we also meet Panora, who is "caught between two worlds"—part human and part spirit.

In the druids Caldecott has traced a spiritual life that could as easily stand as an exploration of Hindu philosophy today. Untrammeled by time or place, their ancient myth is also unrecorded, which has attracted Khu-ren to them from his native Egypt:

> Her people did not capture Truth in words, paint it on papyrus or hammer it on the rocks until it was so fixed and dead, it had nothing of itself left.
> Truth for them was caught in flight, glancing from mind to mind. Always set free again. Never caged.
> All their hidden resources of spirit were used to gain wisdom, and when a Truth was accepted, it was accepted because it had been *experienced*, not because it was written down.[53]

Uniting the surface Reality to all the other worlds—and perceptions of the world—through time and space, her priests offer an existence of ecological balance, of communal identity, and of greatly expanded possibilities of communication within the self, between the self and others, and between the self and the universe—all being part of the same Whole. These values of ecology, community, and communication will provide the balance for many of the worlds within women which we will explore. Caldecott's trilogy stands as a spiritual quest which connects ancient wisdom with future possibilities.

May, conversely, finds in past myths the future manifestations of our present limitations of perception. It is significant that those who choose the one-way trip to her Pleistocene adventure are the misfits of a utopic future. That this future world is much closer to those values mentioned above is implied with our first description of it in the Prologue to *The Many-Colored Land*: "We humans gave up a few cultural fripperies and gained energy sufficiency and unlimited lebensraum and membership in a galactic civilization! Now that we don't have to waste time and lives in mere survival, there'll be no holding humanity back!"[54] In this future the ecological balance is universal, the community is galactic, and communication can also reach the level through metapsychology—as it once had for Elizabeth Orme—of "the beautiful Unity, the synergy, the exultant bridging from world to world, the never-afraid warmth of companion souls, the joy of leading child-metas to full operancy" (MCL:41).

However, such unity is not attractive to everyone. Theo Guderian himself, inventor of the device which sent people back to the Pleistocene Era to Exile, regrets the sacrifice of "our diverse languages, many of our social philosophies and religious dogmata, our so-called unproductive lifestyles . . . our very human sovereignty, laughable though its loss must seem to the ancient intellects of the Galactic Milieu" (MCL:18). Many choose the trip back, accepting Guderian's image of Exile as "a golden time, just before the dawn of rational humankind. A time of benevolent climate and flourishing plant and animal life. A vintage time, unspoiled and tranquil" (MCL:19).

Madame Guderian, however, provides another view for the women who were required to renounce childbearing as a condition of Exile:

But you must accept that this world you seek to enter is not one of life. It is a refuge of misfits, a death surrogate, a rejection of normal human destiny. Ainsi, if you pass into this Exile, the consequences must rest upon you alone. If life's force is still urgent within you, then you should remain here. Only those who are bereaved of all joy in this present world may take refuge in the shadows of the past. (MCL:57)

Not surprisingly, many women changed their minds after this speech, so that four times as many men actually made the trip as women. The women who choose to go among the eight travelers that the series will follow are Elizabeth, who does feel dead without her former communication abilities; Amerie the nun; and the fiercely independent Felice, a Virgin huntress, as Claude recognizes when he hails her as "Diana" (MCL:228).

When they journey into their past, the travelers are surprised to find it populated with aliens from another galaxy. Stranded on Earth by the destruction of their Ship, they have developed a realm of castles and conquest in which the unsuspecting travelers have been cast as slaves, subjected by the psychic powers of the aliens and by the torcs which are bound around their necks.

Clearly prototypes of the golden crescents worn by priests and priestesses in Celtic myths, the golden torcs convey and identify power. They also alert us that May's use of myth will be as a treasury of story and symbol which she can employ. In *The Tall Stones*, Maal had warned Kyla of the danger of starting to believe in the symbol rather than the truth it represents and "worshipping the image": "But when the symbol becomes downgraded into an image of a god that is taken literally, all kinds of misinterpretations of the symbolism can occur" (TS:203). Similarly, in this "death surrogate" of the past, myth is dead and the images are living, as May offers the tall, blond Tanu exotic race as an early version of the Children of Dôn. The small, sometimes deformed exotics called the Firvulag represent the "Fir Bolgs," the three tribes called the "dark Iberians" by the Gaelic "children of light" who worshiped the Children of Dôn (known in Gaelic myth as the Tuatha De Danann).[55] Names of individual exotics further this identification, as we hear of Ayfa ("leader of the Warrior Ogresses"[56]) and Skathe and recall the legendary Celtic queens Aife and Scathach, who were "constantly at war."[57]

Because of this focus on inventing an historical ancestry for Celtic myth, May laces her series with many of the names, the symbols, and the actions recounted in these myths. She has done her research well, some of which she shares with the reader in her discussions of her sources in the appendix to *The Many-Colored Land*. Here she announces her borrowings from folklore, mythology, and fairy tales not only to create the two exotic races but also to provide patterns for the human characters: "the archetypal human characters Aiken Drum, Felice Landry, and Mercy Lamballe are also out of Celtica, via Jung and Joseph Campbell, among others" (MCL:381).

However, as cultural myth becomes historical fantasy, the timeless truths are replaced by the perceived reality of the author's time and place. May offers almost nonstop adventure in her series, but her Tanu and Firvulag rob the myths themselves of their key to "what happens" by being mired in our political, psychological, and scientific understanding of human interaction— "via Jung and Joseph Campbell." Narrowing rather than expanding the possibilities of myth, May deserves the criticism from Baird Searles that "even the divine Tanu are a little too raunchily human at times."[58] Still, these echoes from myth entice us, enriching the worlds her imagination can create and reminding us once more of the insights Jung and Campbell *have* gained through their appreciation of myth. The cultural complexities that May gives her Pleistocene exotics, including the other refugees from the future who make an appearance in *The Nonborn King* and threaten to dominate the saga in *The Adversary*, can tell us much about where and who we are even if they offer little or no clue to what we could be. They certainly do not offer actions we would choose to imitate, however, trapped as they are in a time and space neither of their own heritage nor of their own choice.

While we are revisiting our prehistoric roots, we should include the evolution of myth incorporated into Jean Auel's Earth's Children saga as well. Again we are thrust back to beginnings, although the dark and fair races we encounter are decidedly earthbound and primitive. Yet Ayla, Auel's protagonist in both *The Clan of the Cave Bear* and *The Valley of Horses*, is concerned with spiritual as well as physical evolution. As a tall, fair orphan raised by the short, dark Clan people, Ayla offers the perceptions of the outsider freshly perceiving physical and psychological differences between herself and her adopted society. Later she will find her own people, the Others, who share her physical and psychological characteristics but not her social training. Consequently, her perspective remains both detached because of her differences and committed because of her need to belong somewhere. Through her the reader can experience freshly the contrasting cultures.

The Clan is the more primitive society, dependent on conscious racial memory for their knowledge. While their totemic faith is basically patriarchal, their spiritual leader Creb is assisted by a medicine woman, Iza. Creb also finds in his memories of the far past powerful women who talked to spirits. "The spirits approved then, but they were different spirits, ancient spirits, and not the spirits of totems," he explains.[59] So even in this most primitive society Auel detects an even more ancient myth behind the myths of the Clan, a story of women hunting beside the men and conducting their own ceremonies, of female spirits of the wind (Ooooha), the rain (Zheena), and the mists (Eesha) who make it possible for Ayla at least once to be considered the equal of the men of the Clan (CB:301).

Also in the totemic Clan can be found the values of community, ecology, and communication. In their veneration of the cave bear, they become "aware of their relationship with all life on the earth, and the reverence it fostered even for the animals they killed and consumed formed the basis of the spiritual kinship with their totems" (CB:29). And their communal unity comes from the unique communication they share: "They could recall their racial memory, their own evolution. And when they reached back far enough, they could merge that memory that was identical for all and join their minds, telepathically" (CB:29).

Still, the time of the Clan is passing. A doomed level of humanity, they are blocked from further evolution by their inability to learn what they cannot remember. Only in Ayla's son Durc and the girl Ura who was probably fathered by a man of the Others will their heritage survive.

While Durc preserves the past of the Clan for Ayla, by the Others he would be considered an "abomination"—the sign that she had mated with a beast. The Others do not recognize the humanity of the Clan, so mixed children were seen as "polluted mixtures of spirits, an evil let loose upon the land that even the Mother, the creator of all life, abhorred. And the women who bore them, untouchable."[60] Even here we see the roots of

Shelley's mythmaking in *Frankenstein* as human society rejects the alien and creates a monster.

Yet we can learn to perceive reality differently, and Jondalar of the Others learns to accept the Clan as humans when Ayla explains to him their totemic faith. "Only humans thought about where they came from and where they were going after this life," Jondalar realizes, and it is their capacity for mythmaking which changes his attitude toward the "flatheads" (VH:425). As human consciousness grows, so too does the need to understand the reality in which we exist and to express that understanding in stories. From the fresh perspective offered by Ayla's stories even more than from the mixed genes of Durc comes a blending of cultural heritage.

The Others have not been locked in by nature to their own memories. Like Ayla, they can learn and grow, and their myths reflect this freedom more than do the protective totems of the Clan. In dreams and visions, Jondalar is encouraged to grow and to choose, as he senses when he has the vision of the wavering image of a woman's reflection in a pond of rippling water: "He sensed a divergence, a path splitting, a choice, and he had no one to guide him.... The Earth Mother was leaving Her children to find their own way, to carve out their own lives, to pay the consequences of their own actions—to come of age.... She had passed on her parting Gift, her Gift of Knowledge." (VH:455)

As each grows individually, learning through Journeys and the development of unique Gifts, each "serves the Mother" through those skills. But "Those Who Serve the Mother" with their lives as holy ones are given gifts by Her to become intercessors for their community. In return, they "give up their own identity and take on the identity of the people for whom they intercede" (VH:479).

Whether the spirits and priests are male or female, these early stories of the spirit world as Auel perceives it find their deepest roots in the Mother and offer images of legend and dream to help humanity cope with and relate to the known and the unknown worlds around us. Yet protection is not enough, as can be seen in the doomed Clan; the flexibility of growth and change must be possible, and knowledge is essential in order to make choices. As Jondalar learns through Ayla, Auel's own mythmaking sets the pattern for other breaks from tradition and encourages the inquiring mind to go beyond the memory of what happened to the visions and dreams of what happens—beyond logic to metaphor.

Doris Lessing too ventures back to our earliest beginnings on the planet to initiate her Canopus in Argos: Archives series with the story of our broken planet in *Shikasta*. In her Canopean universe, however, we aren't left to struggle through those beginnings alone. Drawing mostly on Judeo-Christian tradition but also reflecting extensive influence from other sacred narratives and myths, *Shikasta* offers a history of our world which relentlessly uncovers an original sin (embodied in the "Degenerative Disease") which alienates us not only from the superior Canopeans but also from our own potential. On a universal scale, Shikasta is small potatoes in the struggle between the galactic empires of Canopus and Puttiora; on a Canopean scale, human life spans are much too brief to allow for adequate growth. Certainly the absolute truth of myth will not be affected by what happens to one small planet which could easily be wiped out instantaneously by a dis-aster—a fault in the stars—even before it can destroy itself through internal strife. SOWF—the Substance of We Feeling which flows to each planet of the Canopean system providing the supportive strength and understanding so necessary for survival—will continue to flow; less enlightened empires will continue to struggle against even that goodness.

It is only the love Johor and other Canopeans feel for the potential of Shikasta that gives us this opportunity to see ourselves from their perspective. To achieve this perspective, Lessing combines a variety of documents on Shikasta to create what Sharon Spencer calls an "architectonic" novel which offers a "true" picture of our history. As Spencer explains, the structural goal of such a novel is

the evocation or the illusion of a spatial entity, either representational or abstract, constructed from prose fragments of diverse types and lengths and arranged by means of the principle of juxtaposition so as to include a comprehensive view of the book's subject. The "truth" of the total vision of such a novel is a composite truth obtained from the reader's apprehension of a great many relationships among the fragments that make up the book's totality.[61]

The various understandings of Shikasta which offer themselves individually in each of the fragments of the novel are also encased in Lessing's structural fabulation. In her cosmology, the empires governed from the systems around Canopus and Sirius, the two brightest stars in our Southern skies, both take an active part in the growth and development of Shikasta. Sirius, allied to but a lesser power than Canopus, wields political powers that make it seem to be an extension of the possibilities of our own slowly evolving space program. Canopean power is on another level, united by the flow of SOWF and by existence which can manifest itself in any physical form when and if it chooses. Opposed to these united powers is the weaker empire of Puttiora, in which is included the seemingly unimportant planet Shammat. Shammat, however, which thrives on the emanations generated by the Degenerative Disease, is more powerful than the unsuspecting Canopeans could imagine.

Thus, Lessing offers both a physical and a psychic cosmology. The star systems of Canopus, Sirius, and Puttiora share the physical galaxy, while on another plane the SOWF generated by the Canopean system is blocked by the emanations from the Degenerative Disease abetted and desired by Shammat. Between Canopus and Shammat is waged that eternal struggle between good and evil, revealing that on this plane at least Lessing's is a dualistic universe. In such a universe, even the knowledge of the Mother is insufficient; the weak must be protected from the strong. Lessing's universal Necessity demands obedience to keep the SOWF flowing; the Degenerative Disease is individuality—the all-too-human tendency to put the needs of the self before the needs of the community.

This psychic dualism is what separates Lessing's SF myth from most of the other myths by women which we will encounter. Within its boundaries, Lessing still affirms the ideals of communication, community, and ecological—or universal—balance. Furthermore, even Canopeans must bow to the laws of the physical universe because, as the myth of Arianrhod affirmed as well, the real Gods are the stars. In her basically naturalistic universe, Lessing knows that "when the Gods explode, or err, or dissolve into flying clouds of gas, or shrink, or expand, or whatever else their fates might demand, then the minuscule items of their substance may in their small ways express—not protest, which of course is inappropriate to their station in life—but an acknowledgement of the existence of irony.... "[62]

These dis-asters are the unanswerable questions of our perceivable universe; nor can we ask why Shammat—the embodiment of evil—should exist. It *does* exist in Lessing's universe; we should be glad that Canopus exists as well. As did the dark Romantics, as did Herman Melville in *Billy Budd*, Lessing accepts a "depravity according to nature." Consequently, in her universe, we *can* tell the heroes from the villains. Humanity is their pawn; yet, true to the Judaic world upon which she patterns this, humanity also has the privilege of suffering because of this struggle over which it has no control.

If enough SOWF comes through to guide us, however, we would be able to live in tune with the Necessity. Such is the nature of Lessing's prehistoric golden age when Earth was still known as Rohanda. At that time, with the guidance of the Giant-mind imported for us from Planet 10, we lived in a druidic pattern of harmony with our world "where the pattern of stones had been set up according to the necessities of the plan, along the lines of force in the earth of that time." Through our Lock with Canopus ("their Mother, their Maintainer, their Friend, and what they called God, the Divine") we governed our lives by "voluntary submission to the great Whole" (S:25–26).

But even Giant-minds are corruptible. The Degenerative Disease, sent to Rohanda by Shammat, destroys its peace and turns it inexorably into Shikasta, a broken place. It becomes progressively easier to recognize our own history as we rediscover it through the myriad perspectives offered in Lessing's retelling. The return to an existence in tune with the Mother is only possible for the few survivors of World War III, who look back at the turmoil of our past and wonder, "How did we live then? How did we bear it?" (S:364).

For that history has been ours to bear, just as the comfort of
Canopus can be ours to enjoy, which "clears our sad muddled
minds and holds us safe and heals us and feeds us with lessons
we never imagined" (S:364). The many visits from Canopus
throughout that history—which seem to be the stuff from which
our myths were made, as we sing the songs and tell the tales
instilled in us by those we see as the gods—are to tell us to
bear that history as patiently as possible. If we are as completely selfless as are Simon and Olga Sherban, who dedicate
their lives to helping the poor and sick throughout the world
and passively accept that their son George is to be guided by
"visitors" because he is himself a visiting Canopean, we will
be freed from history when we are freed from this life. If, however, we are too attached to this time and place, as is Rachel
Sherban (whose name means " 'womb,' personification of *ra-
chamin*, 'mother-love' or 'compassion' "[63]), we will find ourselves instead in Zone Six and have to come back and do it all
over again until we get it right.

Lessing's pessimistic but historically convincing view of humanity condemns not only us but human life throughout her
posited physical universe to the narrow dualism of the here
and now. Within the psychic framework of the goodness of
Canopus and the evil of Shammat, as Lee Cullen Khanna points
out, "the archetypal struggle is repeated dozens of times in
increasingly realistic human conflicts."[64] This is the most per-
sistent and most depressing reality Lessing weights us with—
the inflexibility of the human mind. If we could learn to accept
and be open to change, as is Canopus, we could recreate the
golden age here on Shikasta, Lessing suggests. For, as Ambien
learns from the Canopean Crystal in *The Sirian Experiments*,
the third volume of Lessing's series, "My guide was changing
again, was showing how it had to change, and flow, and adapt
itself, for all the movements or alterations of the atmosphere
we were submerged in like liquid molded this Globe, or Rod,
or Streak, or Fringe."[65]

To live only in history is to bind ourselves to a limited perception of reality and away from nature. As Ambien sees Shikasta freshly through the influence of the Canopean Crystal,
she recognizes that "the mind of the Northwest fringes, the

mind of the white conquerors" had trapped Shikastan life within "a certain way of thinking": "But now between me and the language of growth and change was this imperious stamp. This pattern. This grid" (SE:277–78). Only the few who commit themselves to the "language of growth and change" still spoken by nature are able to break free from Shikasta and history. Without this perspective even the compassion of Rachel Sherban will not free her because she cannot see beyond the suffering of the present moment and is overwhelmed by it. Her pity is sentimentality; as William Blake told us over a century ago, "Pity would be no more/ If we made no one poor."

Although Lessing achieves temporary utopia within the physical universe as the destruction of World War III cracks the pattern in which people have lived and frees the rest to realign their lives with nature, her Canopus in Argos: Archives series shows a dynamic physical universe in which the Degenerative Disease must constantly be opposed by openness to change. We cannot change the realities of the physical universe, the potential "dis-asters" which threaten us, but we can learn to grow and change with that Necessity, Lessing hopes. What seems to prevent her humans from accepting this Canopean perspective on life is the lack of adequate communication.

Although Lessing does show Shikastans, for instance, returning to a communal life which is in balance with the universal environment, the real key to the survival of that utopic surface reality is communication. In this naturalistic universe where the real Gods might destroy our planet at any moment, life cannot be borne without the singer and the song. It is the artist who broadens our vision and helps us in our "small ways express—not protest" the irony of physical existence. In Lessing's universe, as in "most of these worlds designed by women," Khanna reminds us, art "accompanies moments of significant change."[66] It is the singer who guides us through the growth of human consciousness chronicled in the second volume of Lessing's series, *The Marriages Between Zones Three, Four and Five*, for instance. And it is the misuses of communication which are attacked in her fifth and final volume to date, *Documents Relating to the Sentimental Agents in the Volyen Em-*

pire, where ailing humans are sent to the Hospital for Rhetorical Diseases.[67]

Yet in a world where art is denigrated or ignored, dismissed as "fictions," humanity is trapped in a grid of its own making. Even SOWF cannot reach us. Lessing shows us a world still bound by the Judaic cultural myth which denies human choice and change. To that world she can only offer a protective guidance that promises reward to endurance and obedience. Things will change, Lessing asserts, with or without us. We must be able to step back from our historical moment, to gain the perspective of Canopus, if we are to understand the "language of growth and change" with which nature is still trying to communicate to us.

Humanity's agents of change must come from elsewhere in Lessing's universe. For Octavia Butler in her Patternist series, conversely, we can all be agents of change if we learn to use our potential. What we mean by the human condition is subject to revision, and her blueprint for revision is drawn from our earliest source of myth, Africa. *Wild Seed* is the novel which tells of origins for the Patternists. Set in Africa about three hundred years ago and moving to California during the Civil War, the novel would scarcely seem to be an SF myth or in any way free of our history. Yet Butler's journey into inner space shows us that the same surface reality we thought we knew can be stunningly different from a new perspective. Her changes in that reality won't surface until the near-future setting of *Mind of my Mind*, which was her first published novel.

The story of the gods is the story of the individual, Butler reveals in *Wild Seed*. Anyanwu and Doro exist both in history and myth in these first two volumes of the Patternist series, gods who still "wear a human body." They affect their world on each level of reality, engendering a new "race" and new perceptions of human possibilities. Both of their names mean "sun" in their native dialects, identifying them as the female and male principles of life respectively.

In *Mind of My Mind*, when Anyanwu has adopted the name Emma, or grandmother, Doro mentions that she is "an Ibo woman";[68] so it seems particularly fitting that Sir James G. Frazer has attributed the belief in shape-shifting to her people:

"They think that man's spirit can quit his body for a time during life and take up its abode in an animal. This is called *ishi anu*, 'to turn animal.'"[69] Anyanwu, a wild seed growing free in nature, has learned through an inner quest how to change her body, aging and becoming young again, hunting as a leopard and swimming as a dolphin. Butler's vision of shape-shifting reveals Frazer's error. Anyanwu does not "quit [her] body"; rather, she does literally "turn animal." Symbolizing on one level the adaptations we make to survive (as women make in patriarchal society, for instance), Anyanwu's shape-shifting abilities will be inherited by women in Butler's later novels as well. For instance, it is Alanna's "survival philosophy" in *Survivor*; as she explains, "deception is the only real weapon we have."[70]

Shape-shifting is also the source of the healing power that Anyanwu will hand down to the Patternists. Anyanwu heals herself by turning inward and changing the shape of the injured or diseased part until it is again healthy. The archetypal witch most reflective of its designation by Annis Pratt as the "Craft of the Wise,"[71] Anyanwu is one of many women in fantastic literature who offer healing. From the primitive Clan women whose memories contain the secrets of herbal medicines through Snake in Vonda N. McIntyre's future Earth in *Dreamsnake*, women working with nature open her secrets for the benefit of humanity.

Anyanwu is yet another face of the Goddess, clearly an embodiment of the Mother. She has already been living three hundred years when Doro tracks her down and coerces her into his selective breeding program by threatening to use her children if she refuses. Typical of the black women who follow her, however, Anyanwu stays with Doro not out of fear or acceptance of slavery but out of compassion. In time she comes to recognize the truth in what her husband (Doro's son Isaac) tells her: "I'm afraid the time will come when he won't feel anything. If it does...there's no end to the harm he could do....You, though, you could live to see it—or live to prevent it. You could stay with him, keep him at least as human as he is now."[72]

Doro's selective breeding program is aimed at developing a "master race"—based not on appearance but on psychic abilities. He has himself survived many lifetimes since his Nubian beginnings, when he discovered his ability to take over the bodies of others by taking those of each of his parents in his desperate struggle for survival. Anyanwu thinks of him first as "an ogbanje, an evil child spirit born to one woman again and again, only to die and give the mother pain.... But Doro was an adult.... He preferred to steal the bodies of men" (WS:17).

Anyanwu, however, prefers not to kill. Even when she is attacked as alien to those around her, she tries to avoid violence: "I frighten them when I can, kill only when they make me" (WS:25). Although she can make herself young and beautiful, she usually assumes the less enticing shape of an old woman so that people will leave her alone. Yet, committed to life, she has borne forty-seven children to ten husbands before she meets Doro, and the temptation he offers her is that "If you come with me, I think someday, I can show you children you will never have to bury" (WS:26).

Anyanwu's own religious images, which Doro almost sits on when he comes in, are "my mothers" (WS:28). However, these images serve only to comfort the people who visit her for her help; she knows that "she had only herself and the magic she could perform with her own body" (WS:38). In herself she reveals the potential of the Goddess, while the Godlike Doro has quite a different power, as she knows when she asks worriedly: "What good was that against a being who could steal her body away from her? And what would he feel if he decided to 'sacrifice' her? Annoyance? Regret?" (WS:38). Butler's SF myth retells the story of the confrontation between patriarchy and the Goddess once more. In relation to this confrontation in pre-Hellenic Greece, for instance, Spretnak has noted that

The pre-Hellenic Goddesses are enmeshed with people's daily experiencing of the energy forces of life; Olympian Gods are distant, removed, "up there." Unlike the flowing, protective love of a Mother-Goddess, the character of the Olympian Gods is judgmental. Olympian Gods are much more warlike than their predecessors and are often involved in strife.[73]

Similar comments can be applied to Doro and Anyanwu.

Fantastic literature often reinforces sexual stereotyping similar to that suggested in these mythic contrasts in its characterizations, as Scott Sanders observes in "Women as Nature in Science Fiction":

In much of the genre, women and nature bear the same features; both are mysterious, irrational, instinctive; both are fertile and mindless; both inspire wonder and dread in the hero; both are objects of male conquest.... Men belong to the realm of mind; women and nature, to no-mind. Women are the bearers of life; men are life's interpreters and masters.[74]

In Doro and Anyanwu, however, such dualism cannot be maintained. While she is fertile and close to nature, Anyanwu is also the source of "logic, reason, the analytical workings of the mind" in the novel.[75] She has achieved her shape-shifting knowledge by careful, systematic inner quests, during which she has studied herself down to the atoms. She is both the scientist and the laboratory: "she had spent much of her long life learning the diseases, disorders, and injuries that she could suffer—learning them often by inflicting mild versions of them on herself, then slowly, painfully, by trial and error, coming to understand exactly what was wrong and how to impress healing" (WS:54). Similarly, she learns what nature can provide—what foods are beneficial and which are poisonous—by ingesting small quantities and watching her bodily reactions. She can "clone" a fish or an animal only after she has eaten some of it and studied within her its genetic makeup. Even then, she must consciously decide to shift her shape, and the process is painstaking until each part of her is absorbed and transformed.

Doro, on the other hand, is the Nubian "taboo person" described by Frazer:

The divine person who epitomizes the corporate life of his group is a source of danger as well as blessing; he must not only be guarded, he must be guarded against.... Accordingly the isolation of the man-god is quite as necessary for the safety of others as for his own. His magical virtue is in the strictest sense contagious; his divinity is a fire which, under proper restraints, confers endless blessings, but, if rashly touched or allowed to break bounds, burns and destroys what it touches.[76]

Described as a "small sun," Doro seeks people who are "good prey," who will satisfy his appetite when he devours their lives and assumes their bodies. He can exercise limited control over his appetite if he has fed recently; otherwise his action is instinctive, irrational. He simply occupies the nearest body. Even his seemingly scientific quest for the right people for his selective breeding program is determined by his appetite—latent telepaths and people with high psychic potential are "good prey." In fact, he began his breeding program as one would raise cattle—for food. He still uses his settlements for this, and the followers who love and fear him must come to accept the human sacrifices his appetites demand: "Sometimes such people guessed what was being kept from them, and they ran. Doro took pleasure in hunting them down" (WS:128).

Doro provides a frighteningly literal face of the God to contrast with the metaphorically changing face of the Goddess Butler uncovers; only the balancing power of Anyanwu keeps Doro human in any way, as Isaac had predicted. Countering his destructive power with her power to withdraw from him into death if she chooses, Anyanwu repeats Demeter's victory when he finally acknowledges in response to her withdrawal a human need: "Sun Woman, please don't leave me" (WS:252). Even Doro must learn that "there had to be changes" as he realizes that "he could ask her cooperation, her help, but he could no longer coerce her into giving it" (WS:255). Together the male and female principle balance each other and provide Butler's myth of origins for her Patternist future.

As these women reexamine the beginnings, they provide a foundation for other women writers of fantastic literature by uncovering ancient myth in the cultural myths upon which they hope to build. The face of the Goddess can be seen clearly, overseeing the changes initiated by the New Tribes, as Walton retells the tales of the *Mabinogion*; her survival through the surface of changing religions must be recognized by Morgaine in Bradley's shifting perspective on the Arthurian legends. Caldecott finds in the Druids' sacred circles of stone the same suspension from time and space that Eastern religions offer through meditation today, and Lessing will see those stones as touchstones for realigning ourselves with the Whole in *Shikasta*. But for May—as for Mary Mackey in *The Last Warrior Queen*, in which the goddess Inanna becomes a part of history—time and space expand rather than disappear so that history encompasses the surface of our myths and the underlying patterns become even less discernible. While the truth that emerges in such works is cultural rather than absolute, the perspective provided by fantastic literature and mythmaking still increases our understanding and possibilities, as art expands our awareness of both what happened and what happens to us.

When we go back to the beginning both historically and mythically, however, these possibilities are increased even more. In Auel's retelling of our anthropological realities, the mythmaking process parallels the evolution of human consciousness; in Butler's recreation of African myth, myth and reality combine to provide a new perspective on the world we know and the world it could become.

NOTES

1. Mircea Eliade, *Myths, Dreams and Mysteries: The Encounter between Contemporary Faiths and Archaic Realities*, tr. Philip Mairet (New York: Harper & Row, 1957): 23.

2. Ibid.: 23–24.

3. Marta Weigle, *Spiders and Spinsters: Women and Mythology* (Albuquerque: University of New Mexico Press, 1982): viii.

4. Paul A. Cantor, *Creature and Creator: Myth-making and English Romanticism* (Cambridge: Cambridge University Press, 1984): 103.

5. Robin Roberts, "The Paradigm of *Frankenstein*: Reading *Canopus in Argos* in the Context of Science Fiction by Women," *Extrapolation* 26:1 (Spring 1985): 17.

6. Ibid.

7. Ellen Moers, *Literary Women* (New York: Oxford University Press, 1977): 93.

8. Ibid.

9. Ibid.: 92.

10. Edith Hamilton, *Mythology* (New York: NAL, 1969): 69.

11. Mary Wollstonecraft Shelley, *Frankenstein* (New York: Scholastic Book Services, 1967): 58. Subsequent references are to this edition and will be given parenthetically in the text.

12. Ursula K. LeGuin, "American SF and the Other," in *The Language of the Night*, ed. Susan Wood (New York: G. P. Putnam's Sons, 1979): 97–100.

13. Patricia Monaghan, *The Book of Goddesses and Heroines* (New York: E. P. Dutton, 1981): xiii.

14. Ibid.: xv.

15. Charlene Spretnak, *Lost Goddesses of Early Greece: A Collection of Pre-Hellenic Myths* (Boston: Beacon, 1978): 41.

16. Bob Collins, "Evangeline Walton: An Appreciation," *Fantasy Review* 8:3 (March 1984): 6.

17. Paul Spencer, "An Interview with Evangeline Walton," *Fantasy Review* 8:3 (March 1984): 8.

18. Charles Squire, *Celtic Myth and Legend, Poetry and Romance* (New York: Bell, 1979): 34.

19. Evangeline Walton, *The Island of the Mighty: The Fourth Branch of the Mabinogion* (New York: Ballantine, 1970): 158. Subsequent references are to this edition and will be given in the text with IM:page in parentheses.

20. Quoted by Squire in *Celtic Myth*: 16.

21. Squire, *Celtic Myth*: 252.

22. Ibid.: 261.

23. Ibid.

24. Evangeline Walton, *The Children of Llyr: The Second Branch of the Mabinogion* (New York: Ballantine, 1970): 16. Subsequent references are to this edition and will be given in the text with CL:page in parentheses.

25. Elaine Hoffman Baruch, Introduction to Visions of Utopia in *Women in Search of Utopia*, ed. Ruby Rohrlich and Elaine Hoffman Baruch (New York: Schocken Books, 1984): 207.

26. Evangeline Walton, *Prince of Annwn: The First Branch of the Mabinogion* (New York: Ballantine, 1974): 7. Subsequent references are to this edition and will be given in the text with PA:page in parentheses.

27. James J. Preston, "Conclusion: New Perspectives on Mother Worship," in *Mother Worship*, ed. James J. Preston (Chapel Hill: University of North Carolina Press, 1982): 331.

28. Ibid.: 341.

29. Evangeline Walton, *The Song of Rhiannon: The Third Branch*

of the Mabinogion (New York: Ballantine, 1972): 183. Subsequent references are to this edition and will be given in the text with SR:page in parentheses.

30. Barbara G. Walker, *The Woman's Encyclopedia of Myths and Secrets* (San Francisco: Harper & Row, 1983): 282.

31. Eliade, *Myths*: 23.

32. Preston, "Conclusion": 340.

33. Marion Zimmer Bradley, *The Mists of Avalon* (New York: Alfred A. Knopf, 1982): 266. Subsequent references are to this edition and will be given parenthetically in the text.

34. Squire, *Celtic Myth*: 314–15.

35. Ibid.: 315–16.

36. Ibid.: 323.

37. Ibid.: 369.

38. Merlin Stone, *Ancient Mirrors of Womanhood: A Treasury of Goddess and Heroine Lore from around the World* (Boston: Beacon, 1979): 7.

39. Carol S. Pearson, "Of Time and Revolution: Theories of Social Change in Contemporary Feminist Science Fiction," in Rohrlich and Baruch (eds.), *Women in Search*: 264.

40. Squire, *Celtic Myth*: 336.

41. Squire discusses the identification of the Lady of the Lake, "whom Malory calls 'Nimue' and Tennyson 'Vivien'—both names being that of 'Rhiannon' in disguise," in relation to her seduction and conquering of Merlin (in *Celtic Myth*: 361). In Nimue, the priestess daughter of Lancelet and Elaine, Bradley also shows the seducer of the Merlin, but Nimue loves Kevin enough to commit suicide after she has given him over to the Goddess.

42. Squire translates Arianrhod as "Silver Circle" (in *Celtic Myth*: 261), similar to the "silver wheel" with which Monaghan identifies her (in *The Book*: 26). Monaghan further connects her to the Corona Borealis—the northern lights—and Robert Graves in *The White Goddess* (New York: Farrar, Straus & Giroux, 1948) confirms this, translating it as "The Crown of the North Wind" (p. 98) and not as the "Northern Crown" as does Squire (*Celtic Myth*: 252). None of these sources connect Gwydion with Orion, but Monaghan does say that Arianrhod is a parallel to Artemis, and Orion is the Hunter, a companion to Artemis according to Gertrude and James Jobes in *Outer Space: Myths, Name Meanings, Calendars from the Emergence of History to the Present Day* (New York: Scarecrow Press, 1964: 220). Since Bradley has used the myth of the Great Stag and the Virgin Huntress as the basis for the kingmaking rites played out by Arthur and Mor-

gaine which result in the conception of Mordred, the parallel of the Goddess as Artemis with the hero as Orion seems appropriate here.

43. Preston, "Conclusion": 334.

44. Pearson, "Of Time and Revolution": 264.

45. Preston, "Conclusion": 339.

46. Moyra Caldecott, *The Tall Stones* (New York: Popular Library, 1977): 203. Subsequent references are to this edition and will be given in the text with TS:page in parentheses.

47. Darko Suvin, *Metamorphoses of Science Fiction* (New York: Yale University Press, 1979): 27.

48. Graves, *The White Goddess*: 166–67.

49. Ibid.: 171–72.

50. Ibid.: 172.

51. Thomas Bulfinch, *Bulfinch's Mythology*, a modern abridgement by Edmund Fuller (New York: Dell, 1967): 261–62.

52. Ibid.: 261.

53. Moyra Caldecott, *Shadow on the Stones* (New York: Fawcett, 1978): 71. Subsequent references are to this edition and will be given in the text as SS:page in parentheses.

54. Julian May, "The Many-Colored Land" in the combined edition, *The Many-Colored Land & The Golden Torc* (Garden City, N.Y.: Nelson Doubleday, 1982): 18. Subsequent references are to this edition and will be given in the text as MCL:page in parentheses.

55. Squire, *Celtic Myth*: 68–71.

56. May, "The Golden Torc" in the combined edition: 532. Subsequent references are to this edition and will be given in the text as GT:page in parentheses.

57. Monaghan, *The Book*: 6.

58. Baird Searles, "*The NonBorn King*," *Asimov's Science Fiction Magazine* 7:5 (May 1983): 169.

59. Jean M. Auel, *The Clan of the Cave Bear* (New York: Bantam, 1980): 262. Subsequent references are to this edition and will be given in the text as CB:page in parentheses.

60. Jean M. Auel, *The Valley of Horses* (New York: Crown, 1982): 425. Subsequent references are to this edition and will be given in the text as VH:page in parentheses.

61. Sharon Spencer, *Space, Time and Structure in the Modern Novel* (Chicago: Swallow Press, 1971): xx-xxi.

62. Doris Lessing, *Re: Colonised Planet 5 Shikasta* (New York: Vintage, 1979): 40. Subsequent references are to this edition and will be given in the text as S:page in parentheses.

63. Walker, *The Woman's Encyclopedia*: 839.

64. Lee Cullen Khanna, "Change and Art in Women's Worlds: Doris Lessing's *Canopus in Argos: Archives*," in Rohrlich and Baruch (eds.), *Women in Search*: 272.

65. Doris Lessing, *The Sirian Experiments* (New York: Alfred A. Knopf, 1980): 277. Subsequent references are to this edition and will be given in the text as SE:page in parentheses.

66. Khanna, "Change and Art": 271.

67. Doris Lessing, *Documents Relating to the Sentimental Agents in the Volyen Empire* (New York: Alfred A. Knopf, 1983): 7.

68. Octavia E. Butler, *Mind of my Mind* (New York: Avon, 1977): 95.

69. Sir James George Frazer, *The New Golden Bough*, ed. by Theodor H. Gaster (New York: Criterion Books, 1959): 601.

70. Octavia E. Butler, *Survivor* (New York: NAL, 1978): 118.

71. Annis Pratt, *Archetypal Patterns in Women's Fiction* (Bloomington: Indiana University Press, 1981): 170.

72. Octavia E. Butler, *Wild Seed* (New York: Pocket Books, 1981): 120. Subsequent references are to this edition and will be given in the text as WS:page in parentheses.

73. Spretnak, *Lost Goddesses*: 22.

74. Scott Sanders, "Woman as Nature in Science Fiction," in *Future Females: A Critical Anthology*, ed. Marleen S. Barr (Bowling Green, Ohio: Bowling Green State University Popular Press, 1981): 42.

75. Ibid.: 53.

76. Frazer, *Golden Bough*: 165.

2

New Beginnings: Myths Recreated and Reexamined

Sometimes the best way to understand "what happens" is to let it happen again from the beginning. Might not the surface configuration of the recurring pattern of myth be similar in such tales of "new beginnings" to those in our most ancient myths? In fantastic literature, a writer can take us back to the beginnings or start again in another place, another time. In this new story of origins, the pattern of ancient myth should be discernible. Our cultural myths are adulterated versions of the story told "at the dawn of the Great Time, in the holy time of the beginnings" that Mircea Eliade identifies as the source of myth;[1] they have become fixed in time and place as they were recorded for future use. Would not a fresh experience in that "holy time of the beginnings" give us a fresh look at the ancient myth as well?

To this end, the works we will be discussing in this chapter leave the world we know to rediscover it—in the future, on parallel worlds, or on other planets. The writers shift us in space and time not so that we can confront our futures or the realities of alien races and worlds but so that we can experience the beginnings of a world or a culture. These novels are written from a native rather than an alien perspective—participating rather than observing. Even Simon Tregarth who leaves Earth to enter the Witch World in Andre Norton's novel *Witch World* is not an alien even if the surface reality is new to him. As Petronius has explained before Simon sits on the Siege Perilous which will transport him between worlds, "One takes his seat upon the Siege and before him opens that existence in which his spirit, his mind—his soul if you wish to call it that—is at home."[2]

This is not to suggest that these writers have employed a "mythic method" in their novels. As William Righter has argued, "the moment of insight carried in the inventive adaptability of 'myth,' a notion created for us at least as the vehicle of imaginative flexibility, catching the unimagined conjunction or fresh angle of vision," cannot serve as the foundation of a writer's technique.[3] Fantastic literature does offer a "vehicle of imaginative flexibility," but it cannot create a "moment of insight." It can only provide the process through which such a moment can be reached. It is the mythmaking power of the story itself, and the intuitive image-making abilities of the storyteller, which could create the "unimagined conjunction or fresh angle of vision" within which the reader recognizes mythic truth. I would argue, for instance, that Julian May's attempt to make Aiken Drum, Felice Landry, and Mercy Lamballe in *The Many-Colored Land* "archetypal human characters . . . out of Celtica, via Jung and Joseph Campbell, among others" is doomed to failure.[4] Types she may offer by recreating the surface characteristics and even the analyzed psychological patterns of an identified personality, but such a formulaic approach does not create an archetype which can be considered, as it is defined by *Webster's New Collegiate Dictionary*, "the original pattern or model of which all things of the same type are representations or copies." There is little new about Aiken, or Felice or Mercy; at best they are copies of archetypes which Jung or Campbell or "others" have discovered in myth.

However, if one cannot set out to "write myth," the storytelling process can still produce stories in which we discover the "original pattern or model." What we might find in these novels is the "unimagined conjunction" of or the "fresh angle of vision" on the raw materials of ancient myth—the human consciousness confronting its beginnings.

An important aspect of the novels discussed in this chapter is that they are written by and for contemporary members of Western society. Sharon Spencer has reminded us that

on earth today there exists virtually every historical period in the "progressive" history of man, ranging from the primitive culture of New Guinea to those societies whose technologies enable them to send men to walk on the moon. All these historical periods are *simultaneous*. What has changed is not their existence in time, but our *awareness* of their existence.[5]

We, the destined audience of these novels, belong to the latter societies but have gained an awareness of the simultaneous existence of the former. Such an awareness should help us consider the beginnings created in this fantastic literature as metaphors for our own beginnings—as another route to the understanding of ancient myth by imaginatively "*imitating* the exemplary acts" and thus, as Eliade suggests, "magically re-enter[ing] the Great Time, the sacred time."[6] As Eliade has further observed, "From a certain point of view, we may say that every great poet is *remaking* the world, for he is trying to see it as if there were no Time, no History. In this his attitude is strangely like that of the 'primitive.'"[7] In that poetic/mythic escape from our "Time and History" can be found these worlds within women.

Norton has her character Petronius, who helps Simon escape Earth, provide the rationale for such an imaginative escape in the first volume of her series, *Witch World*. Petronius, recalling from our past the tradition of "stones of great power," identifies the Siege Perilous as such a stone in Cornwall known to Arthur (WW:11). When Simon dismisses this information as "a fairy tale for kids," Petronius argues:

Ah, but who is to say what is history and what is not? Every word of the past which comes to us is colored and influenced by the learning, the prejudices, even the physical condition of the historian who has recorded it for later generations. Tradition fathers history and what is tradition but word of mouth? How distorted may such accounts become in a single generation? (WW:12)

The Siege opens a door between worlds for Simon, and he walks into a primitive world, where he commits himself to service to the witches in the matriarchate of Estcarp. He has walked into a mythic world, and his quest is to come to understand why this world should be his soul's home.

"Will, imagination and faith were the weapons of magic as Estcarp used it," Simon soon learns, and "the end result was that they were extremely open-minded about things which could not be seen, felt, or given visible existence" (WW:35). Witches give up their identity and remain virgins to preserve their inherited Power and their membership in the sisterhood. Only women of the Old Race have this Power—until Simon enters their world and he and they discover his own share in it.

While the Witch people have conflicts with other areas of the Witch World—those ruled by newcomers who remind us of the conflicts in the *Mabinogion* between the Old and New tribes—a balance is maintained until the invasion of the Kolder from "overseas." Continuing our parallel to the Celtic legends as they come alive later in *The Mists of Avalon* might tempt us to identify the Kolder invasion metaphorically with that of the Christians in Britain—and Tregarth's Cornish heritage only increases the temptation. Certainly the Kolder are dangerous here in Simon's "soul's home." We learn that their technique is to "kill the spirit and allow the body, and perhaps the mind, to live" (WW:51), which would make them a threat of metaphysical proportions.

History can offer a parallel to the Kolder, however, if we recall from the contemporary frame of this journey that Simon is a veteran of World War II. His experience helps him recognize the true nature of the Kolder threat, as well as ways to oppose that threat. The Kolder too are from a different time and space from natives of the Witch World. Like the exotics in May's Pleistocene series, they use their advanced scientific knowledge to subjugate the natives, turning them literally into "fighting machines." They are also capable of torturing their prisoners to death. "I have seen such things before," Simon tells his allies, "and that was also done by human beings to human beings" (WW:163).

Simon is referring to Nazi Germany; the resemblance of its

cold, unfeeling force to that of the Kolders is strong. Some have seen Hitler's Nazis as the exaggeration of patriarchal values (even pointing out that Germany is identified as a "Fatherland," while England has always been the "Mother country"); perhaps this is paralleled in the violent opposition of the Kolder to the matriarchate—where "the Power which has held it safe lies not first in the swords of its men, but in the hands of its women" (WW:115). Certainly the Kolder and the Nazis are similar in scientific superiority and examples of inhumanity.

Despite their superior technology, however, the Kolder will lose to the psychic Power of the witches of Estcarp and Simon, whose share of the Power will initiate change. In the world of myth, mind does triumph over matter. At the same time, knowledge initiates change, and the final chapter of the novel is called "A Venture of New Beginnings" (WW:218). "I do not think Estcarp shall remain the same," Simon says. "She must either come fully into the main stream of active life, or she must be content to withdraw wholly from it into stagnation, which is a form of death" (WW:217). One may hear echoes of Avalon here as well, but if the human priestesses of the Goddess withdrew from life, the Goddess Herself could simply take on another surface, another face. In his discussion of *The New Polytheism: Rebirth of the Gods and Goddesses*, David L. Miller argues that "a polytheistic theology will be a feminine theology ... but in the manner of all the Goddesses—the thousand daughters of Oceanus and Tethys, to name only a few. By being many, these Goddesses avoid a monotheistically chauvinistic view of the feminine."[8] Wearing many faces is one way the Goddess can free us from such a "monotheistically chauvinistic view." At the same time, we speak of one Goddess to convey that infinite variety encompassed in the individual and the limitless potential of myth.

Jaelithe at least—the witch who chooses to share her name and her life with Simon—is willing to be an agent of change, to initiate new beginnings. As we learn in the next novel of the series, *Web of the Witch World*, Jaelithe does not lose Power with marriage as witches had done in the past. As a man with the Power is new to Estcarp, so too is a married woman who retains her Power. In *The Forbidden Tower*, part of her Darkover series, Marion Zimmer Bradley tells of similar agents of change—Damon and Callista. Damon challenges tradition to become a Keeper at a time when only women who remain virgins can command that Power, and Callista finds that even after marriage she too has disproved the tradition by retaining her Power. They have rediscovered a truth from the past which offers alternatives to the present. As Damon says, "I want them to know that there *is* an alternative, that if I, working alone and outcast, have found one alternative, then there may be others, dozens of others, and some of these others might even be more acceptable to them than the one I have found."[9] Both Norton and Bradley offer societies where women hold Power, and both initiate change in those societies as a positive dynamic affirming life. Clearly these worlds within women are not advocating a dualistic rebellion—the replacement of patriarchal power with matriarchal power. Instead, each tries to communicate in "the language of growth and change"—with the voice of nature that Ambien recognizes as she watches "how the growth and unfolding of the material of the continent displayed itself in surface contours, and in the disposition of its waters and vegetation" in *The Sirian Experiments*.[10]

Yet in Norton's Witch World as in Doris Lessing's Shikasta, a society cannot hear the song of nature amid the sounds of conflict. Only after the external evil of Kolder is exorcised completely in *Web of the Witch World* do the internal changes really begin for the newly married Simon and Jaelithe and their world. "Well, Estcarp may go as Estcarp," Jaelithe acknowledges, "but perhaps it is now a field in which we sow strange and different seed, and out of that seed may rise a new fruit. This is a time of change and the Kolder have only precipitated turmoil."[11]

The "new fruit" which rises in the next volume, *Three Against the Witch World*, is a set of triplets born to Simon and Jaelithe—Kyllan, Kemoc, and Kaththea. "A man is three things," Jaelithe had told Simon earlier. "He is a body to act, a mind to think, a spirit to feel" (WW:51). In the tradition of symbolic romance—much as Nathaniel Hawthorne has done in Hester, Chillingsworth, and Dimmesdale in *The Scarlet Letter*, for instance—Norton embodies these three parts in the triplets, giving us a human trinity that is both three and one. Setting her novel in the Witch World allows her more freedom than Hawthorne had in Puritan New England to show the three acting in unison, however. *Three Against the Witch World* is narrated by Kyllan, the warrior brother, while *Warlock of the Witch World* belongs to Kemoc (whose gift from his mother is wisdom), and *Sorceress of the Witch World* recounts the story of Kaththea, the witch. As Northrop Frye has defined SF as "a mode of romance with a strong inherent tendency to myth,"[12] so does Norton use her Witch World series to explore through the divided yet united self "the truth of the human heart" and through her structural fabulation of the Witch World the "absolute truth" of myth.

Unlike Lessing, Norton does not see individuality as a degenerative disease, however. The resistance to change that comes when a community tries to preserve its traditional way of life seems more destructive to her. Living in tune with the Necessity demands that human beings truly understand "the language of growth and change." Although Lessing suggests that with SOWF and peace even we humans trapped in time might gain this understanding, only the Canopeans and those who evolve through the levels of human consciousness to share their perspective have that understanding in her Canopus in Argos: Archives series. Even their understanding is imperfect, since they are not gods; for instance, their own motives prevent them from suspecting Shammat of the evil it was capable of committing and spreading. As for the less enlightened humans in her universe, they must accept the guidance of such authorities as the Canopeans or the Providers who direct Al Ith to marry Ben Ata in *The Marriages Between Zones Three, Four, and Five.* "We are not permitted actively to criticise the dispensations of the Providers," the Chroniclers of Zone Three who narrate *The Marriages* inform us,[13] and certainly the Providers prove to have given excellent guidance in the novel. Yet who can we trust to interpret the voice of nature for us?

Norton trusts the individual open to change to have the insight which will help us make the next step in our growth. One step at a time is all she maps out in her series. Jaelithe, who has the courage to initiate change from within her community,

and new but compatible aliens like Simon, who can stimulate
change with what they add from outside the original community, offer promise for the future. Norton's "complete devotion
to the individual and the powers of the individual is the primary characteristic of her content," Roger C. Schlobin has said.
He also recognizes the mythic nature of those characters when
he observes further that she "embraces and stresses an older,
timeless view in creating her characters."[14] We can see this in
the triplets, who embody change in their mixed blood and initiate change in their various aspects of the human adventure.
They are "creatures of process and action, not ending and rest-
ing. Their searches are valuable in and for themselves," Schlobin adds.[15]

Caught between the future and the past of their world, the
triplets take advantage of the time of the Turning—the destructive and almost self-defeating last defense of the witches
of Estcarp which leaves the land itself twisted and broken—to
escape East to Escore. Escore is the first home of the Old Race,
the ancestors of the witches of Estcarp. It has been a forbidden
land, surrounded by a witches' spell that convinces people that
nothing exists in that direction. The triplets help each other
overcome the spell, partly because each offers the other two a
different perspective from which to confront it and partly because their mixed blood weakens the mental block. Still, they
must face crossing the mountains to reach this past of their
people, a psychic as well as a physical challenge. Their willingness to face the unknown of the past is the first step to their
own future.

It is in Escore that the three enter myth and legend—the
foundations of Escarp. Here they explore a central concern of
Norton's fiction—the nature of Power. In the human confrontation with Power, Norton can show the possible beginnings of
our dualistic universe—the creation of pure evil from a world
of natural possibilities which in itself is neither good nor evil.
"How did the ill begin?" is the question to be answered, and
an answer is offered:

With good intentions, not by any active evil. A handful of seekers
after knowledge experimented with Powers they thought they under-

stood. And their discoveries, feeding upon them in turn, altered subtly spirit, mind, and sometimes even body. Power for its results was what first they sought, but then, inevitably, it was Power for the sake of power alone. They did not accept gradual changes; they began to force them.[16]

Norton's Witch World story tells us much about our own reality. The creation of evil through the misuses and abuses of power could be seen as well in the destructive use to which the Kolder put their superscience power. Both sources of power—magic and science—can be corrupted. Each can use or abuse what nature gives us. If Norton's world is more attuned to magic, it is perhaps because her magic is more firmly rooted in nature. As C. J. Cherryh says in her introduction to *Lore of the Witch World*: "Nature is powerful here and those who open their hearts to it and to living things find themselves capable of marvels and involved in an old, old warfare."[17]

Once evil has been let loose on the world, however, it must be confronted by the heroic individual. In each volume of her Witch World series, the hero must recapture the past and combat that released evil to become an agent of change and the future. In this world, as Cherryh further observes, one finds "ancient truths about courage and honesty and duty that involve the highborn and the ordinary, the young and the old, humans and the four-footed kind all in one fabric of magic and mystery."[18]

Norton's hero is, as Joseph Campbell has identified the mythic hero, "the champion of things becoming, not of things become, because he *is*.... Thus the next moment is permitted to come to pass."[19] And he or she is assisted by the powers of good which balance the created evil when the struggle is beyond human capabilities. Particularly in a later Witch World novel, *Horn Crown*, the Goddess shows her face to help those who call on her. Norton's Arthurian fantasy, *Merlin's Mirror*, had brought in the knowledge of the future as known to the half-star-born Merlin to explain our myths; conversely, *Horn Crown* brings our myths to the stars—to the Witch World—to explain theirs. Here we again find the Virgin Huntress and the Great Stag, now as Gunnora and Kurnous, the Horned One. And here, too, Gunnora, as was Morgaine in her recreation of the Huntress and Arianrhod, is a symbol of fertility rather than sterile virginity. That virgin image, represented in classical myth as Artemis or Diane, is embodied in Dians in the Witch World. In *Horn Crown* the apprentice healer Gathea is devoted to Dians until her love for Elron, another outcast who has however earned the favor of the Horned One, teaches her that "in the Maiden lies the Queen" and "in the Maiden awaits the fulfillment of the harvest."[20]

In Gunnora, Dians, and the crone Raidhan, Norton has paralleled the three-person Goddess of the moon which Robert Graves examines, after Her worship reaches Britain, in *The White Goddess*. Raidhan is paralleled in classical myth by Hecate, and both are perverted forms of the Elder or Wise Woman of pre-Hellenic myth. While Artemis in her virgin huntress tradition is also a familiar figure in classical myth, Gunnora's parallel is less well-known. Charlene Spretnak retells this myth of the full moon as Selene.

In Spretnak's pre-Hellenic myths, Artemis, Selene, and Hecate are all recognizable faces of the Goddess. Artemis is the "Goddess of untamed nature and instinct."[21] As Nor Hall defines virgin in *The Moon and the Virgin: Reflections on the Archetypal Feminine*, she is "one-in-herself; not maiden inviolate, but maiden alone, in-herself. To be virginal does not mean to be chaste, but rather to be true to nature and instinct."[22] Nor is Hecate the Hallowe'en witch we conceive her to be today. Rather, she is the wise woman who "shared clues to Her secrets," Spretnak tells us, offering a description which should also remind us of Octavia Butler's Anyanwu in *Wild Seed*: "Those who believed...saw that form was not fixed, watched human become animal become tree become human. ...Awesome were her skills but always Hecate taught the same lesson: *Without death there is no life*."[23]

Neither Artemis nor Hecate comes down to us through patriarchy in this early form. Both are perverted—Artemis into the untouchable virgin and Hecate into the witch. Neither finally serves modern woman as a model to *imitate*. Similarly, the evil unleashed in the Witch World has frozen Dians into the inaccessible Maiden and twisted Raidhan into a witch as-

sisted in her evil by Cuntif, a similar perversion of the Horned
One, Kurnous. Both are "evil, yes—but twisted from another
way long ago" (HC:184). In their perversion we see "the true
nature of evil—it is power which is used to pull apart the
smooth weaving of life and the world" (HC:185). This perversion of the Wise One—of the wisdom of the Goddess—upsets
the balance and brings evil into the world. "Three we are,
nothing in the Lore binding can make it otherwise," Gunnora
tells Raidhan. "But also we are pledged, you, I, Dians, to keep
the faith—or there will be a reckoning" (HC:246).

It is Gunnora who still most clearly shows the face of the
Goddess, yet her parallel Selene is scarcely mentioned in the
later forms of classical myth. Selene, the fertile fullness of the
moon, has horns that "echoed the crescent moon on Her own
crown" because she has taken the Horned One into herself to
become full, Spretnak tells us.[24] Yet this fertile, loving, powerful model for women is unknown to most women today, while
her other two faces are nearly unrecognizable in their patriarchal disguises. In place of Selene, patriarchy offers the Virgin
Mother, whose very virginity makes her impossible for human
women to *imitate*. Yet Mary's virginity has been an important
matter of dogma for Catholicism; in fact, even her conception
was finally accepted as immaculate in 1854. Thus, not only did
Mary become a mother while remaining a virgin, but her own
conception was not "soiled" by natural means. Here, then, is a
Goddess who never really "wears a human body."

In Norton's Witch World, however, Gunnora is still available
as a model for Gathea. Once Gathea chooses this face of the
Goddess to *imitate*, she can go to Elron and "what remained
was priestess and Lady, man and Horn-Crowned Lord. From
their union would come power with which much could be
wrought" (HC:254–55). While Norton's "fresh angle of vision"
lets us see the source of evil in the imbalance created by misused power, it also restores the magic of the Goddess to us. The
individual hero initiates change in a world where evil has been
unleashed; through the individual the balance of community,
communication, and ecology can be restored—with the help of
the Goddess. Reading the images of the Witch World series
reveals a reflection of our world and unveils possible alterna-

tives for our future by confronting the past and acting in the present.

Sydney Van Scyoc and Susan Coon turn to an even earlier beginning in their fantastic literature to confront the Goddess directly, even before She has adopted a human face. On the planet Destiny in Van Scyoc's *Sunwaifs*, settlers from Earth on a planet void of humanoid life must learn to live in tune with their new world, and the powers of that world—the earth itself and the sun—must learn to accept them. From this mutual need come prototypes of the gods and goddesses our myths record. In each of the four novels of Coon's Living Planet series, on the other hand, native humanoid life is protected by Mother Earth herself from outsiders who would invade the planet and ravage its land and its people.

Destiny is a beautiful planet, presenting a welcome face to the pilgrims from Earth who had begun to worry that neither their fuel nor their food would last until a habitable new home could be found. Their thanksgiving to the "Secret Power" is short-lived, however, as "the sky-face of Destiny changed,"[25] announcing a vicious storm which ended in the deaths of four children and many of the bright crybirds they had tried to rescue. "Destiny had thrown her first tantrum for the human party" (SW:5), but it was not to be her last.

This earth mother has a life of her own, as does the planet's sun—a sentient life that acts with motives but that has no other way to communicate with humanity. The sunwaifs of the title will be the mixed children of these powers and the pilgrims, and as the triplets did in Norton's Witch World, this mixed generation will initiate change. These sunwaifs are both human and mythic—each is a god who "wears a human body." *Sunwaifs* offers us one possible "elemental myth" of our origins, in effect allowing us metaphorically "to be present at [our] own making," as Charles Doria and Harris Lenowitz explain is done in the myths they record in *Origins: Creation Texts from the Ancient Mediterranean*: "The very things of these worlds (they are usually fire, air, earth and water) tend to make themselves in various ways and directions, sometimes with, sometimes without the help of gods. The elements themselves in these old stories are animate and divine, the powers of the sensate world."[26]

Struggling against the powers of Destiny, the pilgrims in only one generation had become "a grim society of harsh patriarchs, gaunt women, and frightened children. Their chants and their hymns grew stone-heavy; pleasure became a perversion, worship a duty, suffering a birthright. Only the mystic core of their faith remained untouched" (SW:6). Similarly, on the planet Nelding in her earlier novel *Starmother*, Van Scyoc had presented the patriarchal pilgrims from Earth, led by the First Fathers who had settled the planet, clashing with their new home because of their inflexibility. When Nelding offers them mutants of their crops, they are delighted with the new products, but when she causes mutant children they cannot accept the changes.[27] Butler offers yet another parallel in *Survivor* when her religious Missionaries emigrate to a planet inhabited by furred humanoids who don't fit the Missionary interpretation of the "image of God" in which human beings were created. Thus, these humanoids are "beasts of the field" to most of the new arrivals, and again their inflexibility threatens their survival.[28] In each case, the inability to accept change condemns the pilgrims to suffering.

Yet "the mystic core of their faith remained untouched," Van Scyoc assures us in *Sunwaifs*, and those who can adapt their faith to their new surface reality, as does Headfather Schuster, can preserve that core. Their salvation comes from an acceptance of the world they now live in rather than the attempt to dominate it, and they learn this slowly and painfully through the mixed children.

These children, who narrate the story of Destiny, are shaped by Her as well. "The first recorded sunstorms occurred in the month of our conception," Corrie tells us (SW:11), and these "unusual concentrations of radiation" had caused miscarriages and deformed births already among the animals when the pilgrims recognized and tried to prepare themselves for the effects it would have on pregnant women (SW:13). Out of 362 births, "only six of the entire crop appeared normal, or relatively so: Ronna, Trebb, Nadd, Feliss, Herrol, myself [Corrie]" (SW:14).

Appearances, however, are deceiving. These women and the influences of Destiny and her sun have given birth to the first generation of the gods. Each of the children has special powers and characteristics that reflect nature's gifts, which are revealed as the story unfolds. Deprived of their human parents by the special circumstances of their birth, they recognize Destiny as their mother and the sun as their father. To Corrie is given the vision of "Destiny as it was in the beginning, when my Father was a weak pinpoint in the perpetual night sky and my Mother lay frozen in the deeps of space, swept by cold winds" (SW:100). She is granted the life history of Destiny because her gift is the power of rebirth—and death. Her friend Nira sees in her "the spirit of a huntress in an environment where there is precious little legitimate prey" (SW:91). Yet Corrie is life-giving rain as well, the Goddess encompassing both life and death within her power.

The children, who are "a melding of the powers and weaknesses" of both the environment and the pilgrims (SW:103), come to realize that they were born "to bring the people to the land, to make them truly of the soil, to create the link they could not create for themselves" (SW:187). With their Secret Power to worship and their foreign seeds of wheat and rye, the pilgrims work against rather than with their Destiny. Trebb even argues that "She knows what we did to Earth, Nadd. She realized as soon as she felt us crawling around on her back that we had come to destroy her. And so she fights us" (SW:153). But the children can bring understanding between this earth mother and her new people, and the powers of Destiny can join with the Secret Power of the people to become a Trinity. "And the Three are One," Nadd announces finally, realizing that "we have come to speak for the Destiny powers." It is these godlike children, of the environment and the people, who can "give them voice and intelligence" (SW:211)—can communicate between nature and humanity.

So too do the myths speak to us for nature and humanity. Through SF myth, Van Scyoc recreates the gods and retells nature's history; her metaphorical surface speaks to contemporary attitudes by exaggerating problems of patriarchal rejection of other beliefs and of destructive exploitation of natural resources to provide yet another "fresh angle of vision" on our lives. The planet of Destiny compromises with our invasion, offers us living gods to communicate her needs. Coon's planets will not be as patient.

Perhaps the planets in the Living Planet series are not as patient because they already have native populations which the Earth explorers ignore or reject as animals. Again we make a monster out of what is alien to us, as women writers have shown us doing from Mary Shelley's *Frankenstein* through Butler's *Survivor*. From this perspective, however, it is our narrowness and exploitation which seems monstrous.

Rahne, the first volume of the series, introduces us to a planet that can choose to ignore our existence as well. Only those she chooses can see her City and will be protected through her process of rebirth while she cleanses herself of the destructive presence of the invading humans. The introduction of the novel explains,

Man ascended from the Cradle of Evolution, destroying the unique life form which spawned him. Yet, what we call Nature, Mother of Evolution, does not yield lightly, nor can she escape her creation's ingratitude. But, under the proper conditions, she can try again. Her wounds are severe, her demands great, her anger aroused and her love infinite to those she has chosen. She is Rahne. . . . [29]

Cassilee, in the novel of the same name, is the next living planet, slowly healing herself after she has been ravaged by the "intelligent races" who had once lived and warred on her before they left for the stars. Now the "Star Demons" are returning to use her once more. New Life Enterprises, having never made a proper survey of the planet, yet has certified it free of life and is proceeding to "terraform" it—blasting away whole mesas and buttes and burying alive countless people in the process. Having sent one of its officers, Fancher, for a ten-day mission to the planet surface to get rid of him (he threatens to complain about their procedures), these Star Demons pronounce him dead and continue their restructuring and destruction.

On the planet, Fancher soon learns about the natives who

are being destroyed. With the surviving Betweeners and others, he finally confronts the invaders to let them know that the planet itself will no longer tolerate their presence: "In the ambition to steal Cassilee from her people, you have destroyed thousands of years of culture, taken countless lives, disrupted the geological and ecological balances and incurred the wrath of Cassilee herself."[30] Only violence will convince the invaders that he speaks truly, and in the process he is killed by his former commander. Cassilee avenges him and her own through her telepathic Betweeners, who can draw on natural forces much as could the Witch World people.

The Virgin, Coon's next living planet, adds new mythic dimensions to the creative and devouring mother image of Coon's first two novels. The Virgin has been created by a Great Intelligence—her larger sun—because of his loneliness and his need for love. He has warred with his brother, a weaker sun, throughout time, and The Virgin is physically caught between them. "Eleven times The Virgin was seduced by the weaker sun," we are told,[31] which causes earthquakes and tidal waves as her orbit takes her too near his power. But the "ninety days of chaos" of that part of her orbit are always healed as she comes under the more beneficent influence of the "strong sun who loved her" (TV:7).

The myth of good and evil warring unendingly over their influence on life is only one level of this tale of The Virgin and her lover, however. From among the people who inhabit her, the man Stefen is chosen to be her Champion (a culture hero pattern which will show up again with the fourth and final novel of the series, *Chiy-une*). When outworlders have abused her and upset her natural balance, the planet communicates with and exercises her powers through this Champion. Since the balance of The Virgin is precarious at best, the destructiveness of those species who do not respect nature—who do not believe in the Goddess—and who use their knowledge to plunder and ravage the worlds must be halted.

Although Stefen is the Champion of the land, the Deity which is his sun explains to him that "*it is yourself and the creatures of The Virgin you are guarding and struggling to save, Stefen. Not us. Our time will come in the scheme of Universal events and evolution*" (TV:243). "Our time" refers to when the sun will consummate his love for The Virgin—which will of course result in the destruction of all life on the planet.

Stefen is finally successful, at great cost both to him and to The Virgin, as Enickor will also be a successful Champion for Chiy-une. But Chiy-une must set aside the laws of nature in her struggle to eject those who would tear the ore out of her mountains:

A thousand souls rose on the wind in unison and opposed the natural laws ordering Chiy-une to bare her ore. For those laws applied to the dead worlds, where there was no choice and obedience was inevitable.

All that was and had ever been Chiy-une, from the rangtur to the Quniero and the torna-pok, gave to the whole, and fortified the rock, locking the molecules into place, resisting the power and bouncing it back to the helix ship whence it was summoned.[32]

If the earth itself is a sentient Mother, then it too has choice and can oppose the "natural laws." Respecting other life forms culminates in this Living Planet series to identify the life— the intelligence and feelings as well as the physical reality— of the Goddess, much as did the Old People in *The Mists of Avalon* who could not "bear to see the earth . . . raped by the plow and forced to bear." Looking at human life from such a perspective presents a strong argument for the definition of God or the Goddess as Love. Only love, *The Virgin* suggests, could convince the sun and earth to postpone the consummation of their love for millennia so that human life could evolve and survive.

Such concretization of myth in the surface reality of SF also has the effect of bringing the truth of myth into historical truth. "I wonder and I speculate about all kinds of ideas that our education deems absurd," Lessing asserts. "If I were a physicist there would be no trouble at all! *They* can talk nonchalantly about black holes swallowing stars, black holes that we might learn to use as mechanisms for achieving time-and-space warps, sliding through them by way of mathematical legerdemain to find ourselves in realms where the laws of our universe do not apply."[33] The writer of fantastic literature can begin with the same speculations as does the physicist, and then people the planets or allow human beings to visit them. In this way, "all kinds of ideas" can adopt a place and a time, a possible surface reality which might prevent them from being dismissed as summarily as our own dreams and visions often are. Sigmund Freud and Carl Jung have used the myths to show us that our dreams have important meanings for our waking reality; so too does the writer of fantastic literature present concretized dreams that have similar or even greater importance.

In fact, in *The Snow Queen* Joan D. Vinge uses the theory of traveling through black holes which Lessing mentions to provide a scientific backdrop for her SF myth. Tiamat is another living planet—mother to her children, the Summers and the Winters. Reached by more advanced races through the time-space warp of a black hole, her people are isolated, knowing these aliens only when they visit the planet. Here, too, myth lives again, as we discover Arienrhod ruling Tiamat.

As she acknowledges in her dedication, Vinge comes to her Arienrhod via the folktale of "The Snow Queen" by Hans Christian Andersen and through the treatment of the original Celtic Arianrhod in Graves's *The White Goddess*.[34] The story she tells, however, makes the old myth new in terms of contemporary Western society and its possibilities—in terms of science, politics, and the dualities that define and often blind us. Vinge is a good storyteller, combining disparate elements from her scientific and mythic sources with her own insights to offer a whole greater than the sum of its parts, mapping our present in her "Tale of the Future Past."[35]

Even the name Tiamat tells us that this planet is the Goddess, since that was Her name in Mesopotamia as given in the "Babylonian epic legend, the *Enuma Elish*, the account of the *murder* of Tiamat as the Great Mother of the Sea."[36] The Sea Mother is still worshipped on Tiamat by the Summers (Sumerians?), although such "superstition" is rejected by the more technologically knowledgeable Winters, even though their city of Carbuncle is described as breathing "restlessly with the deep rhythms of the tide, and its ancient form seems to belong to the ocean shore, as though it had actually been born of the Sea Mother's womb" (SQ:20).

Nor can we ignore the pattern of the Demeter myth in the novel, suggested not only by the division of the Winters and the Summers and their cyclically changing influence but also by the name of the reigning "queen" of Carbuncle's "underworld," Persipône. This vegetation myth recounted in the novel has been examined by Carl Yoke, who points out as well the "symbolic descent made by Moon" into this underworld while she is searching for Sparks.[37]

Finally, we are also apprised of the triple goddess of the moon as soon as we meet Moon Dawntreader Summer, who is herself a clone of Arienrhod, whom we already know as a celestial Goddess. The Goddess is many and She is one in the novel, since—as Graves reminds us—we are simply looking at her different faces.[38] These include the major women characters and many of the minor characters as well, such as Elsevier, who comes from the planet Ondinee. Ondine is yet another name for the Goddess as a woman who becomes a stream, and Elsevier herself will be "a sacrifice to the Sea" when she drowns while returning Moon to Tiamat.

The Christianized version of the Arianrhod story offered by Andersen's folktale provides the structure for Vinge's retelling. The boy Kay and the girl Gerda in that tale provide models for Sparks and Moon in several ways not paralleled by the relationship of Gwydion and Arianrhod in the earlier versions. As Gerda must make a cold journey to find Kay in the Snow Queen's palace, so too must Moon rescue Sparks from Arienrhod, Winter's queen, after a journey which takes her off-world through a black hole and back again, a death and rebirth journey which teaches her about the Goddess and her roles as a sybil and the future Queen of Summer. Also, just as Kay's vision has been distorted by fragments from a metaphysical broken mirror which have settled in his eye and turned his heart to a "lump of ice," Sparks's vision too is distorted—by his off-world blood (his father was an alien), his jealousy when Moon is chosen as a sybil and he is not, and finally his despair when he is with Arienrhod. When Moon reaches him, he breaks a mirror and sends "his reflection clamoring down in a hail of splintered ice," and hopefully the evil is dispelled (SQ:415).

Yoke's comments on the use of cultural myths in the work are helpful and enlightening in their details, but they miss the main impetus of Vinge's mythmaking by keeping the Goddess in conflict with Herself:

Arianrhod is loosely transformed into Arienrhod, Blodeuwedd becomes Blodwed, and Moon, who appears in the novel only as a young girl, obviously represents the New Moon, or the birth and regeneration, phase of the goddess. But even though Vinge has adopted their names, she has not necessarily paralleled her characters with the meanings attributed to them by myth. Arienrhod becomes both love goddess and death goddess in the novel, but she portrays love only in its most negative aspects. Blodwed, an illiterate and crude girl who tortures her pets in order to get them to obey her, performs only one important function in the book; she releases Moon in time for her to participate in the footrace that will determine the candidates for Summer Queen.[39]

Yoke is reading in the wrong language here. "Myth and religion are clothed in poetic language," Graves reminds us; "science, ethics, philosophy and statistics in prose."[40] Reading the novel for surface parallels alone will obscure its value as a myth of the rebirth of the Goddess in Moon. A metaphorical reading will show that Blodwed and Arienrhod are again perverted forms of the Goddess, just as were Dians and Raidhan in the Witch World. Blodwed and her crone mother closely parallel the robber girl and her mother in Andersen's tale. Yoke is right that this is not the love goddess Blodeuwedd of Graves's reading of the *Mabinogion*. However, that Blodeuwedd, remember, was an artificial woman created by Gwydion and Mâth from flowers—the "unnatural woman" who provided a model for Bradley's Gwynwhyfar in *The Mists of Avalon*. So too Blodwed is alienated from nature, caging the animals and unable to understand them until her uncorrupted self in Moon restores some of that knowledge to her. Blodwed's "Ma" is called "shaman" by the others, identifying her priestess function even in her fallen state. "I'm the Mother," she asserts. "The earth is my lover, the rocks and the birds and the animals are my children. They speak to me, I know their language." But we are told that "the opacity of madness made porcelain of her eyes" (SQ:258) and know that the Mother has been blinded to her own truths. Rather than become like her mother, Blodwed learns from Moon to "treat animals like human beings" (SQ:329).

Yoke is closer to the mark when he asserts that Arienrhod is "both love goddess and death goddess" revealing only the "most negative aspects" of love. But Arienrhod cannot be understood apart from Moon, her clone and her uncorrupted self. As was the Goddess in Norton's Witch World, Arienrhod has been corrupted by the misuse of power. When she confronts her own self in Moon, Arienrhod tries to justify her use of power in terms of the "creatress and destructress" Yoke has recognized in her:[41] "Why is it wrong to change the world for the better, when you have the power to do it? The power of change, of birth, of creation—you can't separate those things from death and destruction. That's the way of nature, and the nature of power... its inexorability, its amorality, its indifference" (SQ:425). "Real power," Moon counters, "is control. Knowing that you can do anything... and not doing it only because you can." Moon realizes that "becoming Queen did not mean absolute freedom, but the end of it" and that reuniting the Goddess would be only the first step toward a tomorrow that "would never come, if she failed" (SQ:528).

Moon and Arienrhod in Vinge's tale are both aspects of the mythic Arianrhod, dualistically split into her "good" and "bad" faces. That split is already apparent in Andersen's tale, in which the loving Gerda can save Kay from the wicked Snow Queen. Andersen's folktale preserves the Goddess in Gerda's faith, even though she expresses that faith through the Christian hymns and the Lord's Prayer. But even Andersen's images suggest that the dualism of Christianity, embodied in the mirror shattered in the conflict between God and Old Nick, distorts vision and freezes the heart. The Goddess too is fragmented, and her dark version is now white—the ice palace of the Snow Queen—suggesting that the death she represents is an end rather than a beginning.

This dualism will be resolved in Vinge's tale, as her journey

through the black hole—through death and rebirth—matures
Moon so that when she does confront Arienrhod she is able to
identify with her. Graves's comment on Tiamat might prove
useful here in understanding the metaphorical import of the
tale. "The Hebrew prophets knew Tiamat as the Moon-and-
Sea-goddess Rahab," he tells us, "but rejected her as the mis-
tress of all fleshly corruptions; which is why in the ascetic
Apocalypse the faithful are promised 'No more sea.'"[42] In this
dualistically divided Tiamat of Vinge's novel, Arienrhod seems
to fit this description; yet the face she shows and the face Moon
shows are identical.

As the living planets in Coon's novels chose their Champions,
so too is Moon chosen—called—by the Lady—the sybil machinery—to be the agent of change for Tiamat. To this end, she
visits Fate Ravenglass, a maskmaker and nearly blind sybil
who has been forced by the prejudice of the Winters against
the Goddess and Her sybils to "see through a glass darkly" but
who has guided Moon home again. Moon realizes that "this is
why I've come. To make this a real Change, to open the circle ... "
(SQ:384). More is needed than merely the transfer of political
authority from Arienrhod to Moon, which will come with
Moon's victory in the footrace and her selection by Fate in the
masking ceremony. In herself Moon must unite water, earth
and air—Tiamat the Sea Mother, Blodwed the Earth Mother,
and Arienrhod the Starmother (to borrow Van Scyoc's title and
to remind us of her celestial origins as well as her link to the
outworlders)—the spirit, the body, and the mind of the Goddess.
She must also save the mers—those children of the waves reminiscent of Arianrhod's slaughtered son Dylan in Celtic myth—
because she "treats animals like human beings" and respects
other life forms. The blood of the mers had provided unnatu-
rally extended life (and sterility) to Arienrhod and other Winters—and they were hunted and killed by Sparks, which was
partly the source of his despair.

Finally, Moon must bring the knowledge of the Goddess—of
the Old Empire, which is superior even to the "starborn" technology of the outworlders—up from the heart of Tiamat where
the sybil machinery is buried. She will not rule an isolated and
primitive Tiamat because she looks within herself rather than

out to others for true knowledge, and because she is not afraid
to be an agent of change.

Moon rejects the dualism that had divided Tiamat and perverted the faces of the Goddess. "Change isn't evil—change is
life," she asserts. "Nothing's all good, or all bad. Not even
Carbuncle. It's like the sea, it has its tides, they ebb and flow"
(SQ:489). To the three-person Goddess of earth, air, and water
she adds the fire of her love for Sparks. It is this passionate
commitment that comes when the Goddess "wears a human
body." As Graves tells us,

In Europe there were at first no male gods contemporary with the
Goddess to challenge her prestige or power, but she had a lover who
was alternatively the beneficent Serpent of Wisdom, and the beneficent Star of Life, her son.... The Son, who was also called Lucifer or
Phosphorus ("bringer of light") because as evening-star he led in the
light of the Moon, was reborn every year, grew up as the year advanced, destroyed the Serpent, and won the Goddess's love.[43]

Here in the "star son" is the new Prometheus as well as the
Sacred Child, and Sparks fits the pattern perfectly. He comes
to Carbuncle to "grow up," and by destroying the wise Starbuck,
lover of Arienrhod, he fills the vacant role. But that role has
to be given back to gain Moon after he realizes that he has
been loving the wrong face of the Goddess. Even when he is
reunited with Moon, the dualism that has distorted his vison
leaves guilt over the destruction he has been a party to, and
he feels his shame as "one more icy splinter of doubt" (SQ:528).

Vinge has made the myth new for us, as her future Tiamat
speaks metaphorically to our present struggles to resurrect the
Goddess and resolve the dualism that distorts our vision and
chills our hearts toward the Other. Yet she does not reject her
Prometheus or the science and technology he brings; if he is a
mixed blessing, he may still be an agent of change. Nothing is
incompatible with the Goddess if it is offered with love for Her
creatures, Her world, Her universe. The loving ruler serves the
Goddess and her people—and as a sybil Moon cannot lie. Community, communication, and ecology balance in Tiamat once
more.

The Goddess as Sea Mother also rules the worlds of Isis in Bradley's *The Ruins of Isis* and Delyafam in Jayge Carr's *Leviathan's Deep*. On Isis, in fact, the Matriarchate has its own version of the sybil machinery; in the ruins of "We-Were-Guided," the doubts of the settlers of Isis were put to rest when Vaniya prayed for guidance and was answered "by those who dwell here, whom you call Builders. They spoke to me, as they still speak to any woman who will come and kneel before them and seek their counsel."[44]

The Builders prove to Vaniya that the Matriarchate is right, "ordained of old before men had seized power from the women," because "in all the years we have come here to worship, they have spoken to no male.... And thus we *know*, Cendri, ... that the Builders of our race ordained women to rule, and that the Unity was wrong, wrong, wrong!" (RI:209).

Cendri is from the Unity, a scholar studying Isis (or Cinderella as it is called by the Unity, which demotes the Goddess to fairy tale status). Those on Isis assume that Cendri is a Scholar Dame, but it is really her husband Dal who has the higher rank and for whom the study was arranged. Since men cannot hold such status on Isis, the Matriarchate does not suspect the lie which gives Dal the privilege of studying them as no other man would have been allowed to.

Dal is originally from the planet Pioneer, which offers quite a contrast to Isis, a "patrist and woman-suppressive" culture where "all the softer and more scholarly talents were unmanly, and men's sphere restricted to the warlike and competitive" (RI:55). Cendri comes from Beta Capella, a planet not unlike Earth, where "there had been a few—though not many—Scholar Dames—mostly in education and linguistics, but it was not really unusual for women to excel in the social sciences" (RI:7).

On Isis men are referred to as "it" except for specific reference to sexual activity, and they wear an ear clamp or collar tag to indicate which woman owns them and accepts responsibility for whatever damage they may do. The satirical intent of the novel is obvious as women on Isis rationalize discrimination much as it is defended in our society. When the pilot provides a padded seat and straps for Cendri for the takeoff, for example,

Dal is simply wedged in with blankets because "they really don't feel things the way that we do. That is a scientifically established fact" (RI:5).

The inequities of Isis come into question, however, when the Builders speak to Dal. Vaniya cannot understand why they would speak to a man. They respond to her questioning "with a touch of chill that made Cendri tremble with sudden terror," protesting that *"Your mind lied to us. We saw your men only through your thoughts. Now we know that you have lied to us"* (RI:268).

Again, knowledge initiates change, and the Matriarchate must learn both that the Builders are not the Goddess and that man is not inherently inferior to woman. The Builders are instead an alien race "needing to live in symbiosis with another race because of their endless loneliness, desiring love. Pretending to be Gods to get it!" (RI:268). Although their rituals are patterned after those for Isis, the women of this planet that uses Her name must also learn the balance that nature demands. With the loss of their "Goddess" comes valuable information on the earthquakes and tidal waves that have always plagued them. The Builders give this information to the men, simply because, as one of the men tells Vaniya, "you had never asked them for such help and they did not know they could give it until one of us asked to make our needs known, and they found they could answer" (RI:271). Change has robbed them of the divine deity but has given them natural powers they did not have before. So perhaps their Builders are yet one more face of the Goddess after all.

The planet Delyafam in Carr's *Leviathan's Deep* maintains sexual stereotypes similar to those of Bradley's Isis. "Boys" belong to the harems and are clearly subordinate to the women. Yet this planet too worships the Goddess, and its natives, the Delyene, live in harmony with their world. Even the sexual stereotyping seems almost appropriate on Delyafam, because adult males, or Hardyen, have a much shorter life span than the female Delyene. Delyafam has been a peaceful planet until it is discovered by the "Terren" explorers. As humans enter the picture in this novel, again they arrive to destroy and exploit other worlds.

Delyene do not look like their "Terren" visitors with the exception of the Kimassu Lady, who describes herself as "the freak Lady":[45] "In a world of scorching, merciless sun, I have no pigment in my skin. In a world where the ideal of beauty is brilliant orange, I alone am pallid, bleached-pale...loathsome" (LD:16). That the human visitors find only her attractive is ironic and helps make Carr's satirical point about the inflexibility of human perception.

One Terrene, however, becomes an agent of change on Delyafam. To Neill, whose name in one of the old languages of Delyafam actually means "Champion," the Kimassu Lady looks like "a Valkyrie, my tawny-eyed Valkyrie" (LD:22). A Terren reporter after the "real" story of the Delyenes, Neill seems an unlikely choice for the planet's Champion, but he does fill that role. He recognizes and rejects the destruction of Terrens. "We had eaten our world, now we began to eat the universe," he admits. "Nobody can keep track any more, how many planets we've colonized, including—I'm sorry, tawny-eyes—some that already had their own people.... If you resist, they flatten you, and if you don't, they take over, bit by bit" (LD:24).

Terrens justify their destruction of planets and people much as did the invaders of Coon's living planets. They have decided, for instance, to classify Delyafam as a primitive planet because they recognize neither the humanity nor the culture of its inhabitants. Yet, as the report of the Kimassu Lady reveals, Delyafam is far from primitive. Part of Neill's story, which makes it back to Earth through his "amulet" or communication device, are her explanations of the communication forms on Delyafam—their "knotted messages" and their "tapestries and songs and history that went back a dozen-dozen-dozen generations to the First Empress (blessed be her memory!) and beyond" (LD:201). She also reports their skill at building "carefully crafted" boats, their natural technology ("the animals we trained from the sea to live on our walls to give light"), their farming methods, and their "way of worshipping the Goddess (may she reign ever mercifully)" (LD:201).

The Delyene are a people who do not know the meaning of war and who cannot imagine a world that would deny the

Goddess ("To have different religions? Impossible. There is only *one* Religion"—LD:48). They are not attracted to the temptations offered by the Terrens. However, they do begin to realize through Neill the power of these technologically advanced Others. The Kimassu Lady must cut off her hand to rid herself of the band the Admiral had placed on her arm to control her, for instance. She does so without hesitation, and afterward an infection develops there which is slowly killing her.

It does not prevent her, however, from becoming an agent of change herself after Neill dies. From him she has learned what must be done to save her planet from the Terrens. The first step is to make the planet unprofitable for them. She must generate her own followers even, because her perception of the Terren threat is not shared by the governing body of the planet. As was true in Norton's Witch World and Bradley's Isis, both worlds ruled by women and responsive to nature, the established government resists change and it must be initiated by heroic individuals. Even in societies living in tune with "Ancient Harmonies," these worlds within women remind us, change must and should come to keep them vital; fresh perspectives are needed to expand their vision. As the native Jaelithe and the alien Simon initiated change that would be carried out by their mixed children, so too do the Kimassu Lady and what she has learned from the new perspective of the Terren Neill initiate change in this world, and one of the children she produces who are disproving old traditions and changing her world is named Neillson.

Once the Kimassu Lady understands the first step of what must be done, she selflessly pursues her goal even when others tell her she is mad. "Who knows?" she says. "But in my madness I will build. And what I build will—I hope and pray—save us from being crushed under the heel of the Terrene" (LD:212). This image from Genesis has been interpreted in its original form as representing the patriarchal violence toward earlier Goddess religions symbolized by the Serpent of Wisdom (see Graves above as well).[46] The nurturing, natural values of Delyene remind us once more of the balance that seems to be missing on Terre.

Yet Delyene has become stagnant as well, and Neill has

initiated yet another change through his example. The Kimassu Lady has decided to educate her male children—the lumpen. When her friend 'Paysha reminds her that "Boys can't think," she replies, "I wonder. Raise them to think that they can, to rely on themselves, to be independent, and we'll see" (LD:212). One change initiates another.

The People of Cherryh's Faded Sun trilogy are also led by a woman, the she'pan, and are misunderstood by humans. In *The Faded Sun: Kesrith*, the members of this race who are living on the planet Kesrith are nearly all destroyed, leaving only the young she'pan Melein and her brother Niun, a Kel or warrior, alive. Before the human Sten Duncan assists these two, little had been known about the culture of the People beyond the Kel, who hired themselves as mercenaries. In *The Faded Sun: Shon'jir*, Niun and Melein are destined to become experimental specimens for an Earth laboratory when Sten risks everything to free them and provide them a means to return to Kutath. Kutath is the native planet of the People, left far behind long before these two were born.

En route to Kutath, Sten learns "much about the culture of his new friends, although still mostly in terms of the Kel, Niun. He does come to realize the reverence with which the she'pan (which means the Mother) is treated, even if she happens to be someone's kid sister who has never had a chance to take the role on before.

The People call themselves m'ri, while Sten is a tsi'mri, or nonperson. In *The Faded Sun: Kutath*, the final volume of the trilogy, Sten recognizes that on Kutath he is the Other, the alien. Humans do not make the decisions, and tsi'mri are not welcome. Melein, however, accepts Sten and breaks with tradition to bring him to the city they find on the planet. The city seems to be empty of life, but in the Shrine, the "Holy," the she'pan uncovers "a vast room of machinery—bank upon bank" and addresses it: "An-ehon, where are your people?"[47] When the computer replies "Unknown," Melein assures it that she, Niun, and Sten are the People, providing information on her line of descent. When An-ehon rejects Sten, Melein initiates change by ordering that he be accepted as "Duncan-without-a-Mother," the "shadow-who-sits-at-our-door" (FS:194).

An-ehon informs them that other m'ri are alive on Kutath, and Melein knows intuitively that she has come home to give hope to a dying people, to lead them to reclaim the cities they have deserted for lack of water. Trained in exile by the former she'pan, she has overcome the doubts she had and now trusts her training, her knowledge, and her insight—knowing she must combine all three with the computer's help to save and serve her people. "I am the foretold," she tells the she'pan Tafa. "See, and trust your Sight, she'panei; by the mystery of the Mysteries, by the Seeing."[48] When her knowledge and her Sight are in conflict, Melein the Mother trusts to her Sight, to "a she'pan's vision": "She hesitated, reasoning persuading her that he was right; and if there was Sight, he was wrong. She leaned upon it, that inward turning which she had constantly distrusted" (FK:256). Embodied in her, the Goddess serves the People.

On these alien worlds within women, the human is seen as the destroyer, but the Goddess is a part of all people. Since these aliens must also be considered intelligent conscious-nesses, we are forced to look differently at what it means to be "human." A reading of the images in these novels is very crit-ical: to be human is to reject the Other, to ravage the universe, and to exploit its life forms that we haven't managed to destroy. On these other worlds, technology is enlisted in the service of the Goddess, guiding Her people, not pitted against Her. To be human—with the exception of individual Champions who choose change and champion the alien causes as do Neill and Sten—is to be inhumane.

Man's inhumanity is seen to be sex-defined as we return to Earth to discover the all-female societies of the future which try to reject the problem by rejecting men. Joanna Russ's *The Female Man*, Suzy McKee Charnas's *Motherlines*, and Sally Miller Gearhart's *The Wanderground: Stories of the Hill Women* offer post-Holocaust worlds where society has frag-mented and the sexes with it. First "there was increasing sep-aratism, increasing irritability, increasing radicalism," Russ reports in *The Female Man*. Next was "the Polarization; then came the Split. The middle drops out and you're left with the two ends, hein? So when people begin shopping for a new war, which they also seem to do, don't they, there was only one war left."[49]

The final war, between the Manlanders and the Womanlanders, is continuous. What must have been World War III has already "wiped the have-not nations off the face of the earth and made their resources available to us without the bother of their populations; all our machinery was left standing; we were getting wealthier and wealthier" (FM:164). Thus the survivors have already fulfilled the requirements of being "human" by their destructive acquisitions. And although they have separated themselves from the men, the Womanlanders are as much cunning, violent, dualistic enemies of the Other as are the Manlanders. Just as the Manlanders have created females out of their less assertive males ("he—or she—is only a real-man turned inside out"—FM:173), the Womanlanders have bred males as pets from other forms of life. Jael's pet is Davy, a "lovely limb of the house": "His consciousness . . . is nothing but the permanent possibility of sensation, a mere intellectual abstraction" (FM:199).

For a world that rejects such "human" values, Russ must move to the parallel reality of Whileaway. Here the men are dead and the Goddess is revived. The surviving women fill all roles in Whileaway and have brought society back in tune with nature. They have not abandoned technology to accomplish this, either. The education of the children is "heavily practical: how to run machines, how to get along without machines, law, transportation, physical theory, and so on. They learn gymnastics and mechanics. They learn practical medicine" (FM:50).

Whileaway, with no men around, returns us to the more common definitions of human and humane. Their respect for other life forms can be seen as these women "provide human companionship to Whileawayan cows, who pine and die unless spoken to affectionately" (FM:51). What Charnas has said of her own fiction applies to Whileaway as well:

Then with the spectrum of human behavior in my story no longer split into male roles (everything active, intelligent, brave and muscular) and female roles (everything passive, intuitive, shrinking and soft), my emerging women had natural access to the entire range of

human behavior. They acted new roles appropriate to social relationships among a society of equals, which allowed them to behave simply
as human beings—tenderly, aggressively, nurturingly, intellectually,
intuitively, whatever suited a given individual in a given situation.[50]

Charnas presents her all-female world in *Motherlines*, while
the males who survive the Holocaust are treated in *Walk to
the End of the World*, the first novel in what was originally
intended to be a trilogy. The third novel "was intended to provide a synthesis between traditional androcentric culture and
feminist theory" but has never been completed because Charnas feels the time is not right yet: "Someday, maybe, I hope."[51]
Walk to the End of the World does have women characters,
however. These "fems" are trapped in the Holdfast of the men
and used like animals. Yet even the miserable and abused pay
tribute to "Moonwoman" and find such worship a bond among
them. One fem, Alldera, succeeds in escaping and is destined
to join a world of women as she becomes the protagonist of
Motherlines. Thus, she brings a "fresh angle of vision" to the
societies of the free women; yet she can also identify this as
her "soul's home" much as Simon Tregarth recognizes the
Witch World as his in Norton.
Life outside the Holdfasts is not easy, but it is lived in tune
with nature. Not all escaped fems can adjust to its demands;
some of them cannot accept, for instance, that the Riding
Women mate with horses. These horses had been genetically
altered before the Holocaust to breed them daughters, making
their lives without men possible. "My express purpose," Charnas has explained, "was to explore what women might be like
without that domination, living the robust lives of horse-herd-
ing tribespeople."[52]
The women in Gearhart's future all-female society have overcome the need for males by becoming reacquainted with their
own natural potential. This allows them, as Gearhart has noted
elsewhere, to be "sole arbiters of their reproductive function."[53]
Certainly one would not want to have to deal with most of the
males in the world Gearhart envisions, who are ready to rape
and destroy on contact. The women who have left the cities
and retreated to the hill country of Wanderground reject the

values of the society they have known and realign themselves
with nature.

Wanderground harbors a lesbian, communal society in which
the demarcation between human and other life forms is dissolving. Communication is telepathic and other natural talents
have been reclaimed as the women reacquaint themselves with
nature's powers. A society of peace and love in balance with
nature, still the women of the Wanderground have discovered
utopia only in the dynamic terms Lee Cullen Khanna has defined for us earlier in her discussions of Lessing's series.[54] They
too must be open to change, since their society is only part of
a greater whole. For instance, most of the women reject interaction with any men, even the Gentles who have also turned
their backs on the violence of the cities. The women claim sole
identity with nature, who has endowed them with their new
powers, much as the matriarchate on Isis in Bradley's novel
claimed verification of female rule simply because their "gods"
had never spoken to males.

But the Goddess does speak to the Gentles who seek Her in
Gearhart's world, although their power is less easily obtained
and more dependent upon communal effort than is that of the
women: " '. . . worked together for ten months just to get a
chicken hawk's attention.' 'It's got to be in sequence.' '. . . always takes at least four to do it, to lay each strip on top of the
other,' " is the composite explanation they offer the women
willing to meet with them.[55] These women recognize "the significance of what had happened" and worry that the men will
abuse the gift. "Nonviolent? Never," Evona accuses them. "You
know what will happen. You'll use your new power all right.
You'll use it, perfect it, manufacture it, package it, sell it, and
tell the world that it's clean and new because it comes from a
different breed of men. But it's just another fancy prick to
invade the world with. And you'll use it because you can't really
communicate, you can't really love!" (W:179).

Evona must overcome her distrust of all men simply on the
basis of their maleness, if only because change will come anyway: "They will do what they will do" (W:180). Being allies with
the Gentles offers more hope for their world than isolation, and
when this alliance is formed between at least the Hill women

and the Gentles willing to meet, Evona notices that "Actually, the earth looks wise and stubborn tonight. Like she's not about to be raped again" (W:181). The Goddess is not dependent upon the protection of humans; as She had rebelled against man's violence to confer Her powers on the women earlier, She could act again if future changes were not to Her liking.

All-female worlds are a radical treatment of what Russ's two versions of possible futures in *The Female Man* reveal might be a symptom rather than a cause. If the Womanlanders are as destructive as the Manlanders, certainly "maleness" cannot be the only cause of societal ills. Starting all over with only women is perhaps one possibility of rethinking our origins which would seem to offer a route back to the community, communication, and ecological balance that characterizes a Goddess society in these works. Yet Norton, Bradley, and Carr suggest through their worlds that power in the hands of the women can become equally corrupting and narrowing in societies misusing that power or resisting change. Whether or not the power of men— or the men themselves—are eliminated, the society must still be dynamic as well as in tune with nature if it is to offer a surface reality responsive to the values of ancient myth.

Perhaps the reason ancient myth is oral is so that it never becomes fixed into the historical realities of a time and place. Similarly, the wisdom of women in Suzette Haden Elgin's Ozark Trilogy is preserved orally, as the Grannies pass on to each new generation of daughters a heritage of Mysteries while the male Magicians continue to think that governing of the planet Ozark is in their hands. Both in this trilogy and in her most recent novel, *Native Tongue*, Elgin presents women who live within what appears to be a society ruled by men but who maintain communication with each other in ways closed to those men, thereby preserving their own power beneath the surface reality. What men know is encompassed in the history of these societies; what women know is communicated only among the women but still influences the surface realities—in the Ozark Trilogy even controls that reality and preserves its communal and ecological values. A metaphorical reading of this as reflecting the ways women have communicated and preserved their heritage and their power in our society as well seems to be supported by Elgin's use of traditions from the Ozark Mountains region of America as her source of symbolism.

This common body of female tradition is passed down by the Grannies in the Ozark Trilogy. Granny Hazelbide tells the young girls, for instance, "Men are of but two kinds. Splendid—and pitiful. The splendid ones are rare, and if you chance on one, you'll know it. What I tell you now has to do with the *rest* of 'em—as my Granny told me, and her Granny told her before that, and so back as far as time will take you."[56] Granny gives them three principles by which to live. First, if "a man does something properly, that's an accident." Then, "as for the sorry messes they make in the ordinary way of things, that's to be expected, and not to be held against them—they can't help it." Finally, the "third thing—and this is to be *well-remembered*—is that no man must ever know the first two things. . . . Men—all those rare splendid ones—they're frail creatures; they can't bear much" (GJ:258–59).

Women, on the other hand, are quite capable of carrying the weight of responsibility on Ozark, although they selflessly receive no credit for this. The Meta-Magician who really runs things is always identified at birth by the Grannies and given the name Responsible. The power of naming is well attested in myth, as for instance when Arianrhod withholds a name from her son.

The Ozark Trilogy presents a world functioning quite well on what women know, preserving community, communication, and ecological balance through faith in a system of magic. The current Meta-Magician is Responsible of Brightwater. The planet, Ozark, has been settled by residents of that Earthly location who, like the pilgrims who settled Destiny in Van Scyoc's *Sunwaifs*, have rejected the destructiveness of modern society. In their "teaching story" in the appendix of the first volume of the trilogy, *Twelve Fair Kingdoms*, is preserved the story of their exodus, in which they list the destruction of the environment, the creatures, and finally the people that precipitated their departure.

Also included in the appendix is another teaching story called "How We Came to Lose the Bible," which helps us differentiate these pilgrims from those in Van Scyoc's fiction. This story recounts the end of their journey of nine years to find an inhabitable planet. Because of the length of the journey, fuel was gone and they would have died in the water of the Outward Deeps in which they landed if not for the intervention of the natural powers of their new world. Forty "Wise Ones, . . . shaped like the great whales of Earth, but that their tails split *three* ways instead of two," rose up in a circle to catch the Ship on their backs to save them. As they walked ashore the Bible was lost (TF:184–85). It is tempting to see in this story the images of the Sea Mother, the rejection of the patriarchal myth, and the reestablishment of the three-person Goddess to replace the "tails" or tales of dualism.

Elgin's dependence on the American folk culture of the Ozarks, which has retained its faith in magic and the power of Grannies, reflects her own expertise in the field of linguistics and her personal knowledge of the area and its oral traditions. However, it provides an ideal metaphor for the survival of the Goddess as well. Just as Andersen's "The Snow Queen" preserves the Goddess—although divided into Gerda and the Snow Queen herself, so too do these "traditions of the folk" show an ongoing dedication to Her in modern America.

That *The Ozark Trilogy* incorporates the folk traditions as well as the language of the Ozarks becomes apparent when we compare it with folktales from the area recounted in Vance Randolph's collection *Pissing in the Snow*. Even the name of one tale, "Fireworks Under the Bed," recalls the title of Elgin's final volume, *And Then There'll Be Fireworks*. Elgin's trilogy recounts the maturation of Responsible of Brightwater (sexual and otherwise) and the necessary deception of males by the women of Ozark; the folk tale, Randolph comments, "is part of a substantial body of tales and jokes concerned with deception on the wedding night to cover up the loss of the girl's virginity."[57]

Again we find the conflict of cultural values between the surface morality of patriarchy which limits a woman's sexual freedom and an older system of values which defines the "virgin" as "not maiden inviolate, but maiden alone, in-herself." The girl in the tale and the granny she consults clearly accept the earlier system. "Don't you worry your pretty head," the granny-woman says, "because men are all fools, and everything will turn out fine."[58] She gives the girl a little tin snapper to push at the right moment in order to deceive her husband that it is her "maidenhead a-popping." Another girl, learning about the situation, loads the snapper with a giant powder-cap, and the pop becomes the "fireworks under the bed" of the title. Still, the ruse is a success because "the young fellow was so rattled he forgot all about maidenheads."[59] The important elements in this tale—the girl's freedom, the granny's power, and the need for man's deception—are all preserved in Elgin's trilogy.

Responsible is most clearly the face of the Goddess on Ozark, as can be seen when Granny Copperdell hails her return from the sleep the magicians had put her under: "Ah, the Holy One be praised, the Holy One be praised! . . . *Will* you look? It's herself, oh glory be, it's herself! It's Responsible of Brightwater her*self*!" (AT:516). The cost of maturation has been high, another journey of death and rebirth such as Moon had to take in Vinge's tale, but Responsible is now ready to be the Mother to her People. That she is the Triple Goddess is also apparent in her unity with the virginal Silverweb and her sister Troublesome (who is clearly the dark aspect but also the one who saves Responsible).

Faith makes magic work—faith and proper communication. Magic is dependent upon words: formalisms and transformations, granny-speech and formulas properly spoken keep this society healthy and growing. Since names are among the most powerful words, Responsible must live up to hers. At fourteen, she already *is* responsible for her society. Surface communication is just a lot of fireworks to deceive the men while Granny power really governs.

The Grannies are representatives of the Mother, of course, in tune with their new world rather than opposed to it as were the First Fathers and the patriarchal pilgrims of Van Scyoc's fiction. Just as they had accepted the help of the Wise Ones on landing, they appreciate the ability of the native Mules who carry the women instantaneously from place to place. And they will become, through Responsible, the Champions of this planet against the invasion of the Garnet Ring, which hopes to exploit it. As Responsible explains, Ozark "is still rich in ores and forests and land and seawater . . . everything that a crowded system like the Garnet Ring needs and does not have. They have set no controls on their population and no controls on their greed—they will not give us up for a gesture" (AT:518). As Moon had reminded Arienrhod in Vinge's tale, "Real power is control." Responsible clearly shares this insight.

Responsible also knows that only unity will enable the twelve kingdoms of Ozark to withstand the Garnet Ring, a unity that she must carefully maintain through the comsets (communication sets). This communication falters while she is under the spell of the magicians. But the Goddess is sleeping, not dead. Responsible is saved again by the native Mules, who are capable of mindspeech. Working through Troublesome, who must sacrifice her chosen isolation for the needs of the community, the Mules return Responsible in time to achieve the needed unity: "They would show them what a people united could do, how swift and sure a freedom-loving people could move to set up a new and strong government, how quick such a government could move to take care of such petty matters as weather and hunger and disease and disaster and war!" (AT:519).

The cost of a failure of faith and communication to the community is staggering; only a fraction of the population of Ozark has survived the chaos that reigned as Responsible slept. Perhaps Elgin is telling us something about the Sleeping Beauty that needs to be wakened on this planet. Still, *The Ozark Trilogy*, despite its tragedy, is also a delightfully humorous work. Elgin maintains the light satire and human warmth that has marked her Coyote Jones series throughout this SF myth. That light touch, however, is hard to find in her later work, *Native Tongue*. Perhaps it is getting progressively harder to clean up after men.

Native Tongue returns us to our Earth after Americans in 1991 have repealed the Nineteenth Amendment and, in place of the ERA, have passed an article limiting women—because of their "natural limitations"—from participation in government or in "the scholarly or scientific professions." Any outside employment demands that the woman show written permission

from a responsible male.[60] In other words, Elgin envisions a
future America in which women hold the same status as do
men on Isis or Delyafam.

What saves the women from servitude is finally the development of their own language—the ability to express their own
reality, which has been made totally different from that of men
because of the intensely patriarchal social system. Being a
linguist, Elgin is conscious of the relation between language
and culture—language and the way we can conceive reality.
Thus those who initiate this language—the women in the Barren Houses who are no longer useful to the men—are the agents
of change.

As the language changes the women, it makes them seek
independence—at least plan toward it. They do not stop serving
the men; they simply let their bodies serve while their minds
are in the reality of their own language. The men notice the
change and relegate them all to the Barren House as punishment, actually fulfilling their dream of independence in the
process. This is because, as we learn earlier from "The Discourse of the Three Marys," language can alter the way in
which we conceive the world: "Magic, you perceive, is not something mysterious, not something for witches and sorcerers...
magic is quite ordinary and simple. It is simply language"
(NT:242).

When we change reality, we cannot predict what will be the
end result. As Nazareth explains, "We have no science for that.
We have pseudo-sciences, in which we extrapolate for a reality
that would be nothing more than a minor variation on the one
we have... but the science of actual reality change has not yet
been even proposed, much less formalized" (NT:296). Nazareth,
though, *has* predicted this outcome, relying on faith rather than
science: "Faith. That dreadful word, with its centuries of con-
tamination hiding all the light of it" (NT:296). The light of
faith once more is uncovered.

As a doctor of philosophy in linguistics, Elgin knows her
subject almost too well in *Native Tongue*. In the passage quoted
from Nazareth, for instance, the voice of the teacher comes
through. Fantastic literature includes a didactic tradition, and
a tendency to leave the ideas bare of images can weaken the

story. In *The Ozark Trilogy*, we get teaching stories, not lectures, and the message below the devious surface reality can be understood.

In each of the novels discussed in this chapter, stepping back from our time and/or place reveals that power, turned against the Goddess, is dangerous. From these perspectives, "human" becomes synonymous with just such misuses of power. The images of living planets, however, give us a "fresh angle of vision" of the unequal contest that would likely result in an active conflict between humanity and the Goddess. "The longer her hour is postponed, and therefore the more exhausted by man's irreligious improvidence the natural resources of the soil and sea become, the less merciful will" the Goddess be,[61] Graves has warned us, a warning echoed by these writers. The agent of change is needed to champion the Goddess—and this time the change must be *real*.

Norton not only helps us identify that agent of change but also reminds us that true change is gradual rather than manipulated by the misuse of power—that the generation that initiates change will have to count on its children to bring it about. Van Scyoc gives the Goddess children as well, to become her "voice and intelligence" so that humans can learn from them to become a part of their world rather than a destructive parasite on Her back. When the Goddess's children are threatened, as they are time and time again in Coon's series, the Goddess will defend them and Herself against the destructiveness and prejudice that has become synonymous with humanity. "Pity this monster manunkind not," e. e. cummings has told us, and Coon strongly agrees.

But myth can once more help us to a new beginning, Vinge reminds us, if we pay heed to these "Tales of the Future Past." If we do not, we may face the extremes of Isis and Pioneer in Bradley's ironically named Unity or Delyafam in Carr's universe; the enforced sexual separatism that results from a man-made Holocaust that pits male against female in the futures projected by Russ, Charnas, and Gearhart; or the anger of the Goddess herself. But if we need her, as Cherryh suggests in her Faded Sun trilogy, the Mother would cross the dead worlds back to our beginnings to reunite us; She would wake and unite

Her Triple Self to protect us from exploitation as Responsible, Silverweb, and Troublesome do. Faith in magic—words, not swords—can, Elgin shows, still offer new realities.

NOTES

1. Mircea Eliade, *Myths, Dreams and Mysteries: The Encounter between Contemporary Faiths and Archaic Realities*, tr. Philip Mairet (New York: Harper & Row, 1957): 23.

2. Andre Norton, *Witch World* (New York: Ace, 1963): 13. Subsequent references are to this edition and will be given in the text with WW:page in parentheses.

3. William Righter, *Myth and Literature* (London: Routledge & Kegan Paul, 1975): 123.

4. Julian May, *The Many-Colored Land & The Golden Torc* (Garden City, N.Y.: Nelson Doubleday, 1982): 381.

5. Sharon Spencer, *Space, Time, and Structure in the Modern Novel* (Chicago: Swallow Press, 1971): xix–xx.

6. Eliade, *Myths, Dreams and Mysteries*: 23.

7. Ibid.: 36.

8. David Miller, *The New Polytheism: Rebirth of the Gods and Goddesses* (New York: Harper & Row, 1974): 74.

9. Marion Zimmer Bradley, *The Forbidden Tower* (New York: Daw, 1977): 353–54.

10. Doris Lessing, *The Sirian Experiments* (New York: Alfred A. Knopf, 1980): 278.

11. Andre Norton, *Web of the Witch World* (New York: Ace, 1964): 189–90.

12. Northrop Frye, *The Anatomy of Criticism* (Princeton: Princeton University Press, 1957): 49.

13. Doris Lessing, *The Marriages between Zones Three, Four, and Five* (New York: Vintage, 1981): 3.

14. Roger C. Schlobin, "Andre Norton: Humanity Amid the Hardware," in *The Feminine Eye: Science Fiction and the Women Who Write It*, ed. Tom Staicar (New York: Frederick Ungar, 1982): 28.

15. Ibid.: 29.

16. Andre Norton, *Three Against the Witch World: Beyond the Mind Barrier* (New York: Ace, 1965): 130.

17. C. J. Cherryh, Introduction to *Lore of the Witch World* by Andre Norton (New York: Daw, 1980): 7.

18. Ibid.

19. Joseph Campbell, *The Hero with a Thousand Faces* (Princeton, N.J.: Princeton University Press, 1968): 243.

20. Andre Norton, *Horn Crown* (New York: Daw, 1981): 254. Subsequent references are to this edition and will be given in the text with HC:page in parentheses.

21. Charlene Spretnak, *Lost Goddesses of Early Greece: A Collection of Pre-Hellenic Myth* (Boston: Beacon, 1978): 65.

22. Nor Hall, *The Moon and the Virgin: Reflections on the Archetypal Feminine* (New York: Harper & Row, 1980): 7.

23. Spretnak, *Lost Goddesses*: 75–77.

24. Ibid.: 74.

25. Sydney Van Scyoc, *Sunwaifs* (New York: Berkley, 1981): 3. Subsequent references are to this edition and will be given in the text with SW:page in parentheses.

26. Charles Doria and Harris Lenowitz (eds. and trs.), *Origins: Creation Texts from the Ancient Mediterranean* (Garden City, N.Y. Anchor Doubleday, 1976): xxi, xxiii.

27. Sydney Van Scyoc, *Starmother* (New York: Berkley, 1976): 93.

28. Octavia Butler, *Survivor* (New York: NAL, 1978): 5.

29. Susan Coon, *Rahne* (New York: Avon, 1980): 7.

30. Susan Coon, *Cassilee* (New York: Avon, 1980): 244.

31. Susan Coon, *The Virgin* (New York: Avon, 1981): 7. Subsequent references are to this edition and will be given in the text as TV:page in parentheses.

32. Susan Coon, *Chiy-une* (New York: Avon, 1982): 309.

33. Lessing, Preface to *The Sirian Experiments*: vii.

34. Joan D. Vinge, *The Snow Queen* (New York: Dell, 1980): dedication. Subsequent references are to this edition and will be given in the text as SQ:page in parentheses.

35. Vinge uses this as the title of a book Gundhalinu is reading which is written in Tiamatan and is described as a collection of "Old Empire fantasies" (SQ:93). It seems to be her way of pointing humorously to her own use of myth.

36. Merlin Stone, *Ancient Mirrors of Womanhood: A Treasury of Goddess and Heroine Lore from around the World* (Boston: Beacon, 1979): 117.

37. Carl Yoke, "From Alienation to Personal Triumph: The Science Fiction of Joan D. Vinge," in Staicar (ed.), *The Feminine Eye*: 130.

38. Robert Graves, *The White Goddess* (New York: Farrar, Straus & Giroux, 1948): 386.

39. Yoke, "From Alienation": 125.

40. Graves, *White Goddess*: 70.

41. Yoke, "From Alienation": 124.

42. Graves, *White Goddess*: 480.

43. Ibid.: 387.

44. Marion Zimmer Bradley, *The Ruins of Isis* (New York: Pocket Books, 1978): 209. Subsequent references are to this edition and will be given in the text as RI:page in parentheses.

45. Jayge Carr, *Leviathan's Deep* (Garden City, N.Y.: Doubleday, 1979): 16. Subsequent references are to this edition and will be given in the text as LD:page in parentheses.

46. Merlin Stone, *When God Was a Woman* (New York: Dial Press, 1976) discusses this on pp. 199–223.

47. C. J. Cherryh, *The Faded Sun: Shon'jir* (Garden City, N.Y.: Nelson Doubleday, 1978): 193. Subsequent references are to this edition and will be given in the text as FS:page in parentheses.

48. C. J. Cherryh, *The Faded Sun: Kutath* (Garden City, N.Y.: Nelson Doubleday, 1979): 152. Subsequent references are to this edition and will be given in the text as FK:page in parentheses.

49. Joanna Russ, *The Female Man* (New York: Bantam, 1975): 164. Subsequent references are to this edition and will be given in the text as FM:page in parentheses.

50. Suzy McKee Charnas, "A Woman Appeared," in *Future Females: A Critical Anthology*, ed. Marleen S. Barr (Bowling Green, Ohio: Bowling Green State University Popular Press, 1981): 107.

51. Quoted in *Feminist Futures* by Natalie M. Rosinsky (Ann Arbor: University of Michigan Research Press, 1984): 127, n. 4.

52. Charnas, "A Woman Appeared": 105.

53. Sally Miller Gearhart, "Future Visions: Today's Politics: Feminist Utopias in Review," in *Women in Search of Utopia*, ed. Ruby Rohrlich and Elaine Hoffman Baruch (New York: Schocken Books, 1984): 296.

54. Lee Cullen Khanna, "Change and Art in Women's Worlds: *Doris Lessing's Canopus in Argos: Archives*, in Rohrlich and Baruch (eds.), *Women in Search*: 271.

55. Sally Miller Gearhart, *The Wanderground: Stories of the Hill Women* (Watertown, Mass.: Persephone Press, 1978): 178. Subsequent references are to this edition and will be given in the text as W:page in parentheses.

56. Suzette Haden Elgin, *The Ozark Trilogy* (Garden City, N.Y.: Nelson Doubleday, 1981): 258. Subsequent references are to this edition and will be given in the text as TF:page for quotations from *Twelve Fair Kingdoms*, GJ:page for quotations from *The Grand Jubilee*, and AT:page for quotations from *And Then There'll Be Fireworks*, each in parentheses.

57. Vance Randolph, *Pissing in the Snow and Other Ozark Folktales* (New York: Avon, 1976): 42.

58. Ibid.: 41.

59. Ibid.: 42.

60. Suzette Haden Elgin, *Native Tongue* (New York: Daw, 1984): 7–8. Subsequent references are to this edition and will be given in the text as NT:page in parentheses.

61. Graves, *White Goddess*: 486.

3

Fantastic Mythmaking: New Myths

As a primitive art form, as Otto Rank has pointed out, myth-making was "the expression of a collective ideology, perpetu-ated by abstraction which has found its *religious* expression in the idea of the soul." Rank sees modern art, on the other hand, as "based on the concept of individual genius and perpetuated by *concretization*, which has found its clearest expression in the personality-cult of the artistic individuality itself."[1] Grasp-ing this shift from the collective to the individual as the source of art is essential to an understanding of the importance of modern mythmaking in our literature.

As we have seen in the last chapter, the "collective" modern society is seen as destructive, dualistic, and narrow-minded, rejecting the alien consciousness and abusing nature herself at home and elsewhere. In these works, a champion has come forth—an individual from within or outside the community who becomes an agent of change. The community that has grown stagnant is potentially destructive whatever its original value system might have been, as can be seen by the inequities on Isis and Delyafam, for instance. When society resists change, the need for individual genius is evident.

So too have we seen the patriarchal, monotheistic myths as resisting change. Hence, the responsibility for such change lies

with the individual artist. "We have barely started to attempt
to understand literature as a distinctive mode of knowledge in
which the processes, or, better, the desires of the human mind
find their clearest expression," Geoffrey Hartman has said.[2] In
those works I have designated as SF myth in earlier chapters,
individual artists have returned to our earliest myths to retell
the stories which had expressed such desires in the past, to
retell them from the perspective of the present open to the
changes of the future. In this chapter, we will examine fantastic
literature by women which creates new myths to express those
same "desires of the human mind"; when they are successful,
they initiate rather than explicate myth.

The violence of the modern world has ripped through the
fabric of its cultural myths, and when his myths die man feels
lost, betrayed. Myth becomes synonymous with lie—because,
as Suzette Haden Elgin has reminded us, surfaces in themselves often *are* lies—like fireworks under the bed, they are
"full of sound and fury, signifying nothing." However, when
that surface is ripped, the underlying patterns of the myths
might be more clearly recognized rather than destroyed. To
question the "sacred narrative" of cultural myth might lead to
answers. Mircea Eliade, for instance, has taken advantage of
the simultaneity of advanced and primitive cultures in today's
world to study "those societies in which myth is—or was until
very recently— 'living,' in the sense that it supplies models for
human behavior and, by that very fact, gives meaning and
value to life."[3] Myth can provide such models and meaning;
yet the masks of cultural myth can devalue life as well. Blacks
were taught, for instance, that the color of their skin was Cain's
heritage which marked them as inferior; women were told that
as daughters of Eve they were sources of sin. Exploring the
still "living" myths behind these masks helps us rediscover
more positive models. For women, researchers like Merlin
Stone and Charlene Spretnak uncovered earlier faces of the
Goddess which revealed once more that She is an "undying,
mighty being," as Brontë's Shirley had known instinctively;
She has only been waiting for new children to give her "voice
and intelligence."

Therefore, I would argue, discussing the individual artistic creation of a modern writer as a myth is valid. The storytelling process must be reinitiated; the new cultural expression must be stimulated by the agent of change before it can once more begin the process of becoming again. Becoming, not being, is the nature of human existence, and myths must always die to be reborn. "Modern man," Gene M. Bernstein has admitted, "has moved away from the sacred myth incorporating man, nature, and the numinous and accepted the profane or political myth of historical man instead."[4] The Goddess is choosing Her champions to bring him back; women writing fantastic literature are among those champions, whether they uncover and retell the familiar myths from unfamiliar perspectives and thus make them new again or create new myths to embody the "desires of the human mind."

Conscious creation of myth can be seen, for instance, in Doris Lessing's Canopus in Argos: Archives series. The second volume particularly, *The Marriages between Zones Three, Four, and Five*, concentrates her mythmaking by expanding a psychic cosmology within the space and time cosmology which governs the series as a whole and affords metaphors for her observations on contemporary reality.

Lessing's journey through inner space has its concretization in the Zones established around Shikasta, her parallel for Earth. Each Zone seems to parallel a level of consciousness which reflects the individual's attachment to earthly concerns. Closest to Shikasta is Zone Six, from which a consciousness is reborn into earthly existence. Trapped here are those who cannot divorce themselves from history in its most immediate sense—their personal feelings keep them tied to what and who they were. These are souls who must be reincarnated to try again to survive and serve on Shikasta, as do Ben and Rilla in *Shikasta*.

At least this umbilical cord is severed as the soul achieves the levels of consciousness embodied in Zones Five, Four, and Three of *Marriages*. Beginning with our most primitive and warlike attitudes in Zone Five, we move through the patriarchal political inequities (closest perhaps to those of today's society) of Ben Ata—soldier and king of Zone Four—to the peaceful, orderly, almost androgynous land ruled by Al Ith in

Zone Three. Submitting to the Necessity that governs the actions of all who occupy these Zones, Al Ith gains insight and comes to desire the heights of the snow-covered mountains (reminiscent of the Himalayan home of ascetic hermits who meditate away the problems of this life) of Zone Two. Zone One, we know, is the threshold of universal existence and understanding.

As the title suggests, Lessing focuses in this volume on marriages—on the relationship of the sexes in terms of the perpetuation of the race. Al Ith must marry Ben Ata both because her Zone Three is becoming stagnant—hence sterile—and because the women of Zone Four need her as a living myth—a model for their behavior to give them hope of overcoming the attitudes of their Zone toward women. When Ben Ata has learned as well from her example, he must then marry the warrior queen of Zone Five to pass on that knowledge and to confirm his own growing realization of the negative potential in his past attitudes toward women.

Marriages is very much a "teaching story," preserved and repeated by the "Chroniclers and song-makers" of Zone Three. Ben Ata and Al Ith become agents of change under the direction of "the Providers."[5] Lessing's more pessimistic view of human capabilities still keeps control in a benevolent power rather than in the hands of the individual. Only with this guidance can the human consciousness be trusted to accomplish a positive change in her universe. Each must submit to the Necessity and act on faith, and in the end all will accept and understand: "For this is how we all see it now" (M:245).

If Lessing does not trust the individual consciousness, she does trust the Goddess, however. Ben Ata learns from his marriage to Al Ith that women too have souls to be perfected; when he is remarried to Vahshi, the warrior queen, he can accept her imperfections and try to be a good influence on her as Al Ith has been on him. "Well, Al Ith," he admits, "I had to love her—after knowing you!" (M:244). The Zones too have grown by acceptance of each other, and a continuous exchange of ideas keeps them from stagnating.

Al Ith has graduated even further, learning to love other life forms and what lies beyond the physical world as she contemplates Zone Two. Her sister Murti, who now rules in her place, recognizes the change, and Al Ith is relegated to the freedom of a small shed near the border of Zones Three and Two. Although guards are posted between her and the rest of Zone Three, she soon serves as a model here as well. Her admirers

all had the same characteristic—not visible at all at first, but then, as you got to know them, it was like a brand. Each one suffered from an inability to live in Zone Three as if it was, or could be, enough for them. Where others of us flourished unreflecting in this best of all worlds, they could see only hollowness. Fed on husks and expecting only emptiness, they were candidates for Zone Two before they knew it, and long before the road there had been opened up for them by Al Ith's long vigil. (M:243)

Although their initial stimulus comes from outside themselves, individuals still champion the Goddess in Lessing's venture into inner space. The songs sung and stories told from Zone to Zone affirm the values of communication, community, and ecology as the insights of Zone Three are infused into Zones Four and Five. Unity maintained by communication among diverse elements and openness to change characterize the healthy attitudes Al Ith and Ben Ata rediscover for the people of the Zones.

Still, the ultimate good Lessing posits is beyond "this best of all worlds" of humanity. Al Ith and her followers yearn for the icy perfection of the mountains of Zone Two, perhaps to leave the body behind as will the Representative of Planet 8 in a later volume of Lessing's series. It is not the future Moon would understand in Vinge's *Snow Queen*, as she wins Sparks from icy perfection to human interdependence, or Simon in Norton's Witch World, when he warns the witches of Escarp against isolation as "a form of death." But if death is "but the mid-point of a long life," as Robert Graves suggests in *The White Goddess*,[6] then Lessing has truly opened the future— and the universe—to the evolving consciousness of humanity. Lessing offers glimpses of that universe as she conceives its possibilities in the other volumes of the series.

Ursula K. LeGuin uses the mythmaking capacities of SF

myth to confront more immediate social and political problems in *The Left Hand of Darkness*. Both Lessing and LeGuin elicit reader involvement in mythmaking in these works: Lessing has her story narrated by the "Chroniclers of Zone Three" whose "songs and tales are not only known" in their own Zone but have also spread to Zones Four and Five by the end of the tale (M:245); LeGuin introduces the myths and tales of Gethen into her own tale in several pivotal places.

LeGuin's is not a Canopean but a Hainish universe, referring to the people who had originally "seeded" the other planets with human life. It is now joined by the Ekumen, a loose unity of worlds which is offering membership to Gethen, or Winter as the Ekumen calls it. Gethen has the distinction of being the one planet upon which a genetically altered seed was planted, producing androgynous humans. To a Gethen, whose physical makeup relegates sex to the few days a month when one is in *kemmer*, human sexuality is a perversion. Since the Gethen can emerge in kemmer either as male or female, only locked into female if conception takes place and then only until shortly after giving birth, our sexual stereotyping is—pardon the pun—inconceivable.

Consequently, through her structural fabulation of an androgynous reality, LeGuin forces Genly Ai to confront his inherent sexism while providing the reader a look at human behavior without the distortion of the fragments of that sexist mirror. Ai is the envoy from the Ekumen whose very name forces us to identify with him as a "gentle" representative of the "I"—of the human. He must complete two important journeys in this novel—a physical journey through Winter, during which he learns the surface realities of a nonsexist (but definitely political) world, and a psychic journey, which culminates in his shared trek with Therem Harth rem ir Estravan across the Gobrin Ice. The latter serves not only Jung's process of "individuation," which, as Peter Brigg has argued, allows "the finding of the answers to existence within the self from whence the conscious ego emerged and to which it must return in order to achieve psychic wholeness."[7] This psychic journey is also shared—with an alien intelligence on an alien world.

The journey archetype is common to literature, as the individual encounters a series of events which externally reveal the nature of the society in which s/he must function, so that self-realization and social definition are reached simultaneously. The *Bildungsroman*, for instance, is usually structured around such a journey to reveal the maturation of the protagonist within a given society. Since, however, SF can alter its external reality, the psychic journey in SF myth can take place in a surface specifically created in which to examine human responses rather than to demand acceptance from the individual.

The shared journey through such a metaphorical surface also takes on new dimensions in this genre because the fellow traveler can be admittedly an alien. That LeGuin is very concerned with the theme of alien encounter is apparent in her remarks introducing *The Altered I*:

I was moaning about the way many sf writers skip blithely over the problem of alienness, just tacking a few tentacles or queer mating habits onto a standard Anglo-Saxon Cardboard Man and calling it a Pxzquilchian Native. When we get culture-shock just from visiting a different human society, what will it be like to meet a real alien? Will we even recognize truly alien intelligence when we meet it—have we already failed to do so, in the Cetacea? The question of communication is infinitely complex and stimulating, and instead of glossing it over with "translation machines" sf writers might face it, and draw strength from that very complexity.[8]

That she sees alien encounter as a metaphorical equivalent for the treatment of women as aliens in patriarchal society is also discussed in LeGuin's article on "American SF and the Other."[9] Genly Ai recognizes his alienation from women when he must refuse Estravan's request for a description of women. "I can't tell you," Ai admits. "In a sense women are more alien to me than you are. With you I share one sex, anyhow ... !"[10]

Ai's physical journey across Gethen, particularly through Karhide and Orgoreyn, reveals much about human inadequacies when confronting the alien. Apart from the sexual differences, Karhide seems very much like the United States, while Orgoreyn is suspiciously close to the Soviet Union in its bureaucratic secrecy and communistic claims. Yet Ai tends to give gender definition to each, perceiving Karhide in female terms because of its variety and apparent disorder—even madness—and Orgoreyn in male terms because of its standardization and "steady, subdued" people (LH:82).

Ai distrusts Estravan, who is a true agent of change and friend of the Ekumen, because of the deviousness of his words and actions in his efforts to preserve *shifgrethor*—"prestige, face, place, the pride-relationship, the untranslatable and all-important principle of social authority" (LH:10). Karhidians "tell the truth, but tell it slant," as Emily Dickinson would say. Ai is "annoyed by this sense of effeminate intrigue" (LH:6) and thus misjudges Estravan.

Although Gethen is hauntingly familiar, the androgyny of its humanity offers a satirical comment on our sexual myopia. Furthermore, its perpetually cold climate demands more communication and communal effort simply for survival. When nature turns a cold shoulder, humans must turn to each other. The pattern of the psychic journey as a shared experience of alien encounter is the basis of this SF myth. As Ai and Estravan find themselves isolated from both societal and natural comforts as they cross the glacier, they must overcome personal alienation to survive. In the process, they achieve a level of communication which can transcend external definitions and bring mutual understanding. Theirs might be considered a journey of Breaking the Ice.

Confronting isolation and hardship together teaches Ai and Estravan the relatedness of supposed opposites—of aliens—a lesson echoed by the Handdara philosophy LeGuin creates for Gethen. As Estravan explains of the Handdarata, "Maybe they are less aware of the the gap between men and beasts, being more occupied with the likenesses, the links, the whole of which living things are a part" (LH:167–68). Ai has heard a similar philosophy expressed in Tormer's Lay, from which LeGuin takes her title:

> *Light is the left hand of darkness*
> *and darkness the right hand of light.*
> *Two are one, life and death, lying*
> *together like lovers in kemmer,*

like hands joined together,
like the end and the way. (LH:168)

"Like the end and the way," the journey and the goal are one. Ai and Estravan are trying to unite their worlds, to open communication between Gethen and the Ekumen, and their journey across the ice teaches them how to communicate with each other. Each must learn about the self and the Other in this demanding isolation in order to survive at all, and each learns more about the self because of getting to know the other. While Ai cannot rise to the physical resolution of differences—with his sexual bias, he cannot accept Estravan as female while in kemmer—he does achieve psychic acceptance of this alien, learning that the very differences become "the bridge, the only bridge, across what divided us" (LH:178). The acceptances of differences between individuals is the source of love.

Ai and Estravan also achieve a unity of communication—of "mindspeak" on the journey. Significantly, Estravan hears Ai's message in the voice of his dead brother and lover Arek. Ai will meet their son Sorve Harth after the journey and will see in him "the flash of my friend's spirit" (LH:215). Although Estravan initiates change, it is his child who will realize it, who asks for tales of "other worlds out among the stars—the other kinds of men, the other lives" (LH:215) from Genly Ai.

Thus for Estravan "life and death are one" when his spirit is embodied in the next generation and his goals are shared. Estravan and Ai are committed to life rather than death as they flee across the ice. As creatures of time and history, we are always fleeing death—as individuals and as a species. And eventually death will come: "the sun will devour itself and shadow will eat light" (LH:171), LeGuin reminds us halfway through the journey in "An Orgota Creation Myth." But human life is in "the middle of time"—the time of the journey rather than the end, and the journey that is life provides an opportunity for the self and the Other to achieve honest communication, to find in their very differences the bridge of love which unites them in a community that accepts rather than denies or eliminates differences. To dissolve differences is to die as we know human life; that step must wait for the enlightenment

of Lessing's Canopeans. For Genly Ai and Estravan, accepting
differences leads to understanding; LeGuin manipulates their
environment to provide the needed isolation from external influences in which such an acceptance can be achieved.

Gaining perspective through a successful alien encounter
and reinstating communication, community, and life fitted to
its environment as central values for human behavior are the
primary accomplishments of LeGuin's mythmaking in *The Left
Hand of Darkness*. Through SF myth she has also offered the
concept of a nonsexist world, of a world which preserves rather
than rejects differences as links between people, and of a world
which finds no contradictions in uniting seeming opposites. The
right hand is not the left hand, nor is death life, but each is
part of a greater whole in which life and death are one and left
and right work together. Nature delights in differences, never
even duplicating a snowflake; yet the parts blend together in-
distinguishably in a snowbank, for instance. LeGuin too envisions a world where differences can bring delight but not
division, where people can learn to understand and appreciate
the alien, as does Genly Ai.

Sydney Van Scyoc structures quite a different surface reality
on the planet Brakrath, the setting for her Daughters of the
Sunstone trilogy. Brakrath does not have to endure the cold of
Gethen because of the power of its barohnas, women who can
"take the sun" into themselves and offer its warmth to the
valleys they govern. As we have found in other societies ruled
by women, these valleys survive in tune with their world, and
the individual sacrifices for the survival of the community.
Each palace daughter of the barohnas must pass a test of endurance in the mountains to earn the power of the sun and the
stones. Few survive the test.

Yet, if Brakrath is a world more blessed by and in tune with
the Goddess than was Gethen, it holds a similar lesson for
humanity. Here too we will find the alien encounter, the agents
of and need for change, and the importance of songs and tales
to preserve and communicate human values. For Brakrath is
in danger of stagnating; its people must be wakened to their
own possibilities and to the universe which surrounds them if
Brakrath is to remain a "good place" to live. Again, utopia

must be "the capacity to see afresh—an enlarged, even transformed vision."[11]

The story that weaves itself through this trilogy picks up
generations after the tensions Van Scyoc had examined in *Starmother* and *Sunwaifs*. Earthexodus, which had sent humanity
to settle various planets, also provided the first settlers of Brakrath. But the struggle against their new home was long ago
resolved, and the mutated humans are now Brakrathi. As the
sunwaifs were the "voice and intelligence" of Destiny, the barohna, or daughters of the sunstone, are intermediaries between nature and humanity on Brakrath.

But learning to live with the environment is not enough if
we are only in tune with our own small corner of the universe.
The people of Brakrath must become aware of the Other—in
their own world and in the universe—and be able to change
without ripping the fabric of their society in the process. Brakrath thus metaphorically reflects the contemporary need to
change perspectives—from national to international, from
worldly to universal, from androcentric to an expansion of consciousness that can, as LeGuin has already suggested, "recognize truly alien intelligence when we meet it." Surely
humanity that cannot even bridge the differences between the
sexes has a long way to grow.

In *Darkchild*, the first volume of the series, Van Scyoc offers
her own Breaking the Ice journey to provide the psychic landscape in which a potential barohna confronts an alien and both
become agents of change for Brakrath. In the second volume,
Bluesong, their children spread that change out of the valleys
to the desert nomads of the planet, and both societies benefit
from the increased communication and understanding between
them as the Zones had benefited from similar exchanges in
Lessing's *Marriages*. Finally, in *Starsilk*, one of the children
and a Brakrathi outcast—a "winter-child" and hunter from the
mountains—leave the planet to learn of other worlds and other
songs to bring back with which to fulfill the hunter's pledge to
"Waken the people" of Brakrath.[12] In each volume, a young
man and a young woman confront the alien in themselves and
in each other to become agents of change for their world.

That Brakrath is "sleeping" is apparent in the winter imagery and the cultural traditions revealed in *Darkchild*. Because of the severe winters, the people of the valleys have learned to take "sleepleaf" and hibernate until the spring. Exceptions are the barohna, who goes to the mountains until she has stored enough of the sun's power to come back again and thaw the fields, and her palace daughters, who stay alone in the palace. Khira is the only surviving daughter—six have already died facing their challenge—and is isolated in the palace for the winter. This winter, however, she is confronted by an alien whom she names Darkchild. As in Norton's Witch World and, to a certain extent, in LeGuin's Gethen, change must be initiated by an alien and by a native who learns to love him.

Darkchild does not come to Brakrath by his own choice, however, or as an envoy bringing the hope of unity with a larger human community. Rather, he is a "Rauthimage," an illegitimately conceived clone of Birnam Rauth, a famous explorer. Hundreds of such clones have been produced by the Benderzic, unnatural themselves in that they live on a fleet of ships rather than on any planet. The Rauthimages are set on planets as tools of the Benderzic, recording their impressions so that the Benderzic can sell the information or exploit the planets themselves, enslaving or destroying the natives. In the Benderzic we see the inhumanity of imperialism which drives the planets in Coon's Living Planet series to defend themselves and their people.

Nor is Darkchild the first alien to land on Brakrath. Already in residence is a team of Arnimi scholars who peacefully study the planet as they have studied life throughout the universe. Yet neither the Benderzic nor the Arnimi are seen by the Brakrathi as models of a "superior culture." The Benderzic are rapacious and devious; the Arnimi are cold and noncommital. Both are technologically superior, but in the process each is isolated from nature and humanity. Both, for instance, deny Darkchild any humanity, as the Arnimi recommend that he be put out into the snow to die because "he has no right to independent existence."[13]

Darkchild is, however, the first "successful" alien encounter. Although he is seen as "a data-gathering instrument, nothing more" by the Benderzic (D:130), Khira recognizes and learns to love his humanity. Both Khira and Darkchild also confront the alien within themselves on this Breaking the Ice journey. Darkchild must learn to act independent of and then to accept the "guide," the part of his mind programmed by the Benderzic; Khira needs to understand the "stone in her heart" that is part of her makeup as a potential barohna. The psychological importance of their adolescent struggle to uncover and unite their own identities can be seen as the human need for both history and myth. Darkchild and his guide are the struggle between superego and ego, the social programming there to protect us from the threats of natural drives. Darkchild, however, has been robbed of his memories—his history, and his guide is without faith and rejects feeling—is without myth. Van Scyoc repeatedly shows the need to unify history and myth, to preserve the individual and the community, to blend tradition and change if we are to grow.

Khira too tries to come to terms with her inner selves. If Darkchild has been a tool of science and history, she is in some ways a tool of tradition and myth. Each tries to understand what it means to be human in this world where the greater-than-human powers seem overwhelming. Although Khira will initiate change in tradition—will take Darkchild as a permanent mate in a society in which one-year mates are the norm—it will wait for her daughter Reyna to rewrite the myth in *Starsilk*. With her love, Darkchild will also resolve his conflicts, but Khira must learn to accept both his human and alien characteristics to give him that support. As the wise Kadura advises her, "If you support him, even that aspect of him you like least, you will strengthen him to deal with his inner difficulty" (D:169).

Learning to bridge the gap between the self and the Other also teaches Khira how to govern: "You must learn to put on the face you want him to see—the accepting face" (D:170). To rule the self or others, as we have learned from Moon in Joan Vinge's *The Snow Queen*, is to maintain control. Controlling the surface is seen by Van Scyoc, as it was seen by Elgin in the Ozark trilogy, as necessary to maintain societal balance. The "lie" here is not practiced for itself, however; the face is always the goal toward which you are striving. "But after a time it will no longer be just a face. You will no longer be making a pretense. Eventually the act becomes the reality, Khira" (D:170). One might compare this to the survival technique of "shape-shifting" in Octavia Butler's Patternist series as well.

The act becoming the reality is the basis of change. In the past, the stranded survivors of the Earthexodus ship had been able to accept Brakrath and "under the force of change, a diverse people gradually became a single new race of hardy, fair people" (D:37). Some even learned to communicate with the alien intelligence of the redmanes, much as the women on Elgin's Ozark interacted with the Mules. But life is a process, demanding continual change, and centuries of tradition have caused them to isolate themselves in valley, desert, and mountain with little communication between them. Each group has legends of the other groups which separate them, much as cultural myths separate our world.

Myths, too, must change—must be seen as symbol and metaphor rather than graven image. Khira's sister, Mara, for instance, was doomed by worshipping her mother. As Khira's sister Alzaja explains to her, "You've heard stories of people who took gods, people who went out of the valleys carrying stone images and never came back. Our mother was Mara's god, and Mara thought worshipping her was enough" (D:21). One must prepare and act individually for myth to live. Stones might be given life, as Khira and her mother can do as barohnas, but life must not be trapped in stone. Stone images can become destructive, as they do in Caldecott's Sacred Stones trilogy; waiting for the gods to save us can become self-defeating, as it is for the souls in Zone Six in Lessing's Shikasta.

Teaching stories, legends, must be explored as is history and tested with new experiences to understand what they mean for our time and place. Thus Khira was named after Khirsa, who had penetrated the legend of the silverwings, so that she too would "look for the truth behind whatever legend you might hear" (D:17). In Starsilk, Khira's daughter Reyna will recognize the same desire in the hunter Jauren: "He wanted to look behind the familiar tales. He wanted to touch the past, to grasp its scent and its texture. He wanted to track the legendary figures from flesh to the place where myth claimed them. Because what was sung and whispered in the halls was legend. Only the scrolls exposed the human flesh behind it" (SS:631–32). History is not enough, however; new songs must also be sung, and alien songs must be listened to, as are the bluesong and the starsilk which lend their names as titles to the other two volumes of this trilogy.

Darkchild and Khira initiate change on Brakrath, producing the first palace son in Danior and resettling Darkchild's Rauthimage brother Jhaviir on Brakrath to father the first palace daughter of mixed blood, Keva. In *Bluesong*, Keva with Danior's help will become the first barohna for the desert nomads, reviving communication between this patriarchal society and the bahronic valleys and dispelling false myths for both cultures about the nature of the other. Finally, Reyna and Juaren will trace Darkchild's history to the planet where Birnam Rauth's awareness still exists in *Starsilk*. On this alien world, history and myth unite, and Reyna and Juaren are able to bring what they learn back to Brakrath in the tales and songs of Rauth's life-silk.

As Reyna has learned from her experience, communication comes with song, not technology. Although the Arnimi Verra has provided equipment which can ease the search for knowledge, finally Reyna must sing her song to the alien sithi and the Unseen, and both she and Juaren must reach out and try to understand the aliens to achieve understanding. If the Arnimi miss this communication, Reyna concludes, it is because they are "never listening to the land and the people, only to instruments" (SS:695). As Birnam Rauth summarizes in the epilogue to *Starsilk*, "he had learned to find humanity in alien creatures. He had discovered the alien in himself. And he had learned that sometimes the alien and the human are so far separated by perception and experience that it is difficult to speak across the gap" (S:696). We must be open to experiences, to perceive things differently, if we are to understand even the alien within ourselves. Van Scyoc gives us songs and tales to achieve this understanding, but she reminds us that the song must always be made new by each new singer if true com-

munication and understanding is to be achieved. Ours is a
world in the process of becoming, and we must change with it
to grow.

The inhabitants of the future Earth we visit in Pamela Sargent's *Watchstar* also feel they have evolved a utopia but have
instead become stagnant. Van Scyoc has reminded us that both
myth and history must be reckoned with in our lives: if myths
offer timeless patterns, they must still govern our behavior in
a world of time and place. To deny part of ourselves is to live
with an alien within; the encounter, when it comes as it inevitably must come, can destroy both self and society. "The fabric
of valley life—how easily might it disintegrate?" Reyna had
worried when she began to realize that change must come to
Brakrath (S:568–69), and she knew that new myths would be
needed to replace the traditions they had known. She found
these in "Birnam Rauth's stories of all the people and places
that lay beyond Brakrath. His was the voice that could rouse
them, his the tales that could wake them" (S:694). In *Watchstar*,
Daiya must be an agent of change for her society but has no
new songs to sing them. The bare history of their myths destroys many of the people; only those open to change survive.

On the surface, the society of the Merging Selves seems to
be built securely on the principles of communication, ecology,
and community. Yet this community is preserved at the cost
of infanticide. Children born as solitaries, with no psychic powers, are put to death, Daiya is told, because

if they lived, they would become the victims of those with normal
minds. They would be outside society, separated from the Net. They
would threaten the world with their separateness and eventually they
would have to be killed anyway. It had happened in the past. Individuals had warred with themselves and with the world, separated
mentally from one another, separated from the world by machines,
apart from God and nature.[14]

Solitaries are thus destroyed not for what they will do but
for what the villagers are afraid that *they* would do to these
vulnerable individuals. Rather than learning to control their
power, as Andre Norton and Joan Vinge have reminded us is

necessary, they try to control the world around them instead, to alter it so that they will not confront any test of their powers and beliefs.

Yet these same people require their children to survive an ordeal to become one with the community. The ordeal is not a physical challenge only, for which the children could train, as was the test for barohnas on Brakrath. Rather, these children are given no clue as to how they should prepare except that "it is your character that will be tested, your ability to become a Merging One" (W:10). Daiya is used to this lack of information; her questions and those of other children always seemed to be answered only by the vague assertion that "the Merged One had ways not easily expressed" (D:10). Curiosity was discouraged and could be punished by isolation.

Daiya, however, has difficulty accepting everything on faith—even the very existence of God, although others like her friend Harel see her questions as "meaningless abstractions, ideas of no importance" (W:14). He resists any change in their lives. Clearly, change in Daiya's society must be initiated by an alien encounter. So it is, as Daiya confronts Reiho, a solitary who lands his aircraft near her while she is in the hills training herself for the ordeal. She cannot imagine how solitaries could form a community and communicate; Reiho wonders how any people could exist without history. All Daiya knows or feels she needs to know about the past is what all her people know: "There were those like us and those not like us and they fought long ago. Then there were only those like us" (W:26). She knows even less of any but this ancient history, because in a society that does not change "the passing of time is an illusion, a warp in eternity. What else is there to say?" (W:26).

If one has the truth, why should one change, Daiya explains to Reiho. But, as Mark Twain suggests, innocence untested is not innocence; so too truth untested may not be truth. To avoid knowledge and to accept truth solely on faith, then to destroy those who do not fit that concept of truth, is the pattern of life in Daiya's village.

Yet Reiho and Daiya learn that they were both descended from the same past. For Daiya, Reiho cannot be considered human at all. Not only is he a solitary, but also his people have used science to "modify" humanity—adding artificial skin and organs, supplementing what Nature has given then with what science could add to make them able to survive in other environments once they left Earth. Daiya despairs as she imagines "her world torn apart by these beings, these creatures who had been cast out and should have died" (W:34).

On the other hand, Daiya sees nothing unnatural about the powers she and her people receive from "God," until she learns that the real source of those powers are giant computers buried under the mountains. Daiya had recounted a legend of their origins to Reiho that "these mountains were touched by the Merged One, by God. A web was woven, and people were caught by it. They were no longer solitary selves, and in their fear they tore at one another, almost destroying themselves and the world" (W:95). Preserved in the legend is enough of their history that Daiya cannot avoid the knowledge of the computers once she confronts it.

Confronting that knowledge, however, destroys many in her village, especially the older ones. Reiho, too, is destroyed by their violent resistance to the change; and, although the advanced science of his world can give him back his life, he can never reclaim what Daiya calls his soul. He will remember the life of the Reiho she knew, but he will never feel that the memories are his own. Science can only go so far; there are still unanswerable questions.

Daiya has lived in a world of mythic powers that rejects any knowledge of science and history; in Reiho's world of advanced technology, the concept of the soul has no place. When the worlds come together, it is Daiya who survives as an agent of change because she has the power to combine the two worlds in herself. She does not reject her world: "We can dream the world as well as see it, we can ripen the wheat and fruit, shape the water, see through what is only visible with the eyes, and touch minds, while you must live blind and twist the substance of the world into strange shapes. Now we shall have knowledge too, and we may become something you will never be" (W:174). Knowledge that science and technology can offer cannot create "souls" or the models for human behavior discovered by living in tune with nature and each other, nor does knowledge destroy these truths. Myths, but not myth, can be threatened by increased knowledge; the mythic mind of the poet in each of us grows with that knowledge, expands with the evolving consciousness of humanity just as the child matures as its consciousness expands.

But one must accept such knowledge as does a child, open to possibilities and strong in faith. Daiya's villagers have become inflexible; even the survivors can no longer match her growth. Thus she lives on the edge of the community much as do Al Ith and her followers in Lessing's *Marriages*, and those who can grow and divorce themselves from the past come to her. Her friends in the village light a watchfire—a watchstar—for her. She is no longer confined to the narrow Net of minds of a single planet; now she can touch the Homesmind computer on the comet; now she hears the voices of other stars. Ready even for the consciousness that "Her body was only a shell," she begins to understand and desire the possibility of merging with those stars one day—of finding a universal definition for the Merged One which she had begun to doubt before new knowledge offered her a fresh perspective (W:183). She can recognize her God in the machine (the *deus ex machina* of Greek drama?) without losing faith, just as Moon could accept the buried computer as the Sea Mother in Vinge's novel; she can understand that the mind of the computers could have been what was originally meant by the metaphorical designation "God's mind" in the legends (W:175). If humanity strives to model itself after gods, who is to say that a previous cycle of life had not achieved that goal at least inasmuch as they can offer guidance to the next cycle, guidance preserved in computers even?

Such questions are unanswerable from the current perspective of human consciousness, however, and asking them before that consciousness is expanded or at least opened to change by champions of new knowledge and singers of new songs is to court destruction. Homesmind reminds Daiya, for instance, that she is still part of her world and has only begun to explore it. Despite its narrowly enforced prejudices, Daiya's world is still more open to change than is the technological world of Reiho. There the knowledge accumulates in machines rather than people; and in people, feeling and sensation are slowly being eliminated by their modifications. Like the Arnimi who study Brakrath, they are in danger of "never listening to the land and the people, only instruments." They deny the comprehensive understanding of myth and are left with only the limited explanations of science. Daiya's world need only give up their cultural myths and rediscover the timeless myth which provides them the power of nature and the strength of unity. If they can accept the new song and the new singer, they can grow.

Denial of the alien within, however, leads to death—the actual death experienced by the older generation when the truth of the computers buried in their own world becomes inescapable and, earlier, the ongoing death of a denial of consciousness, as the computers under the mountains tell Daiya when they ask her to wake her people. What value is consciousness if we do not use it as far as it can take us in understanding our world and our universe? The villagers may dread change, but at least they don't reject it completely. Her grandfather Cerwen tells Daiya that she can live near although she must remain outside the village so that the change caused by her presence, her "separateness," will be gradual enough not to destroy them. The agent of change, Sargent reminds us, must often sacrifice the comfort of communal identity as a price for new knowledge. Juaren had told Reyna in Van Scyoc's *Starsilk* of the price of lifelong isolation he had paid for his understanding of Brakrath's need to be awakened; he is even willing to pay with his life to provide Reyna with the knowledge she will need to waken the people. Only Reyna's song—her attempt to communicate with the alien intelligence—saves him from paying that price. As his aunt had told the native American champion Tayo in Leslie Marmon Silko's novel *Ceremony* (a novel which celebrates the flexibility of native American mythmaking), "It isn't easy. It never has been easy."[15]

In Daiya we see the price exacted from the agent of change, which should remind us that the Son who brings light—the Prometheus with his gift of mixed blessings—also must endure torture until he is freed by the next hero: "Because of his unselfish devotion to the cause of humanity, Prometheus drew down upon himself the anger of Olympian Jove."[16] Hercules will release Prometheus from this agony, just as Gwydion releases his son Llew Llaw Gyffes—another god of light—in Celtic legend. That our women writers have shown us light that comes from daughters rather than sons reminds us where the Son himself came from and suggests that an even earlier version of the myth might have concerned a female giver of gifts—a Pandora—as helper to humankind. Charlene Spretnak describes Pandora, for instance, as the "giver of all gifts" who provides the new humans given life by the Mother with fruit, seeds, and "two flat stones"—the flint from which fire is made.[17] This Pandora *is* an earlier Prometheus.

If Pandora becomes a male to be tortured, then a Son to be sacrificed, we might argue that both the Virgin Mary and her Son are symbols of the Goddess—as Mother and as Maiden. Certainly the values attached to Jesus are similar to those we have found associated with other faces of the Goddess. In the next SF myth we will be considering, God does seem to have sent a daughter to humanity. In Elgin's *Star-Anchored, Star-Angered*, Drussa Silver comes to the future planet Freeway, where the population is supposed to "know that religion has almost nothing to do with spirituality and is simply a matter of economics."[18]

In the thirty-first–century universe of the Tri-Galactic Federation, mindspeech is a common acquirement, but Elgin creates her protagonist Coyote Jones (a precursor of Indiana?) as a mind-deaf "cripple." While Jones is the "strongest projective telepath in three galaxies" (SA:45), he has only shared the intimacy of direct mind communication with one person—the mother of his daughter in Elgin's earlier Coyote Jones novel, *Furthest*. It is his handicap which qualifies Jones for assignment to Freeway to uncover the truth about Silver. If she is a fraud, he will not be receptive to her powers of illusion.

Jones is an unusual "secret agent" in other ways as well. Unlike the usual hero of space opera, he is, as the ruling Council of Eight on Freeway discovers, "basically an ignorant man, he is known to be given to emotional excesses of various kinds, ... he is excessively fond of women, I understand, and a perfect fool about children" (SA:31–32). Bungler that he often is, Jones really cares about other people. He is also concerned with his soul, as was first seen in Elgin's novel *The Communipaths*, in which he tried to join the religious Maklunite community—and failed. As Dean O'Halloran points out to him before he goes to Freeway, the main difference between the Maklunites and the followers of Drussa Silver (who call themselves Shavvies) is that the former demanded sainthood of its members while the latter is "a religion of the people. All people" (SA:158).

While Silver herself seems perfect—even physically—and is able to convince Jones and her other followers that she is indeed divine, she does not want to be worshipped. Knowing that for some people the image is needed temporarily, she preserves that image for them, however, by not having sex with Jones but explaining that "there is nothing about divinity that is incompatible with either creativity or love" (SA:120). That many will never grow beyond the worship of her image is rightly recognized by Analyn the Singer as Silver's failure: "No true faith can come of such division, she told us; no salvation can come of such ranking. Women have always known that. Transcendence must come of union, not of separation" (SA:154).

Union with the Goddess is evident in Silver's preaching. *All* the Shavvies seem capable of what those around them describe as miracles—walking on water, for instance. Yet Silver has only offered them new knowledge about what humanity is capable of when it can gain fresh perspectives on reality. "It is a matter of understanding where the *spaces* are in things," she tells Jones. "There's nothing supernormal about it" (SA:121). Expanding their ability to perceive reality allows Silver to offer her followers freedom from the limits of their society and its technology. "I am going to show you what is *real*," she tells Analyn the Singer, "so that you will remember forever, and so that this dream-structure set up by human beings cannot ever again confuse you" (SA:86).

Analyn is the representative of the Old Faith, but she is not tied to its social role in the economy. She is the Singer, communicating with no words the beauty of her faith, while the parson preaches the necessity of tithing. While she and her Holy Sword will be the instruments of Silver's death, she is still another face of the Goddess—the death/crone. And so that

the preachers of the Old Faith cannot use her in opposition to
Silver as yet another image for people to worship, she becomes
a mind prostitute, choosing the ice of Arianrhod (whose name
is also Silver—Silver Wheel); when she breaks the lamp, Jones
can see "the vicious shards dropping all about her like a rain
of murderous ice." "It's very difficult indeed for them to claim
me as their Messiah, as the Holy Champion of the Old Faith,
when I spend my days as public whore," she ironically assures
Jones, and he notices that "her eyes were ice-honed, like the
music, bitter-clear" (SA:153–54). In the context of the Old
Faith— "a branch of Neo-Judaeo-Christianity"—the face of the
Goddess we see is that of a sorceress, a witch, a whore. Divinity
in its true guise is destroyed.

Yet the impact of Silver's teachings will last long after her
image is rightly forgotten, as Dean O'Halloran knows, because
"all the Students coming out of the Multiversities in other
words—are Shavvies" (SA:159). The Students, the finest thousand minds picked from the trillions in the three galaxies, will
be agents of change with social power, as they are the leaders
of the future in science, politics, and the arts (SA:159). Thus
can the values of the Shavvies eventually bring together social
and spiritual realities, history and myth. Furthermore, this
"religion of the people" encourages full expression of the potentialities inherent in each individual and yet offers the love
and support of the community even in failure. "Our community
rallies round to help us do better the next time and to assure
us that if we are weak, so is every one of them," Jones is told
(SA:158).

Communal faith, preserving the world we live in and expanding our perception of it rather than promising us another,
is communicated through the intimate and honest expression
possible with mindspeech. Its Messiah is a woman, also filling
Mary Daly's description of the Antichrist as "the surge of consciousness, the spiritual awakening that can bring us beyond
Christolatry into a fuller conscious participation in the *living*
God."[19] Elgin's invented source, Ann Geheygan, in *Woman
Transcendent*, explains why it should be a woman: "The state
of surpassment, in which the spirit moves beyond the ancient
boundaries and can no longer be affected by fear or pain or an

other illusory perception, comes only with great difficulty to the male human" (SA:113).

But if woman is the bringer of light, the gift-giver, she does not limit that gift to other women. She is a culture hero, offering "a religion of the people," of those pagans of the heath. Nor is she offering answers only to be taken on faith as part of a life beyond the physical; the Goddess offers the human potential available immediately to the person capable of "surpassment." We must learn to see in the many new and old ways in which reality can and must be perceived. Asking new questions elicits new answers, and the unanswerable questions of what lies beyond this life can wait at least until our consciousness has expanded to that level. Coyote Jones learns not to ask them; when Analyn asks him why Silver permitted herself to be murdered, he offers only a rhetorical "Who can know?" (SA:155). The living myth, not the stone image or even the temporary explanation of the legend, had entered our world through Drussa Silver, the Goddess offering Herself as an agent of change to stimulate the next step in human evolution. Even the male, mind-deaf Jones can understand and receive that message, because even the weakest individual is of value to the human community. Besides, Jones is open to caring, to the insights of women, and to the future because he is "a perfect fool about children."

Harder to reach is the despairing protagonist of Joanna Russ's SF myth, *And Chaos Died.* That this too is a novel about "surpassment" is suggested in the quotation from Chuang Tzu with which Russ opens: "The eye is a menace to clear sight, the ear is a menace to subtle hearing, the mind is a menace to wisdom, every organ of the sense is a menace to its own capacity."[20] Jai Vedh, a blue-eyed blond of Hindu descent on his father's side, has turned to the hard, flat vacuum of outer space in his rejection of what his senses have told him about existence. Space is but a "big cousin" to the void within him in this standardized future in which "every place was then like every other place" (AC:9). Vedh must have a new beginning rather than a model to imitate; he must learn new ways to be human.

His rebirth is accomplished through the wreck of the spaceship he is in when he has his breakdown; his healing will take

place on an unnamed planet inhabited by former Earth people
who had been taken there "long, long ago and taught . . . the
rudiments of going Inside, for such things don't come by nature"
(AC:188). Vedh's psychic arrival on the planet, given before
the physical landing, is replete with birth imagery. The escape
capsule is described by the Captain, who accompanies him, as
an egg, in which he is surrounded by "white hard walls" and
"tubing and webbing also white—what a blessing!" (AC:23–
24). Once they land, the egg/ship cannot be repaired; "No, the
shell's cracked. Wide open" (AC:22). As in the legend of the
silverwing explored by Khirsa in Van Scyoc's *Darkchild*, the
cracked shell tells us that the silverwing has flown, that the
soul must learn to fly before its power can be called upon.

The cosmic egg echoed in this creation imagery is of course
common to Chinese and Vedic mythology both of which are
referred to in the novel, as in Russ's quotation from Chuang
Tzu and the Hindi heritage she provides for Vedh. Now Judaic
myth is introduced with the entry of Evne, whose name suggests that she is both the Goddess as Eve and as Ev(eryo)ne.
Evne thus achieves in herself that unity of living myth which
Silver described as the real source of transcendence. In this
garden paradise, Evne comes "holding a green apple in each
hand" (AC:34), but only Vedh seeks her knowledge. While the
Captain "cannibalizes" the ship to build a radio, Vedh recognizes that these people do not want to be rescued. "You would
guess eggs if you saw the shells," Evne compliments him on
his perception, again by comparison with Van Scyoc's tale suggesting that Vedh is at least capable of perceiving both physical
and psychic reality (AC:35). Learning that Evne is a doctor,
and that she has diagnosed both himself and the Captain as
sick "in the head," Vedh alone asks to be cured (AC:35).

Vedh is also introduced to the Mother face of the Goddess in
Olya, next to whom Evne "was hardly a woman at all" (AC:40).
With her magnificent body, Olya is the very vessel, cauldron,
grail, pot, horn of plenty by which the gifts of nature have been
variously symbolized, as Vedh is aware when he notices the
Captain's strong attraction to her (AC:41). Yet Olya and Evne
are facets of each other, as is symbolized by the later appearance of Olya's black mole on Evne's face. Vedh, a homosexual

who has "never liked women," is terrified of this "giantess, a mountain goddess" capable of "killing trees right and left," as his dreams reveal; he needs to receive her gifts through the "delicate, flushed, dim-eyed and shivering" mediatrix of those dreams (AC:51).

As Albert Wendland has acknowledged, Russ brilliantly creates through her storytelling "the interpretive viewpoint of a telepath or a new means of perceiving our world" so that "we get the new alien *perception* presented as the conceptual idea, a concentration on new views."[21] Vedh is healed by being reborn into this world where humans are telepaths, with a full range of psionic abilities and a resultant unity which allows them to lend their full potential of power to any one when necessary.

This new perception terrifies Vedh, and at first he rejects the adults who "were gods and the children heartless" (AC:63). He must gain new knowledge to accept new visions, and he gains that knowledge when he journeys to the "library" with Evne. Here in the heart of the garden he loses his "virginity" and faces his fear of life itself as embodied in the creative act of hetereosexual love. As he "of his own free will...dove into it and ploughed it, ruined himself, gathered himself together" (AC:84), he confirms his fears of losing the self when he cannot "remember his own name." Then he finds that self returned freely to him when Evne offers "*Jai Vedh Jai Vedh Jai Vedh Jai*" and discovers in the reborn self an openness to all life, even to the consciousness of the plants and hills (AC:85–86). In communal life and in the unity of love is found, not lost, the value of the individual.

The "library" itself, this storehouse of knowledge, appears to be merely a "circle of stones," which Vedh recognizes as "The Henge," thus adding Druidic myth to Russ's compendium of symbols. He also learns as did the Shavvies "the spaces in things" when he sees Evne walking into a boulder within which is the library, concretized in marble, the size of a gymnasium (AC:78). Inside are books that talk, that are organic, and that are engraved in metal. This machinery beneath the surface of the Garden suggests again that the return to the Goddess is not a return to the primitive. It is rather, as Samuel Delany has pointed out, "advanced technology hidden behind a rural facade," just as the expressionless faces of the people hide "not human communication in good faith, but *ordinarily invisible* communicational pathways (some form of ESP)."[22] The Goddess is not limited by our cultural blinders; she does, however, demand a world in which nature and technology are compatible.

Vedh, with his new perception, must now return to Old Earth to judge whether or not the Goddess can still survive there. The Goddess as Evne accompanies him, and we discover a future there which might be considered a utopia by some standards. Here too the surface reality appears to be a garden of suburbs and parks. Yet only the facade is maintained, as Vedh discovers while "he lay...breathing unpleasantly warm and slightly stinking air and wondering why the layer of earth under him was so thin" (AC:114). This is a garden devoid of life; "only in the central desert were there any animals at all: insects, and toads, and of course, some birds" (AC:124).

Beneath this deceptive surface are the overpopulated cities, in which aimless people try—or no longer try—to order their lives. Because of the "Great Work Change...people's lives are entirely what they make of them" and "credit is practically unlimited, actually. Things change hands, that's all" (AC:131). Yet with all the time and things anyone could ever want, the humans on this planet are in danger of becoming things themselves. Again myth is perverted, as Vedh discovers when he wakes up "in the lap of the Earth-Mother" who is calming him to be sacrificed by a neo-Aztec cult (AC:138). Russ has chosen her symbols well, for the history of the Aztec religion includes mass human sacrifices to the sun god Huitzilopochtli. Yet this Aztec myth itself, which describes the god beheading his sister, Coyolxauqui, and killing most of the four hundred Huitznahua, has been interpreted as representing "the conquest of the multitudinous peoples of the south," of the Toltecs, by the Aztecs.[23] The androgynous dual god of the Toltecs and "such ancient precepts as the repudiation of human sacrifices and war, which emphasized the superior morality of the Toltecs," were also overthrown.[24]

In yet another mythology Russ has found appropriate symbols for her SF myth. Here too the violent ritual is preserved and the ancient myth is perverted. Little seems to be savable in this future Earth, with the possible exception of the children. Ivat, who with his bow and arrow is to be the weapon of death of this religon just as Analyn the Singer was assigned that role for the Old Faith in Elgin's novel, is in himself worth the salvation Vedh would offer him. Vedh becomes a new god for Ivat to follow, the "Sun Nut" (AC:151). He promises the boy that "I will love you and teach you to be a dragon and a tiger. ...Man, you will *love* your way to Heaven!" (AC:159–60). Caught in his destructive time and place, however, Ivat must grow through hell and madness to earn his chance for rebirth in Vedh's Heaven.

Earth itself is not savable in Russ's future, and the "Conference" at the end of the novel reminds the reader both of the trial which is the climax of Lessing's *Shikasta* and of Franz Kafka's *The Trial.* The name of Evne's fellow telepath, Joseph K, further brings Kafka to mind, and this trial also ends in death. Yet death, as Graves had affirmed, can lead to rebirth, and everyone on Earth is taken into Limbo, from which to be reborn, beginning with Ivat: *"One more out of Limbo: Our work is cut out for us"* (AC:188).

This trial has judged the guilt of our present perception of reality, not the guilt of the body. Bodies are necessary to "go Inside," as Evne and her people had discovered. They were taught this level of perception because the beings that taught them had given up bodies, replacing them with durable mechanical substitutes in an attempt to live forever. Evne is human and she will die. The possibilities inherent in humanity begin with biological reality even though the goal seems to be an expansion of mind and spirit. Even Lessing's Earthborn Canopean George Sherban in *Shikasta* could not at first see beyond the "thirty bladders full of piss, and thirty backsides full of shit, and thirty noses full of snot, and thousands of sweat glands pouring out grease" at his parents' party (S:214).

The beauty of the body is reaffirmed by the power of sexual love to transform in this novel, just as that power is honored in the Vedic myths. The beauty of the mind is apparent in the idyllic existence on the nameless planet of telepaths, which Joseph K. reminds Vedh is "just life" (AC:189)—Russ's last word on Paradise. But the beauty of compassion, of caring, is also essential. Since these telepaths are human, not gods, and since their Paradise is natural, not divine, change and process are necessary here as well. *"You're better than I,"* Evne tells Vedh. *"You'll have to get used to it. Change me"* (AC:186). She had put the people of Earth in Limbo rather than killing them because of the compassion she was learning from Vedh.

Beginning again with new perceptions of reality, in a world where history and myth are compatible and technology is in tune with nature, with the ability to communicate fully with each other as a united community and yet to maintain individual identity and worth—such a world seems impossible to reach without the intervention of "someone" to teach us. Yet, in two other SF myths, *Woman on the Edge of Time* by Marge Piercy and *Mind of My Mind* by Octavia E. Butler, such worlds can be imagined as expansions of our present reality and can find their concretization in our future on Earth itself. Both novels, in fact, begin with the *least* Edenic aspects of today's world, choosing minority female protagonists in urban America and vividly depicting the concrete realities of life in a contemporary American ghetto.

Consuelo Ramos is the middle-aged, Mexican-American protagonist of Piercy's novel, surviving on welfare in El Barrio, the primarily Puerto Rican ghetto of New York City. Even that existence seems preferable to her commitment to Bellevue and then return to Rockover State Psychiatric Hospital for incarceration and experimentation. The dehumanization of Connie's experiences is thoroughly explored by Piercy, and the little light that begins to seep into her life with Luciente, a mind visitor from the future, is first seen by Connie as part of her illness.

If Luciente and the future possibilities she represents are hallucinations, Piercy quickly convinces us that they are still far preferable to the surface reality in which Connie is trapped at present. Luciente may be merely the undying hope within the most exploited human being, but the light she brings reveals a world in which community, communication, and ecological balance can be fully realized, in which the individual is a valued part of the community and also contributes to the survival and well-being of that community.

Communities in Luciente's reality consider themselves extended families, although these families are not structured along the lines of patriarchal hierarchies, as Carol Pearson observes.[25] Ethnicity is determined geographically rather than racially, so that all the residents of Mattapoisett, Massachusetts, in Luciente's time of 2137 are Wamponaug Indians.[26] Even individual names are open to change, as Jackrabbit explains: "When I was born, I was named Peony by my mothers. . . . When I came to naming, I took my own name. . . . But when Luciente brought me down to earth after my highflying, I became Jackrabbit. . . . When Luciente and Bee have quite reformed me, I will change my name again, to Cat in the Sun" (WE:77).

Jackrabbit has referred to his "mothers" because in this version of 2137 children are born in hatcheries and have three parents of either sex co-mothering them. As with feminist utopias by other writers, Piercy's future Mattapoisett has offered alternatives to the sexual biases of today. While hers is not an androgynous world as is Gethen, it does encompass a variety of sexual expressions without conflict. As Joanna Russ has observed in her study of thse utopias,

Classless, without government, ecologically minded, with a strong feeling for the natural world, quasi-tribal in feeling and quasi-family in structure, the societies of these stories are *sexually permissive.* . . . The point of the permissiveness is not to break taboos but to separate sexuality from questions of ownership, reproduction, and social structure.[27]

Russ has accomplished similar aims in *And Chaos Died*, in which Vedh meets Evnika, Evne's daughter by parthenogenesis.

Juxtaposing journeys to her utopic future with increasingly vicious and dehumanizing experiences in Connie's present allows Piercy to make a strong statement about the inadequacies of that present while immediately offering alternatives (many of which Connie reluctantly recognizes as having roots in her cultural past). Discriminatory practices against and among minorities, women, the old and the very young, the poor, and the insane characterize Connie's society.

Insanity, in fact, is presented as a social label that often is rooted in prejudice and sexism. As Phyllis Chesler has pointed out in *Women and Madness*, in our society madness and confinement are "both an expression of female powerlessness and an unsuccessful attempt to reject and overcome this fate. Madness and asylums generally function as mirror images of the female experience, and as penalties for *being* 'female,' as well as for daring *not* to be."[28] Caught in a double bind, women are easily labeled insane. Furthermore, the "irrational" ways of knowing also prompt such labeling in our "rational" society. Thus Lynda Coldridge, who first appears in Lessing's *The Four-Gated City* and more recently in her *Shikasta*, is confined to an asylum because she is able to perceive more of reality than can most of us. "Nearly everyone has been brought to believe that the 5 percent is all there is," she explains to Doctor Hebert in *Shikasta*. "Five percent of the whole universe. And if they think anything else, they are peculiar" (S:182).

Connie is "peculiar," a "catcher" in Luciente's terms, but the "dreams" she catches from Luciente are not nearly as destructive or insane as is her waking life. In the former she is welcomed into a community of friends; in the latter she is confined in a state mental hospital which accords subhuman treatment to the poor and where an experimental operation on her brain is in progress. Not surprisingly, she comes to recognize the doctors as her real enemies. She identifies "the satisfied twinkly blue gaze of Dr. Redding" in the enemy craft about to attack her as she flies with Hawk and Luciente in their future world; she has also seen "pasty Dr. Morgan" piloting the floater, and "dodging about in the back seat,...meticulous Dr. Argent glowered" (WE:336).

The mistreatment in the state hospital is only the most immediate attack against Connie in her waking life, as is symbolized by the other enemy floaters she observes in the battle of the future:

As she stared to left and right she saw that they were piloted and manned by Judge Kerrigan, who had taken her daughter, by the social worker Miss Kronenberg, by Mrs. Polcari, by Acker and Miss Moynihan, by all the caseworkers and doctors and landlords and cops, the psychiatrists and judges and child guidance counselors, the informants and attendants and orderlies, the legal aid lawyers copping pleas, the matrons and EEG technicians, and all the other flacks of power who had pushed her back and turned her off and locked her up and medicated her and tranquilized her and punished her and condemned her. (WE:336)

Her "dreams" reveal to her conscious awareness the struggles she has tried to endure as a powerless female at war with the powers of her world. They also suggest to her a dystopic future based on those powers in which men and women become more machine than human and sexual stereotyping is intensified. These insights combine with Luciente's explanation that Mattapoisett is only one of many possible futures to convince Connie that the only way she can become an agent of change is to act now.

Connie chooses to wage her own battle by poisoning the doctor. She, like Analyn the Singer, hardens herself, becomes ice, so that she cannot be a tool of the way things are, of the Old Faith. She too must pay a price to become an agent of change, however; she sacrifices her own connection with the light of Luciente's future: "She could no longer catch. She had annealed her mind and she was not a receptive woman. She had hardened" (WE:375). As the barohnas of Brakrath know, to gain the power of light they must take stone into their hearts.

Connie will never know the results of her actions, but she has committed herself to the initiation of change. Piercy offers us a possible future with clear roots in our historical reality which could revive the values of community, communication, and ecology—could offer a new face to the Goddess. On the other hand, she foresees a dystopic future if we continue the prejudices, the dehumanization, and the destructive uses of power common to contemporary society. She turns to a seemingly powerless individual in her search for a champion to initiate change, and the individual discovers that even she, victim that she has been, has power if she chooses to use it.

Similarly, the waste products of our ghettos are reevaluated and salvaged in Butler's chronological sequel to *Wild Seed*, *Mind of My Mind*. The novel follows the pattern of a novel of development or initiation. However, while such novels with male protagonists are considered as *Bildungsroman* and chronicle growth and maturation, Annis Pratt has characterized the similar novel with a female protagonist as *"Entwicklungsroman*, the novel of mere growth, mere physical passage from one age to the other without psychological development" because of the limitations put on women as they mature into a patriarchal society.[29] She does identify an important exception, however: "In the genre of science fiction women authors are sometimes able to project visions of worlds where heroes dare *not* to be female, transcending the gender limitations characterizing more conventional novels."[30]

In *Mind of My Mind,* Mary will transcend those limitations, not by daring *"not* to be female" but by daring to deny such limitations on any individual, male or female. A product of the selective breeding initiated by Doro in *Wild Seed*, Mary is the culmination of his genetic experiments in human psychic potentialities.

Still, as a contemporary black American woman, Mary must also struggle against the poverty and violence common to "the multiple alienation of sex, class, and race" which, Pratt has admitted, "intensifies physical and psychological suffering for the young Black woman."[31] She grows up in a California ghetto with a prostitute mother and finds it necessary at times to protect herself from unwanted men by wielding a cast iron skillet. But Mary is exceptional due to her "breeding," and her "transition" from adolescence to selfhood leaves her an active telepath controlling minds of others like her through a Pattern.

In giving birth to the Pattern, Mary gives birth to a new society in which she is the most powerful figure, and gives rebirth to thousands of "latent" telepaths who are Doro's as well as our society's discards. They have been suffering from their uncontrollable reception of human pain from everyone around them until her ability to borrow strength from the Pattern aids them through their transitions to control or cancellation of the telepathy.

However reluctantly, Mary has inherited her ability to survive from her maternal side, from her mother Rina and her ancestress Emma (Anyanwu of *Wild Seed*). Now she must be the teacher, the agent of change, as well as the mother to "her people" in the Pattern, teaching them to develop constructive uses for their individual skills. Frances Smith Foster argues that Mary, despite her name, cannot fit the stereotype of the Black Madonna defined earlier by Daryl Dance. However, she does admit that Mary combines the traits "not only of Eve and Madonna, but also of God and Satan" into "a new kind of female character in both science fiction and Afro-American literature."[32] That new character in SF has been described by Phyllis J. Day as follows:

The new women of science fiction, then, whether witch or Earthmother, are real people, strong people, and they are integral to and often protectresses of Earth and ecology. Moreover, they are part of an organic whole, a return to our premechanistic past, and they represent a force against man in his assumption of the right to dominate either women or Earth/nature.[33]

Much of this applies to the women in the novels we have discussed, although the "premechanistic past" may only be the interpretation our limited perspective puts on a world where technology and ecology comfortably coexist. Mary, daughter of godlike Doro and descendant of Sun Woman Anyanwu, is also such a woman. As the child of these two agents of change, Mary will combine the male and female principles of the life-giving sun and be the Champion to realize the fruition of change in her society. Complete in herself with the heritage of Anyanwu's healing compassion and creative motherhood balancing that of Doro's relentlessly searching spirit and physical need for "good prey," Mary gives birth to a physical and psychic Patternist society.

All life lives by devouring other life; nature asks only that we give back when we must take, which Mary does. When Doro comes after her to destroy her and the Pattern, she does take his life, but she does not want to destroy. Actually, through her Doro lives on by being absorbed into and strengthening the very community he has dedicated his life to establishing. Through his death, therefore, he is reborn as part of the Pattern; only his individual, destroying self is dispersed.

Usually, in fact, the Pattern is a source of enhanced indviduality, as Mary can really offer rebirth to those who draw their strength through her from the Pattern to enable them to successfully survive transition: "Karl lived. The family lived. ... Now we were free to grow again—we, his children."[34] Doro is gone; the male god is absorbed into the new reality, the new pattern. Nor does Emma choose to survive her male counterpart; the Goddess has taken a new face, a new living myth for the changes that will come.

In her new role, Mary is indeed the Triple Goddess. The Maiden has become the Mother as well, and the Elder must practice her wisdom to help her family. This "third figure of the triad, who has often been gynophobically perceived as 'devouring mother' or 'crone,' " Pratt argues, "represents the older mother's knowledge of the best moment to fledge or let go of her children, a moment that, if precipitous or delayed, can lead the maternal element to become destructive."[35] As Mary draws strength from her people through the Pattern to combat Doro, she learns that letting go too late kills them. But Mary is not Doro: "I'm not the vampire he is. I give in return for my taking" (MM:210). Mary is whole in ways Doro never has been, which even he has recognized: "She was a symbiont, a being living in partnership with her people. She gave them unity, they fed her, and both thrived. She was not a parasite, though he had encouraged her to think of herself as one. And though she had great power, she was not naturally, instinctively, a killer. He was" (MM:217).

In Mary, Butler has found one of the "new ways of thinking about power" for which she had turned to the genre of SF.[36] As we will learn in *Patternmaster*, the person at the center of the Pattern can draw on the power of all Patternists, but she is slowly being drained of her power, her very life, as well. She sacrifices her freedom to serve as their leader; she pays the Champion's price.

Yet Mary is hated and feared at first, embodying as she does that overwhelming power of the Goddess which Jai Vedh had recognized and feared in Olya. Does submission to the Pattern, the community, the Goddess, mean loss of self, of individual possibilities? Does it mean merely a glorified slavery? Day has commented on the patriarchal fear of strong women which seems to underlie Vedh's fear: "These capable women with power are most often called witches and considered deviant from their society. They are usually feared and hated by other tamed women, as well as by men."[37] Even her husband Karl fears Mary at first, and the latents she tries to bring through transition often struggle against her. Yet all benefit from what she gives individually and as the focal point of their community. "I don't write about heroes," Butler has said. "I write about people who survive and sometimes prevail."[38] These survivors *are* the heroes of new societies, as is Mary.

Through Mary, Butler transmutes Afro-American heritage into a new face of the Goddess and achieves a societal Pattern which also fulfills her aim of bringing "together multi-racial groups of men and women who must cope with one another's differences as well as with new, not necessarily controllable, abilities within themselves."[39] Telepathic abilities are not distributed by race, by gender, or by religion. Mary is black; Karl is white. While the latents are dependent upon the Pattern, they might come into it with the same prejudices as any other contemporary American.

Yet submission to the community of the Pattern makes possible the greatest individual development these latents could ever hope to have. Many would never have developed into active telepaths or healers without the Pattern. Instead, they would have continued not only in the misery and confusion of what their society would consider madness but in enmity toward each other as well, as can be seen in the Cain and Abel of this potential Paradise, Clay and Seth. An "abnormally sensitive" latent, Clay has no control over his psionic gifts before the Pattern, and without the protection of his brother Seth he "would be insane or dead by now" (MM:70). Since Seth protects rather than kills him, Clay is contemplating suicide because "he was just becoming less and less able to tolerate the pain of living" (MM:71). While the Pattern does not make him an Active, able to control and use those powers, it does relieve him by removing his mixed blessing, thereby freeing both Seth and Clay from an ultimately destructive brotherhood and letting each develop independently.

Adults not in the Pattern, with no telepathic ability, are called Mutes. Since they are easily and unknowingly manipulated by the Patternists, they *are* in danger of becoming slaves, or "pets" as Karl considers his Mute girlfriend. Unlike Daiya's society in Sargent's *Watchstar*, however, the Patternist society finds a place for their "solitaries." Although they never really know the true character of their community because they are unaware of the telepathic control, Mutes provide a service of central importance as child rearers. Telepaths make very bad parents, especially in the latent stage when they take out their frustrations on the vulnerable young or simply lose themselves in the escapes of sex, drugs, or alcohol while the children suffer from neglect. Since the latent period can continue as late as middle age, being able to foster the children out to Mutes preserves the community.

Mary, the new Goddess in a near future, can expand the inherent possibilities of humanity for each of the Patternists: "In the two short years of its existence the Pattern had given these people a new way of life. A way of life that they valued" (MM:214). She is the ruler and the servant of her people, and as telepaths they can be sure of this: "I let them feel the emotion I felt. . . . I wanted them to see how important their safety was to me" (MM:214). Nor does power in this society depend upon the desecration of nature; human beings are one of our world's primary resources, and these "societal discards" had been wasted before the Pattern. Butler's society is similar to Luciente's future Mattapoisett in that each depends upon "a mobilizing of inknowing resources—mental" which can offer constructive uses of power (WE:56).

If the retelling of our cultural myths and examination of women's worlds has uncovered the face of the Goddess for the earlier writers we have discussed, the creation of the new SF myths discussed in this chapter has given the Goddess quite a face-lift and discovered new, even alien, faces she might be wearing. Yet the ancient myth that unites these worlds within women is still the same, offering a pattern in which the individual and the community, men and women, self and alien Other, nature and technology, magic and science, and myth and history unite to enrich each other. The left hand and the right belong to the same person; the myth and the history can tell the same story if we can learn to listen. In the best of all possible worlds, the underlying myth and the surface reality show the same face; as our worlds strive to emulate that world, we can learn to "put on the face you want him to see—the accepting face," and to know with Van Scyoc's Kadura that "after a time it will no longer be just a face": "eventually the act becomes the reality" (D: 170). Not only human behavior but also social behavior can find a model to *imitate* in ancient myth.

Lessing has shown in her SF myth that isolation can lead to sterility and that we earn our next level of human consciousness only by living in and giving to the world when Necessity demands changes. LeGuin has removed the blinders of gender to show us that self and alien can maintain differences and yet reach mutual understanding through love if they begin breaking the ice individually and find ways to communicate honestly. On Van Scyoc's Brakrath, the alien from within us and from outside must be confronted if we are to initiate change in ourselves and our world; then we must listen to the land and the people to learn new songs to sing and tales to tell to make that change work in our expanding universe without destroying the fabric of our lives. Sargent shows the destructiveness of closing ourselves off to new knowledge even when we feel content with our world, limiting ourselves to myths which can be destroyed by change rather than opening ourselves to universal possibilities. Elgin offers us yet another woman Champion willing to sacrifice herself to expand our possibilities, while Russ forces us to earn new knowledge through rebirth and then to examine what we think we know from new perspectives. Piercy and Butler bring the promises of the stars back to Earth and suggest ways we can find the face of the Goddess in our own future, ways in which we too can become agents of change by expanding our own attitudes to accept new perceptions of reality. Each woman reminds us that life is a process in which even the worst among us can get better and the best need our communal support. To sing new songs is not to destroy the ancient harmonies but to give them new expression.

NOTES

1. Otto Rank, "Life and Creation," in *The Myth of the Birth of the Hero and Other Writings*, ed. Philip Freund (New York: Vintage, 1964): 146.

2. Geoffrey Hartman, *The Unmediated Vision* (New York: Harcourt, Brace & World, 1966): xi.

3. Mircea Eliade, *Myths, Rites, Symbols*, ed. Wendell C. Beane and William G. Doty, Vol. I (New York: Harper & Row, 1975): 3.

4. Gene M. Bernstein, "The Mediated Vision; Eliade, Levi-Strauss, and Romantic Mythopoesis," in *The Binding of Proteus*, ed. Marjorie W. McCune, Tucker Orbison, and Philip M. Withim (London: Associated University Presses, 1980): 163.

5. Doris Lessing, *The Marriages between Zones Three, Four, and Five* (New York: Vintage, 1980): 244. Subsequent references are to this edition and will be included in the text as M:page in parentheses. See Barbara Hill Rigney, *Lilith's Daughters: Women and Religion in Contemporary Fiction* (Madison: University of Wisconsin Press, 1982): 82, for one view of Al Ith's "fortunate fall."

6. Robert Graves, *The White Goddess* (New York: Farrar, Straus & Giroux, 1948): 57.

7. Peter Brigg, "The Archetype of the Journey in Ursula K. LeGuin's Fiction," in *Ursula K. LeGuin*, ed. Joseph D. Olander and Martin Harry Greenberg (New York: Taplinger, 1979): 46.

8. Ursula K. LeGuin, Introduction to *The Altered I*, ed. Lee Harding (New York: Berkley, 1978): 9.

9. Ursula K. LeGuin, "American SF and the Other," in *The Language of the Night*, ed. Susan Wood (New York: G. P. Putnam's Sons, 1979): 97. "Isn't the 'subjection of women' in sf," she asks, "merely a symptom of a whole which is authoritarian, power-worshipping, and intensely patriarchal?"

10. Ursula K. LeGuin, *The Left Hand of Darkness* (New York: Walker, 1969): 169. Subsequent references are to this edition and will be given in the text as LH:page in parentheses. Cf. also Franz van der Bogert, "Nature through Science Fiction," in *The Intersection of Science Fiction and Philosophy*, ed. Robert E. Myers (Westport, Conn.: Greenwood Press, 1983): 65, on the " 'sexed' nature" of Gethen.

11. Lee Cullen Khanna, "Change and Art in Women's Worlds: Doris Lessing's *Canopus in Argos: Archives*," in *Women in Search of Utopia*, ed. Ruby Rohrlich and Elaine Hoffman Baruch (New York: Schocken Books, 1984): 273.

12. Sydney J. Van Scyoc, "Starsilk," in *Daughters of the Sunstone* (Garden City, N.Y.: Nelson Doubleday, 1984): 567. Subsequent references are to this edition and will be given as SS:page in text.

13. Sydney J. Van Scyoc, *Darkchild* (New York: Berkley, 1982): 130. Subsequent references are to this edition and will be given in the text as D:page in parentheses.

14. Pamela Sargent, *Watchstar* (New York: Pocket Books, 1980): 7. Subsequent references are to this edition and will be given in the text as W:page in parentheses.

15. Leslie Marmon Silko, *Ceremony* (New York: NAL, 1977): 272.

16. Charles Mills Gayley, *The Classic Myths in English Literature and in Art* (Lexington, Mass.: Xerox College Publishing, 1939): 11.

17. Charlene Spretnak, *Lost Goddesses of Early Greece: A Collection of Pre-Hellenic Myths* (Boston: Beacon, 1978): 48–52.

18. Suzette Haden Elgin, *Star-Anchored, Star-Angered* (New York: Daw, 1979): 31. Subsequent references are to this edition and will be given in the text as SA:page in parentheses.

19. Mary Daly, *Beyond God the Father: Toward a Philosophy of Women's Liberation* (Boston: Beacon, 1973): 96.

20. Joanna Russ, *And Chaos Died* (New York: Ace, 1970): 5. Subsequent references are to this edition and will be given in the text as AC:page in parentheses.

21. Albert Wendland, *Science, Myth, and the Fictional Creation of Alien Worlds* (Ann Arbor: University of Michigan Research Press, 1985): 130.

22. Samuel R. Delany, "The Order of 'Chaos'," *Science-Fiction Studies* 6:3 (November 1979): 334. Delany presented a greatly expanded version of this study at *Women Worldwalkers*, a symposium at Texas Tech University in January 1983 in which I also presented a paper on Russ and Elgin. Our discussions were very helpful in clarifying this novel for me.

23. Miguel Leon-Portilla, "Mythology of Ancient Mexico," in *Mythologies of the Ancient World,* ed. Samuel Noah Kramer (Garden City, N.Y.: Doubleday, 1961): 462.

24. Ibid.: 465.

25. Carol Pearson, "Women's Fantasies and Feminist Utopias," *Frontiers* 2:3 (1977): 52.

26. Marge Piercy, *Woman on the Edge of Time* (New York: Fawcett, 1976): 100. Subsequent references are to this edition and will be given in the text as WE:page in parentheses.

27. Joanna Russ, "Recent Feminist Utopias," in *Future Females*, ed. Marleen Barr (Bowling Green, Ohio: Bowling Green University Popular Press, 1981): 76.

28. Phyllis Chesler, *Women and Madness* (New York: Avon, 1972): 39.

29. Annis Pratt, with Barbara White, Andrea Loewenstein, and Mary Wyer, *Archetypal Patterns in Women's Fiction* (Bloomington: Indiana University Press, 1981): 36.

30. Ibid.: 35.

31. Ibid.: 33.

32. Frances Smith Foster, "Octavia Butler's Black Female Future Fiction," *Extrapolation* 23:1 (Spring 1982): 37.

33. Phyllis J. Day, "Earthmother/Witchmother: Feminism and Ecology Renewed," *Extrapolation* 23:1 (Spring 1982): 14.

34. Octavia E. Butler, *Mind of My Mind* (New York: Avon, 1977): 220–21. Subsequent references are to this edition and will be given in the text as MM:page in parentheses.

35. Pratt, *Archetypal Patterns*: 172.

36. Quoted by Veronica Mixon in "Futurist Woman: Octavia Butler," *Essence* 15 (April 1979): 12.

37. Day, "Earthmother/Witchmother": 14. See also Pratt's discussion of the "Craft of the Wise" in *Archetypal Patterns*: 175–76 and Margot Adler's study, *Drawing Down the Moon: Witches, Druids, Goddess-Worshippers, and Other Pagans in America Today* Chapter 8: "Women, Feminism and the Craft" (Boston: Beacon, 1979).

38. Mixon, "Futurist Woman": 12.

39. Quoted by Curtis C. Smith (ed.), *Twentieth Century Science Fiction Writers* (New York: St. Martin's Press, 1981): 93.

4

Fantastic Mythmaking: Transformed Patterns

"Fantasies," says Rosemary Jackson, "image the possibility of radical cultural transformation through attempting to dissolve or shatter the boundary lines between the imaginary and the symbolic."[1] In the works we have been discussing, the imaginary *is* the symbolic, and the concretization of "radical cultural transformation" is not merely representative but definitive as well. In fantastic literature, these writers have offered radical alternatives to today's culture which depend upon the extension and expansion of already accepted possibilities. "A mobilization of inknowing resources" such as Marge Piercy offers in her future Mattapoisett and a reclamation of natural resources need not be incompatible with knowledge provided by science and technology nor with workable social structures. They do seem to be, however, incompatible with that knowledge and those structures as they are utilized today. "We can only know what we can truly imagine," Piercy's Luciente has told Connie (WE:328), but in the imaginings of fantastic literature we can dissolve what might be artificial barriers between us and what is indeed knowable. From another vantage point in space and/or time, we not only gain perspective on what is and what was but also open new perspectives on what can be and might have been.

Beyond the significance of the structural fabulation and creation of alien perspectives in fantastic literature, these works must also be considered in terms of the mythic purposes of the novel as a form. Eric Gould argues that

the novel always implies some set of assumptions about the nature of the divided self in society and about the problems of its discourse. The concept of the novel, that is, is positively mythic in scope even before classical, religious, or totemistic mythologies lend its plots their meaning. In fact, it would seem that mythologies could not enter the novel, and be something more than merely functionalist motifs, unless the novel as a genetic system had a history and a set of appropriative needs of its own, allowing a repetitive attempt to get beyond history and, like a true "science of the concrete," accommodate everything to itself.[2]

Therefore, even in novels which do not obviously involve myth, the archetypal patterns undergirding the story—the plot or "mythos"—might be equally reflective of this discourse between the self and society. That society may be internalized as the superego (as it was in Sydney Van Scyoc's *Darkchild*) or externalized as the alien or Other, the historical moment and place, or the universal possibilities by which the self is confronted. In her study of *Archetypal Patterns in Women's Fiction*, Annis Pratt has examined yet another form of mythmaking intrinsic to the novel. She argues that novels by women are unique in their utilization of patterns common to women which can be best identified with pre-patriarchal archetypes.

The four major categories Pratt identifies for women's fiction present (1) the development of the female central character as a young girl entering womanhood, (2) her courtship and marriage or (3) her alternative choice of sexual freedom or celibacy, and (4) her transformation and rebirth in maturity. However, Pratt has also concluded that in each of these four stages, the women characters are "disrupted by social norms dictating powerlessness for women."[3] In other words, the discourse with a patriarchal society puts women at a decided disadvantage: "Young girls grow down rather than up, the socially festive denouements appropriate to courtship and marriage fictions are often subverted by madness and death, Eros and celibacy

alike are punished with tragic denouements, and when a rebirth journey is attempted, the reward of personal power makes
the conquering hero a cultural deviant."[4]

If Pratt is accurate in her assumptions, the lack of growth
(or social acceptance of growth) in women characters seems to
be reflective of the devaluation of the Goddess. As Marta Weigle
has suggested, the women in myth with whom most of us are
best acquainted are negatively portrayed or are applauded for
passive, submissive qualities and willing sacrifice of sexual and
other freedoms.[5] These are the women I will identify with Toni
Wolff's category of the "hetaira." Wolff has analyzed the archetypal components of the feminine as consisting of four op-
posing aspects; the amazon, the mother, and the medial are
the other three. In relation to the Triple Goddess archetype,
these three aspects are easily identifiable as the Maiden, the
Mother, and the Elder or Wise Woman respectively, as is reflected in Wolff's analysis of them.[6]

Who, then, is the hetaira? Taken from the word for concubine,
hetaira refers to the companion of men, to the woman defined
by patriarchy. She is most often in women's literature portrayed as her "father's daughter"; in fairy tales she might well
be the stepmother who has taken the real Mother's place as
the father's wife. The force of this social definition has distorted
the other three aspects of the feminine and limited their meaning, as we discussed earlier in relation to the forms of the
Goddess found in Andre Norton's Witch World series. These
aspects are like phases of the moon, and the same person can
express any of them at any time in her life. Thus, being a
Maiden does not preclude either sexual activity or the "sight"
of the wise woman; being a mother does not mean the sacrifice
of personal and sexual freedom; being the wise woman does
not put one beyond the creative urge. The Mother is not synonymous with maternity, so this aspect does not just disappear
when one is beyond the childbearing years.

With the omnipresent influence of patriarchal definition,
however, the Maiden has been seen as sterile, her sexual freedom confined by the glorification of virginity and her personal
freedom granted only inasmuch as children are allowed some
freedom from gender specification—as a tomboy, for instance,

which in the word itself reminds her that this is behavior more appropriate for males. The mother is, as Pratt points out, particularly enclosed in the patriarchy for the simple necessity of being able to identify the father of her children. When inheritance passes from father to son, the mother cannot be allowed sexual freedom. This is reflected in the presentation of Lilith, Adam's first wife, in cultural myth and in our literature.

In Jewish tradition, Lilith comes down to us as an evil seductress, a she-demon who steals men's seed and creates illegitimate children—the Lilin or night-demons. Jealous of legitimate offspring, Lilith is said to threaten women and kill children.[7] Although her epithet is "the beautiful maiden," she is also known as a harlot and a vampire who enslaves men.[8] According to later Kabbalistic texts, Lilith is identified one minute with the serpent Leviathin and seen as the symbol of "mere fornification" and in the next minute with the Matronit, wife of God.[9] Raphael Patai has argued that the two are simply different faces of the Goddess: "God is one, but the Goddess, who is part of him, is two: the Matronit and Lilith.... Although the God and the Goddess are one, innumerable strands of attraction and repulsion run back and forth between them, and likewise between man and the deity ... and the two aspects of his female component constantly struggle for man and in man."[10]

The tangled web of tales about Lilith is like the tangled web of her beautiful hair, her most commonly noted feature, and the former traps the human imagination as surely as the latter is supposed to entrap the heart. In the Walpurgisnacht scene of Goethe's *Faust*, for example, we are warned against "Adam's first wife" and the "allure of those fair tresses,"[11] which is all she wears. Poets from Dante Gabriel Rossetti to X. J. Kennedy dedicate poetry to her; playwrights from George Bernard Shaw to Le Roi Jones give her continuing life.

Yet the sexual threat Lilith poses has its real danger in the legal ramifications of any offspring she might have. That she is primarily a threat to the validity of patrilinear descent is obvious in the Kabbalistic attack on her "demon" children: "All the illegitimate children that a man has begotten with demons in the course of his life appear after his death to take part in the mourning for him and in his funeral. . . . The demons claim their inheritance on this occasion along with the other sons of the deceased and try to harm the legitimate children."[12] This then is the danger of allowing the Mother her own identity beyond her role as the legitimate parent of a man's sons. The Wise Woman, on the other hand, offers us the survival of irrational knowledge in a supposedly rational world. The dualistic attitudes of patriarchy devalue that knowledge and call the wise woman a witch.

What is left is Bloduewedd, the artificial woman created to be the wife of man. Small wonder that women writers find a conflict between their intuitive perceptions of themselves and of their relationship to the world around them and the limited perception they are taught by their society. Seeking the new perception of the individual is their first step in seeking the new perception of reality itself which will make them agents of change.

With its imaginative freedom, fantastic literature is able to offer new perceptions to the female protagonist, so that these novels can go beyond the pessimism Pratt has noted in other fiction by women. The same archetypal patterns emerge transformed in fantastic literature to reinstate feminine power, just as the cultural patterns we have examined in the last chapter reinstate the Goddess on a communal level. It is this transformed woman who can be the agent of change, who can embody the Goddess in her own self. The young woman can change her society rather than be changed by it, courtship and marriage can offer magic and rebirth rather than madness and death, the alternative choice of Eros or celibacy can find acceptance in a community that encourages individual growth and expression, and the reborn woman can be recognized as a culture hero rather than a "cultural deviant."

By allowing its writers to manipulate societies as well as characters, fantastic literature can mirror the inner rather than the outer woman and concretize her experience in a world of expanded possibilities. "Doctor Hebert says that I feel myself to be useless. (But I am. Anyone would see that at once.)," Lynda Coldridge begins in Doris Lessing's *Shikasta* (S:182). Yet with Dr. Hebert's support she will discover that hers is the correct perception of reality and that she too will be an agent of change.

Maturation of the young woman in novels of development by women, Pratt has determined, follows three patterns, usually to negative conclusions. The first pattern of meeting a "green-world lover" usually ends in the death of that natural sensuality, which Pratt relates to the dying god of early myth such as in the Ishtar/Tammuz myth.

The Demeter/Kore myth provides the second pattern of "rape and theft" of the growing woman and of nature itself by men. However, Charlene Spretnak reminds us that such violence cannot be found in earlier versions of the myth and suggests that it "was added after the societal shift from matrifocal to patriarchal."[13] Potentially, therefore, this need not be the negative pattern it is in Pratt's analysis; daughters can learn and grow away from mothers without violent separation and desecration.

The third and final pattern which is described as "growing up grotesque" by Pratt is also flexible; by whose judgment is the growth pattern grotesque? Phyllis Day's comments on the denigration of strong women as witches in our literature is worth remembering here.[14] As Pratt points out, women are not the heroes of our society; nor are they admired if they display the heroic qualities of intelligence, personal and sexual freedom, "allegiance to nature," and the desire for "meaningful work" as men would be.[15]

Thus, when we consider the patterns we already find the potential for the transformation possible in fantastic literature. The love of the green world of nature, the heritage of maternal knowledge and assertion of individual growth, and the realization of strong personal qualities could be the end to which the respective patterns lead. In two novels by Tanith Lee, *The Birthgrave* and *The Silver Metal Lover*, such transformation begins to take place.

In *Birthgrave*, which was Lee's first novel, we find, as Marion Zimmer Bradley asserts in her introduction, a woman who "takes her destiny in her own hands, neither slave nor chattel. Her adventures are her own. She is not dragged into them by the men in her life, nor served up to the victor as a sexual reward after the battle."[16] Awakening as an adult in the heart of a volcano, this nameless woman knows only that a disembodied voice, Karrakaz the "Soulless One," accuses her of inevitable evil and tempts her to suicide. "Recollect, you should have been powerful," Karrakaz says before convincing her that hers is the face of "a devil, a monster, a mindless thing, unbearable to look on" (B:10). Only one hope is held out: the existence of her "soulkin of green jade" (B:10). Symbolically, however, we are confronting the divided self; the waking ego is driven and derided by the alien within, Karrakas as the voice of social condemnation, and is seeking her own spirit or soul.

This social condemnation illustrates the "growing up grotesque" pattern in which the young woman finds herself. Yet she resists the criticism, deciding that her "instinct for freedom was too strong, too terrible," and runs for her life, steps ahead of the molten lava following her as she begins her journey of individuation (B:10). It is important to remember here that the volcano is a symbol of the Goddess of Fire as Pele in Polynesia, Maueea in New Zealand, Fuji in Japan, and Chantico in Mexico. As Pele she is "often said to be seen as a woman shortly before an eruption" who "was known to fancy handsome young chiefs, and to enjoy joining in the holua sled racing and other sports."[17] In bringing again the mixed blessing of fire, the Goddess as culture hero is both feared and welcomed.

Our hero, however, must remain nameless and faceless for most of the novel, temporarily succumbing to the image of herself as grotesque that Karrakas establishes in her mind. As she pursues her adventures through several definitely patriarchal societies, however, the people she encounters remember the Goddess even when she does not. They often worship this woman who wears a mask and masters men and their skills. Moreover, to the skills of the warrior she adds healing powers and a remarkable gift for language acquisition. Her adventures with Lord Vazkor to unite the cities still loyal to the race of which she is the last survivor show her commitment to her community as well, so that we see the values of community, communication, and ecology embodied in her actions.

Her first lover, Darak, is her green-world lover, taking her through the forests and offering her the "solace, companionship, and independence" which Pratt has identified with the pattern.[18] Despite his rather feeble attempts to dominate her which seem to reflect the expectations of the patriarchal structures in which they live, his support helps her grow in skills and self-awareness. The pattern of his death is not avoided, however, in this novel; he is destroyed at his moment of social triumph as punishment for his antisocial history.

The transformed pattern of the Demeter/Kore myth can be seen in our hero's relationship with the healer Uasti, her source of feminine power. "I thought I had been one with Darak, in my fashion, forgetting oneness does not come from the body alone," she realizes. "Now I became one with the strange old woman of the wagon people—by an almost imperceptible process that sprang from understanding" (B:152).

But her journey will not be free of the negative aspects of this pattern either. The rape-trauma pattern comes into her life with Vazkor especially, who has tried to usurp her place as leader of her race by a kind of black magic training in her Goddess skills.

Finally, reborn after destroying the unjust claims of Vazkor to her power, she must wander alone, through oppressive and supportive societies, to confront her "grotesqueness" and transform it. By an interesting *deus ex machina* (though really a *dea ex machina* since the Goddess is the power source) which shatters temporal and spatial limitations by pulling a spaceship into this primitive reality, the hero discovers that totality of self for which she has been searching. She, Karrakas, and the green jade are rejoined as parts of the same self, beautiful and powerful and worthy of admiration rather than condemnation.

True to contemporary realities, Lee has brought her hero through the patterns of female maturation which devalue, exploit, and rob her of supportive love. She has not stopped there, though. Her protagonist is assisted in her maturation process by the support of Darak and Uasti and the natural strengths of the the Goddess within herself, which often need only to be believed in to be of use. Literally, Lee has achieved Pratt's goal for women's fiction of reclaiming the Goddess and "casting aside the gynophobic masks that have obscured her beauty, her power, and her beneficence."[19] Lee creates an emerging woman who chooses her own path and earns equality with men even in patriarchal society. Through self-acceptance she finally recognizes the power inherent in the female, in herself. As she finally asserts, "I am alone. No one stands beside me. I have no Dark Prince to ride in my chariot, to walk with me, to hold me to him. I have no one. And yet, I myself, at last, I have myself. And to me, at this time, it seems enough. It seems more, much more, than enough" (B:408).

In Lee's later novel, *The Silver Metal Lover*, the title character Silver (acronym for Silver Ionized Locomotive Verisimulated Electronic Robot) offers a unique embodiment of the green-world lover who supports sixteen-year-old Jane in her search for self. If the Goddess can appear in the modern world as a buried computer, why can't her Son, the sacrificial god, appear as a robot? So he does, and if Silver is definitely artificial and unnatural in origin, yet he provides the values of the archetype for Jane.

True to the social purpose of fiction, Jane must plunge into her society, leave her bright home in the clouds and her protective mother Demeta to move to the slums of Tolerance Street. In the city, the urban blight and threatening quakes, generated by an orbiting asteroid which has already destroyed a third of the world's population in Lee's future reality, effectively convey Pratt's rape-trauma pattern. No wonder Demeta, true to her name, has withdrawn to the clouds after this rape of the green world. The Old River is so polluted that "every apartment there has a warning notice cut into the window frame which says: The Surgeon General has established that to open this window for more than ten minutes every day can seriously damage your health."[20]

Jane could *watch* nature through the sealed window walls of her mother's home, but the comfort of nature comes to her ironically through the clouds and rainbows which Silver paints on the walls and ceiling of their slum apartment. As human beings destroy the environment, Lee seems to suggest, those we designate as subhuman or less recreate it. And why won't robots be considered another life form worthy of respect, just as we learned on Van Scyoc's Brakrath to acknowledge the humanity of the Rauthimages?

If Jane gains solace from Silver's artistic recreation of nature, she also gains companionship from his presence. Silver is programmed to find his joy in making others happy. "So are humans, actually, to a certain extent," he reminds her (SM:77). An androgynous, Christlike figure, Silver teaches Jane about herself and about love. "My joy was his joy," she marvels. "I'd been crazy to say what I had, that he couldn't love. He can love all of us. He IS love" (SM:89).

Demeta, on the other hand, is definitely a demented form of Demeter, the Mother face of the Goddess, as is revealed in her attempts to program Jane in the "growing-up-grotesque" pattern. Denied Kore's role, Jane complains to her: "Mother, why did you call me 'Jane'? I mean, why not Proserpina? That was Demeta's daughter in the legend, wasn't it? Didn't you think I'd be glamourous enough to be called Proserpina, Mother?" (SM:140).

Engendered by artificial insemination, delivered by a machine, and raised mechanically by the latest psychological, sociological, and cosmetic guidelines, Jane is more a machine than the robot she loves. As she learns to find "my pleasure in his pleasure. So I knew what he'd known before, the joy in my lover's joy" (SM:164), Jane is finally learning a human definition of self. In her love for Silver and her earned acceptance into the urban community, she transforms plain Jane into "Jain," a self-defined woman beautiful with her own ash-blonde hair, her own slight frame rather than the "Venus Media" type she had been cosmetically induced into recreating, and her own pain when society destroys her doomed lover. Like Karrakaz, Jain finds herself alone (SM:227); unlike Karrakaz, however, she won't stay that way.

Lee has brought Jain through the grotesque pattern by letting her discover her own beauty and singing talent, through the rape-trauma pattern by offering her painted rainbows and communal love in the slums of the city, and through the death of her green-world lover by resurrecting his soul—the soul Jain herself had given Silver by loving him unselfishly in return for his freely given love. The Mother as Maiden gives human life to the Son, and when he dies again for the sins of this world his love lives on.

Love comes back to support Jain through the *dea ex machina* of a seance set up by Clovis (whose very name suggests that he is an imperfect substitute for Silver in his loving friendship with Jain). With this support, Jain faces life on her own, returning to the slums and to her singing, even confronting her mother with a commitment "to learn, to grow, to gain experiences and sights and sounds and truths and friendships." Although her initial motivation is her love for Silver, wearing the accepting face and opening herself to change promises further growth: "If I still feel like that when I'm old. If I still feel like that in another year" (SM:239).

In both novels, Tanith Lee brings the novel of development through the social restrictions which have straitjacketed other women writers. By using the structural fabulation possible in fantastic literature, she revitalizes the archetypes and rediscovers the Goddess (seemingly in the least likely places to those with limited perception) and lets her women accept their own power and potential.

Still, most women entering adulthood will not remain alone, even supported by a loving memory. What are their alternatives to what Pratt calls "enclosure in the patriarchy"?[21] Pratt sees in the novels of marriage both complicity and escape into madness, social protest, or even death. Only in SF does she see the potential for equality: "the only possible abrogation of sexual politics is to project other worlds of being."[22] Such other worlds as Gethen with its androgynous population or Joanna Russ's all-female Whileaway offer drastic solutions for this "gender despair." Less drastic is the world of Darkover in the fantastic literature of Marion Zimmer Bradley; yet it provides ample opportunity for Bradley to examine and offer alternatives to such patriarchal enclosure. Although some of the societies on Darkover reflect or even intensify the sexual stereotyping found in contemporary societies on Earth, the structural fabulation of another planet allows her to create alternate societies as well.

Especially in the three novels of the Darkover series which record the adventures of Jaelle, a native Darkovan, and Magdalen Lorne, a Terran born on Darkover, Bradley examines representatives of women's roles in several social levels and divisions on Darkover. These novels include *The Shattered Chain*, *Thendara House*, and *City of Sorcery*.

In *The Shattered Chain*, Jaelle's aunt, Rohana Ardais, begins the journey which will be extended in the other two novels from an examination of Darkovan roles for women through the unity of all women and possible recovery and rediscovery of the Goddess in the *City of Sorcery*. Rohana is a Comynara, a member of the ruling class of Darkover; yet she is more completely defined through her wifely and motherly duties as the hetaira. She sees an exaggerated travesty of those duties in the life of her kidnapped sister, Lady Melora, who had been carried away to the Dry Towns where married women actually wear chains. Risking her own life to rescue Melora, her daughter Jaelle, and her unborn child from the slavery of Jalek's household, Rohana seeks the support of the Free Amazons, a sisterhood which, through its independence from male protection, has earned its own social role.

Even before Melora and her unborn child die on the arduous journey, Rohana begins to examine her own roles. As a Comynara, Rohana has inherited the gift of *laran*, psionic powers used only by women who accept the isolated and virginal lives in the towers. *"Why must women have to choose between the use of laran and all the other things of a woman's life?"* she asks herself, questioning this willing sacrifice of feminine power.[23] She even begins to wonder, concerning Melora's fate,

Did Jalak really change her life so much? Do any of us have choice, really? At our clan's demand, to share a stranger's bed and rule his house and bear his children ... or to live isolated from life, in loneliness and seclusion, controlling tremendous forces, but with no power to reach out our hand to any other human being, alone, virgin, worshipped but pitied.... (SC:88)

"A tendency to speculate," Nathaniel Hawthorne muses in *The Scarlet Letter*, "though it may keep woman quiet, as it does man, yet makes her sad."[24] Certainly, Hester Prynne's sadness about women's roles in that romance seems a precursor to Rohana's Darkovan concerns: "Indeed, the same dark question often rose into her mind, with reference to the whole race of womanhood. Was existence worth accepting, even to the happiest among them? As concerned her own individual existence, she had long ago decided in the negative, and dismissed the point as settled."[25]

Ultimately Rohana will affirm her own commitment to the enclosure when she explains to Jaelle "that everything in this world has its price, even such serenity as I have found after so many years of suffering" (SC:273). Her commitment to a life which provides her with "everything but freedom" (SC:273) echoes the same submission to the Necessity which prompts Al Ith to marry Ben Ata in Lessing's *Marriages*. Supposedly the Providers do know what is best for the people of the Zones, but who in power has ever failed to make that claim?

The young Jaelle provides a contrasting view. To preserve her freedom, she chooses to be reared by the Free Amazons rather than by her aunt, and even later in the period covered by *Thendara House* she will again refuse Rohana's invitation. "*I am not a slave, and I do not want my daughter enslaved,*" she thinks. "*I want to live for myself, not for that arrogant caste which rejected my mother and abandoned her to slavery, then rejected me because I was my father's daughter as well as my mother's.*"[26] Yet as she matures Jaelle also finds the sisterhood confining for her. She falls in love with Peter Haldane, a Terran raised on Darkover and thus himself caught between two worlds as much as is Magda, his ex-wife. Jaelle chooses to marry Peter and work with him at the Terran HQ, hoping to unite their societies.

Yet another contrast is embodied in Magda, known also by her Darkovan name Margali. On a mission for the Terran HQ to rescue Peter, Magda is coached by Rohana on how to pass for a Free Amazon and thus be able to travel alone through Darkover. However, her disguise does not convince the group of real Free Amazons she encounters, a group of which Jaelle is a part. Because she has pretended membership in the sisterhood, Magda is required to join by taking their oath. Jaelle becomes her oath-mother, and this combined with later shared experiences lead them to become freemates, a commitment a

Free Amazon can make of her own free will which carries the
weight of marriage inasmuch as the freemate is the appointed
guardian of any children she might have.

It is Jaelle who realizes the "enclosure" aspects of Terran
society. As she tells Peter, "I believed, for a time, that women
among your people were more free than mine. Now I know that
there is really not so much difference between Terra and Darkover. My foster-mother told me, once, that it was better to
wear chains than to believe you are free, and weight yourself
with invisible chains" (SC:286). Conversely, it is Magda who
first recognizes that Jaelle has matured and is making a responsible choice in marrying Peter. Yet the ideal of a marriage
of equals for Jaelle or a life independent of gender roles among
the Free Amazons for Magda is not so simply resolved while
both Terra and Darkover remain primarily patriarchal societies. Although she tries to maintain her individual identity,
the Jaelle we meet again in *Thendara House* finds the Terran
world defining her as Mrs. Peter Haldane. When Jaelle conceives a child to please Peter (which by its motivation rather
than the act is a betrayal of her Free Amazon oath), she only
succeeds in increasing his already growing need to "own" both
her and the child.

After nearly killing Peter in her efforts to escape the "enclosure" their life has become, Jaelle recognizes her own unresolved complicity with that enclosure. "They don't chain us,"
she marvels. "We chain ourselves. Willingly. More than willingly. We crave chains.... Isn't that what it means to be a
woman?" It is now Magda, who has grown in self-awareness
during her year with the Free Amazons, who reassures Jaelle.
"Of course not," she replies firmly. "It means—to be in command of your own life, your own actions" (TH:389).

But even on Darkover, the new world is still one step beyond
the known world. Not with the socially ambivalent Peter or
the socially independent Free Amazons do Jaelle and Magda
overcome internalized patriarchal constraints. They must
make another journey to find the agents of change on Darkover.
With the help of the personal gift of power each discovers in
herself of the telepathic *laran* and the gift of love each offers
the other, both women find and become a part of an alternate

society, the Forbidden Tower. This community, working with the "Soul of Darkover. Or the Dark Sisterhood" (TH:411), introduces the young women to others who place the value of the community and of the "centuries" above any individual time or person.

Yet in this clearly Goddess-oriented community, individuality is preserved. *Laran* is not confined to women, nor do women have to sacrifice *laran* when they give up virginity. Men and women alike choose to commit themselves to being "instruments of fate" as do Al Ith and Ben Ata in Lessing's *Marriages*. As Andrew explains to Magda, "There isn't one of us here who hasn't had to tear up our old lives like waste paper and start over again. . . . It isn't safety, or security. But . . . we've got each other. All of us" (TH:414). While again "it isn't easy" to be an agent of change, individual sacrifice and communal love provide necessary support for growth in a society that works with the "Soul of Darkover." Here community, communication, and ecology take precedence over the domination, aggression, and material possessions that seem to govern patriarchy.

Love can also provide a bridge between self and other, as Ursula K. LeGuin demonstrates in *The Left Hand of Darkness*. On Darkover, Jaelle and Magda establish a Bridge Society to facilitate communication and understanding between Darkovans and Terrans. In *City of Sorcery* they will make a Breaking the Ice journey as well to build bridges among the aliens who accompany them and between themselves and an earlier, perhaps native Darkovan society.

This Breaking the Ice journey carries Jaelle and Magda into the frozen wastelands beyond the "Wall Around the World" which defines the limits of the known parts of Darkover. Accompanying them are the Darkovan Camille, the Terran Vanessa, and a dark-skinned alien, Magda's boss Cholayna Ares. They are searching for a missing Terran, Lexie Anders, and her Darkovan guide, Rafaella. Lexie has become lost pursuing a legend—a sign of life beyond the "known world." She is also pursuing Magda's legend. As Cholayna explains to Magda, "She came here and immediately found herself up against the Lorne Legend."[27]

The legendary City of Sorcery toward which all these women are traveling supposedly contains descendants of native Darkovans. Jaelle and others like her are descended from the first Terrans who had settled this planet. The face of the Goddess known to the Free Amazons and the Dark Sisterhood of these Darkovans is only one, but beyond it might be yet another unseen face. Entrance to the City of Sorcery, however, is not easy to attain. Perhaps Jaelle finally accomplishes it through her choice of "a good death, saving her friend from dying before her time" (CS:300). As the priestess who approaches the travelers suggests, death may not be the end we think it is: "Thee thinks death a punishment for wrong-doin' an' life the reward for good, like a cake to a good child or a whip to a naughty one. Thee is a child, little one, an' thee canna' hear wisdom" (CS:300).

This priestess allows some of the travelers the choice of journeying with her to the City of Sorcery, but that choice involves total commitment to this unknown. Madga and Camille choose to follow the priestess, while the rest go back. Of the latter, Cholayna was also offered the choice of the journey; the wisdom of this new Sisterhood was not deceived by her alien appearance. "Sister from a far world," the priestess explains to her, "you have all your life sought wisdom beneath every strange sky. You hold life in reverence and you seek truth. The Sisterhood has read your heart from afar. If it is your will to enter, you too may come, and seek wisdom among us" (CS:304). Only her sense of unfulfilled duty and responsibility in this life deter Cholayna from the journey.

Clearly, individual choice still governs this communal commitment; the alternative must be chosen, not thrust upon, the person. Magda too is asked, *"What is thy truest will?"* (CS:304). But the journey which takes her from this life takes her out of the novel; Bradley does not yet allow us to follow. In this trilogy of novels from her Darkovan series, however, she has examined the nature of and possible alternatives to enclosure in a patriarchal society. Her insight into how slight the differences can be within that society reveals that whether or not chains are visible they may still be forged in the minds of the people. "You must walk another road," Estravan reminds us when we visit LeGuin's Gethen, and Jaelle and Magda search for those roads on Darkover. Their journeys to the Forbidden Tower and to the City of Sorcery offer hope of change. The world itself may have secrets we have yet to discover—or recover, if we did know them before. On Darkover, in other words, we hear echoes of the human search for self and for the Goddess, not an escape from what and who we are. Love supports us on the journey that is our life in this time and place, and the possibilities suggested through fantastic literature remind us that if the Goddess cannot be found enclosed in the patriarchy then we can choose to "go elsewhere."

Yet love, especially in its erotic forms, has been denied women unless it should happen to occur within that enclosure. Pratt has shown that in "women's fiction only marital love earns social praise, and even then the marriage is more appropriately without passion."[28] Certainly the medieval tradition of courtly love considers passion an extramarital affair. Erotic fulfillment and equal marriage must evolve elsewhere too, Pratt intimates. Love between women and satisfying lives as single women are handled indirectly or negatively in women's fiction, only presented positively in what Pratt calls the novels of the "new space."[29] Fantastic literature offers such a "new space."

Joanna Russ has particularly concerned herself with roles for women not functioning through, or even sometimes in relation to, men. In *The Female Man*, Russ examines the erotic freedom of expression natural to Janet Evason, who was raised in the all-female Whileaway; the sexual servility of Jeannine, a product of a Hitlerian parallel world; the violent rebellion of Jael Reasoner, that survivor of the War Between the Nations, the Polarization, and the Split of Manland and Womanland; and the contemporary confusion of our own Joanna. Clearly all these women are different faces/phases of the same self: "I said goodbye and went off with Laur, I, Janet; I also watched them go, I, Joanna; moreover I went off to show Jael the city, I Jeannine, I Jael, I myself."[30]

Before the self splits so drastically in *The Female Man*, Russ asserts the singleness of her first hero. Alyx, the prototypical Amazon of the early stories and of Russ's first novel, *Picnic on*

Paradise, jealously protects her unique role: "The attitudes that are not detachable from my special and peculiar skills. If I have anything to say about it"[31] and "there is only one of me, my dear, only one, and there never will be any more" (PP:154). Later, Irene Waskiewicz in *The Two of Them* will sound like a direct descendant of Alyx, although she does not seem to be as content with her singleness as was her predecessor. "When we go back to the Center," she tells her partner Ernst Neumann, "I want to change partners. I want a female partner next time."[32] When this earnest new man assures Irene that "there aren't any women as extraordinary as you," she comes back with "let them recruit some" (TT:141).

Not interested in being a legend, a stone image, Irene calls for human sisterhood, and she will give up her unique personal power by the end of the novel for a commitment to the young girl Zubeydeh. Irene's is the vision of all women coming together, even of her own mother Rose from whom she had willingly escaped in 1953 to join Ernst: "Perhaps life would be supportable with Zubeydeh on an uninhabited island: Zubeydeh and Rose and Chlöe and one of the nameless women from R & R. They can call it Paradise Island" (TT:144). Ideally, Irene would create her own Whileaway on the legendary island of the other Wonder Woman of comic-book fame, on the island of the Amazons.

But Paradise is no picnic, as Alyx had already discovered. Thus Irene returns to the less attractive reality of Joanna's world, coming back to Earth as did Jai Vedh and trying to start again with her new perspective and her new "daughter." Russ repeatedly tries to salvage something from her historical moment. Sisterhood, not superwomen, a simple commitment to love and to the future is needed to become an agent of change in the real world: "Now it'll take longer than one woman's lifetime; now she'll never get to it except the hard way; a civilian attacking from the outside. A nobody. An unimportant and powerless person. She has no idea yet that she can find other unimportant and powerless people" (TT:179).

True change does take generations. As Norton has reminded us in her Witch World series, evil entered the world when the people "did not accept gradual changes; they began to force them."[33] Marge Piercy and Octavia Butler both suggest that "unimportant and powerless people" can be agents of change. Yet regaining the faith necessary to draw on hidden and denigrated powers is not easy. No wonder Irene first feels that "she wants it back, even with Ernst attached to it, even with the lying and being snubbed and being thought mad: there really is nothing else" (TT:178). Life outside the enclosure of the patriarchy is not easy.

Yet out of this seeming nothing, something seems to form, as Irene learns through her dream. Irene regains faith in the Goddess, who wears the face of Zubeydeh "brooding behind her veil like the Spirit of the Abyss; Zubeydeh is waiting for something to happen." And something does happen: "for the first time, something will be created out of nothing" (TT:181). Russ commits her single hero to the community of women. Irene must join the countless "other unimportant and powerless" people to effect any change in society and to support each other.

These agents of change will be the *Extra (Ordinary) People* of Russ's recent novel/short story collection, which is composed of teaching stories joined by comments between the "tutor" and the "schoolkid" on how (and whether or not) the world was saved.[34] The vision of a world in which the self and the community are united has haunted Russ before; in *And Chaos Died* Evne embodies both Eve and Everyone, and in the female Whileaway as much personal freedom as is compatible with communal goals is encouraged. A similar vision emerges in this work. In the future of "Bodies," the terms male and female no longer have meaning; in the past of "Souls," the love the Abbess Radegunde leaves for the young male narrator, Radulf the Happy, bridges the time and distance between them so that "when I am in real sorrow or distress I remember her fingers touching my hair and that takes part of the pain away, somehow" (EP:56).

"Souls" is set in medieval Britain, and the "sight" that the Abbess leaves to her Norse conqueror when she goes is her own telepathic clarity of vision into the real conditions of the pitiful world in which they live. Radulf cannot see this as revenge because "all you did was change him into a good man" (EP:58), but we have already discussed the danger of new knowledge to inflexible visions. The setting of "Souls" reminds us once more of our Celtic Goddess, and Radulf identifies the Abbess as "a woman of the Sidhe." Radulf also refuses to believe Father Cairbre's teachings that these "grotesque" fairy folk were "wanton and cruel and without souls" because he has known the Abbess to have "more of a soul with a soul's griefs and joys than most of us" (EP:56–57).

Through these people, human and therefore extra (ordinary), Russ commits herself to sisterhood (read with the same generic weight as brotherhood). And if "the book should be full of real politics," as the writer in "Everyday Depressions" suspects, what historical movement today, contained as it would be within patriarchal society, would be appropriate?

Oh Susanna, what wishest thou? Marxism-Leninism? Too doctrinaire. Women's Studies? Too respectable. Lesbian separatism? Too unrealistic. The "women's community"? Too incestuous. Anti-racism? Too narrow. Cultural anarchism? Too crazy. Gay liberation? Too many realtors. Doing nothing? Too bourgeois. Marxist-Leninist academic lesbian feminist socialist culturally anarchistic separatist anti-racist revolutionaries? Too few. (EP:159)

The end of "Everyday Depressions" lists the "unanswerable questions" which LeGuin has cautioned us not to answer, but it also lists the questions we *can* answer: *"Does Life Exist?"* To this question, the writer responds, "Well, yes. It does."

Life is, well life is ... like this & like that & like that & like this & like nothing & like everything.
That's what life is.
Live, if you have the time. (EP:160)

Life itself is the only answer we know.

Pratt's fourth and final category, which allows for the rebirth of the middle-aged female hero, leaves more room for optimism even in traditional fiction by women. As Pratt explains, older women are in many ways beyond social usefulness and have often given up on their expectations of society. Their transformations therefore become personal rather than social, because they no longer have to achieve that part of individuation which aligns them socially.[35] However, in fantastic literature not only can the female hero begin the quest for identity earlier in life; she can also transform her society or find another society in which the self she discovers can be an accepted and integral part of the community.

Octavia Butler is concerned with rebirth and social transformation in *Survivor* and *Patternmaster*. An examination of these novels reveals both quest patterns which Pratt has associated with the novel of transformation of the self: the mythic quest for the grail and the psychological individuation journey through one's own nature, past, and unconscious.[36] In Alanna's story in *Survivor* the latter journey is more apparent, while Teray the future Patternmaster and Amber the healer complete the other quest in *Patternmaster*.

Butler's only novel set on another planet, *Survivor* presents a group who have designated themselves as the Missionaries of Humanity because of their deification of the human image. Consequently, they are blind to any other form humanity might take—to the humanity of the native Kohn, for instance, furlike creatures of various hues who live in tune with their world. These Missionaries are not part of the Pattern discussed earlier in *Mind of My Mind*; those telepathic members of the community on Butler's future Earth have found themselves unable to endure the separation and isolation of space travel. Such alternatives, however, can be chosen by the Mutes who do not fit into the Pattern.

Unfortunately, these Mutes have carried their prejudices to the new planet, prejudices that extend to Alanna as well, an Afro-Asian who had survived on Earth as a "wild human" after her parents had been killed while protecting her from a Clayark attack. The Clayarks, once human as well, are mutant results of a disease brought back to Earth by the first space travelers, and that widespread infection has drastically changed Earth society in the intervening years, as we shall see in *Patternmaster*.

As a wild human and because she is not white, Alanna is not accepted by most of the Missionaries even though their leader Jules Verrick and his wife Neila have adopted her. On Earth these "religious" people felt quite justified in killing wild humans as if they were animals; in their new world they attribute bestiality to the Kohn as well, since they are not reflective of the "divine image." Again we see a people who work against rather than with the world in which they live and who believe they have the right to deny status to other life forms because of their religion's definition of what is human.

The Kohn known by the Missionaries include the green-furred Garkohn natives with whom they had peacefully lived and the blue-furred Tehkohn. When Alanna, some Missionaries, and some Garkohn are abducted by the Tehkohn, Alanna alone survives. The Garkohn, she then learns, have tricked the Missionaries into sharing their addiction to the native meklah fruit, which has since become the staple diet of the Missionaries. The other prisoners who died in the Tehkohn camp suffered withdrawal from the drug; Alanna probably owed her own survival to her wild human brushes with starvation and her incredible will to survive.

This experience teaches Alanna that all is not good in nature; the green world can offer poison as well as nourishment. If we do not have the individual capacity to test it ourselves as does Anyanwu in *Wild Seed*, then we need a guide, a green-world lover. The Missionaries accept the Garkohn's deception as truth; Alanna has learned better and will now be guided by the leader of the Tehkohn, the Hao Diut. However, she challenges his advice and learns as much as she can on her own, participating in her own education and satisfying herself as to the quality and trustworthiness of the guidance she is given.

Diut rules the Tehkohn because he is the darkest blue; before him, the Hao Tahneh, a female, had ruled, showing that Butler has once again created a society in which sex is not the determining factor. It is hard not seeing a satirical dig in her hierarchy of blue fur (blood?), however. Still, Diut does offer Alanna knowledge of and participation in a society native to the planet, living in tune with it by constructing a communal dwelling which "mimicked the mountains around it in its interior as well as its exterior."[37] The Tehkohn fight without weapons and respect the animal jehruk "as their wild relative and they took pride in its ferocity" (SV:110). Whereas the Missionaries reject mutant Clayarks and wild humans, these creatures they consider "beasts of the field" even acknowledge and admire their "wild relative."

Still, Diut must learn from Alanna the limits to his own power in their relationship "where differences existed but were ignored" (SV:114). This alien encounter too can build a bridge with love, and Diut fathers Alanna's daughter. On his world, it is Alanna who is the alien, who must prove that the Missionaries are "human"—that, as she explains later to her adopted father, "we were rational people, Jules. That we could think and learn. That we were not animals!" (SV:159).

Drawing on her memories of Earth survival, Alanna finds herself able to fit in to the Tehkohn society. The shared knowledge of the green world, of working with nature, is lost on the Missionaries, whose walled settlement mars the natural landscape and whose narrow definition of humanity walls them off from the Kohn. But Alanna is "rescued" by them from the new home she has found, and in the process her daughter is killed. Symbolically and literally, the Missionaries destroy the new life she has begun with Diut. This return to her past, also a part of the pattern Pratt has described, allows her to confront her parents and teaches her to commit to her own insight and judgment.

While Neila could accept changes in her daughter, Jules cannot condone the blasphemy of Alanna mating with an "animal." Although she does all she can to help her parents accept the new knowledge and fresh perspective she has gained from the Tehkohn, they reject the change and the agent of change. The inflexible society is dooming itself, but Alanna must complete her inner journey and define herself if she is to survive and grow. She tells her father, "I haven't lost my self. Not to anyone" and assures her mother that "in time, I'll also be a Tehkohn judge. I want to be. And I'm Diut's wife and your daughter. If . . . you can still accept me as your daughter" (SV:170).

Thus Alanna completes her quest for selfhood and chooses that self above any social identity which would deny her humanity or her individuality. However, she willingly chooses to commit to the society which does not place such limitations on her, and which is itself open to growth and change. Diut has grown and changed from knowing her, for instance. He scarcely seems ideal when he begins their relationship more as a rape trauma than a green-world lover pattern. Later he beats Alanna as well, but the conflict here is in perceptions of power. Diut expects respect and obedience to his blue color. When Alanna resists violently, choosing as would Anyanwu in *Wild Seed* to die rather than to submit, Diut learns to change his concept: "I did not beat her again. Not once. And most of the time, she obeyed. When she did not, we talked—sometimes very loudly. But in spite of our disagreements, our nights together became good again. I lay with her contentedly and her knife remained in its sheath" (SV:115).

Unfortunately, Alanna finds the Missionaries less open to change. Their prejudices limit their humanity and their possibilities for survival, and Alanna, already an alien in the eyes of most of them, joins the alien society to find the humanity they lack. However, Teray in *Patternmaster* is much more open to change. The female hero of this book, the healer Amber, chooses to prepare Teray to fill the position of Patternmaster rather than to pay the price of her freedom which accepting that responsibility herself would entail. The grail quest pattern, which Pratt borrows from Jean Markale, underlies the journey Teray and Amber take in the novel. For Markale, the goal of this quest is the reestablishment of a supportive, protecting society after the former ruler has become impotent, which must be accomplished by an androgynous and compassionate individual.[38] The deterioration of the kingdom is symbolized by the mistreatment of women, and the grail itself is yet another appearance of the cauldron of the Goddess. We have encountered that cauldron in Bradley's retelling of Arthurian legend and have heard the richness of the Goddesslike Olya in Russ's *And Chaos Died* related to it. Evangeline Walton has pointed out in her retelling of its history as given in the *Mabinogion* that it offers rebirth as well, just as the darkness of the grave was seen as a return to the mother's womb, the first step toward reincarnation.

In these contexts, the quest for the grail is indeed a quest for the Goddess, achieved by a compassionate individual (like

Sir Galahad in Bradley's version) who can see through history to myth. If the quest is successful and the questor becomes the new ruler, we have symbolically returned the Goddess to the world, whether her new face is male or female. That agent of change can bring the society back in tune with the values of communication, community, and ecology and can offer expanded perceptions of reality.

In *Patternmaster*, Teray's father Rayal is the ailing ruler, but his older brother Coransee is also seeking to replace their father. Patternist society has deteriorated since its founding by Mary in *Mind of My Mind* due to the extended illness of Rayal, and Coransee reflects that deterioration. He has violated Teray's prospective wife Iray, demanded his Housemaster's right to sexual favors from the independent Amber, and allowed the mistreatment of other women under his care (as Teray discovers when the beaten and abused Suliana seeks his aid). Rayal, suffering from Clayark's disease, is unable to intervene; only Teray stands between Coransee and the power of the Patternmaster.

Teray has the appropriate "androgynous" qualities of the successful questor, as can be seen in his protection of Suliana and others like her, in his willingness to recognize human potential in the feared and hated Clayarks, in his unwillingness to kill except for survival. Yet Teray is young, lacking the necessary knowledge or the skills to succeed in his quest.

Amber has both. Knowledge has literally been transferred to her by her older friend and lesbian lover, the Housemaster Kai (which might remind us that Kai was Arthur's "housemaster" in legend). Kai has also given Amber the necessary support to bring her own powers through transition as a healer, being for her the green-world lover of the maturation pattern. Even more importantly, however, Kai has been Demeter to Amber's Kore, passing on female knowledge to the next generation.[39] With this heritage, Amber now encompasses in herself the Triple Goddess—Maiden in her independence, Mother in her healing powers, and Wise Woman with her new knowledge. Only with Amber's aid can Teray hope to become the next Patternmaster; she offers that aid freely because she sees in him the true knight of the Goddess, promising to bring a more beneficent, androgynous, and humane rule to Patternist society.

Thus it is Amber who heals Teray after his struggle with Coransee; it is she who provides him with motivation to continue his quest when he is ready to give up: "Abruptly, Teray urged his horse forward to pull alongside Coransee. He could not abandon the woman, could not let her be drawn back into captivity without even trying to help her. She had helped him."[40]

Not only Amber's healing ability but also the Pattern itself can symbolize the grail, since it offers rebirth to the latents who draw strength from it. Yet, as Walton has recounted in *The Children of Llyr*, when the Cauldron was stolen and misused, it produced only soulless soldiers who fought to their deaths much like the soul-robbed victims of the Kolders in Norton's Witch World series. Good can be twisted into evil; the Pattern too, which takes as well as gives, could be a destructive rather than a constructive power in the hands of the wrong Patternmaster. Even Amber's healing power is ambiguous in its potential uses: it enables her to kill with great efficiency as well as to heal. As in Norton's Witch World, power is good or evil depending upon how it is used. The Goddess has her dark aspects, and sometimes killing takes place in the healing process, just as bacteria die in our bodies.

Butler can face the darkness as well as the compassion of the power she offers her symbiotic leaders, because their strength lies in the strength of their people. Teray is chosen as new Patternmaster because he is a healer as well, a necessary gift for a Patternmaster. As Rayal tells him, "*Without that method just now, you would have killed at least three of the people you just took power from*" (PM:159). Any change, Butler reminds us, is costly.

At times, indeed, death can be a welcome door rather than a blank wall, if we can see it as such. Rayal has had to make those life-and-death choices for others as the Patternmaster; as he observes after the death of Coransee, "*I wouldn't have sacrificed one of Jansee's sons if he hadn't had to die.*" He is ready to make the choice for himself as well once he has found

Teray to preserve the quality of the Patternist society: *"When the need arises next, young one, the Pattern will be yours. That will kill me, too, but at least I'll die alone—not take thousands of people with me. . . . Hurry and get here. You have no idea how tired I am"* (PM:159–60).

So too in Lessing's *The Making of the Representative for Planet 8* must the fifty people who will comprise that Representative learn that death is a rebirth into a more expansive life in the Canopean universe. Their journey, a trek northward to their polar ice with Johor, their Canopean guide, is both a rebirth journey and an alien encounter, a Breaking the Ice journey in which the resolution of the differences between self and alien Other comes on two levels: the Representative becomes part of Canopus, and the inner self becomes the outer self while its "huddle of bodies" is left behind.[41]

This rebirth from the individual into the communal is achieved by a shift in perspective, which Johor teaches on the journey. From this perspective, the composite Representative looked back and recognized their human bodies as "webs and veils of light, saw the frail lattice of the atomic structure, saw the vast spaces that had been what in fact we mostly were— though we had not had eyes to comprehend that, even if our minds knew the truth" (MR:117–18). Now free to leave that level of human consciousness for the next, "we, the Representative, many and one, came here, where Canopus tends and guards and instructs" (MR:121). Breaking the Ice between alien and human can conceivably lead to bridging the gap between life and death—can reveal death as the rebirth promised in myth.

Yet rebirth can take place within *this* journey as well, within the time of our lives, and the effects of that rebirth can enable us to be agents of change. Maybe it can even help us to initiate changes in our society that will reinstate the values of the Goddess. An interesting version of this pattern can be detected in Kate Wilhelm's novel, *Juniper Time*, in which the young woman protagonist must first complete her own rebirth journey and then, with the strengths she has gained, offer a golden grail to her sick society.

Point of view in *Juniper Time* is shared between this woman,

Jean Brighton, and her childhood friend Arthur Cluny. Both
are children of astronauts; both have grown into a near future
Earth of overpopulation and drought to find themselves watching their world end with the proverbial whimper rather than
the usually projected big bang. That this is a deteriorating
kingdom again is obvious in the results of the rape of America
which are now being felt in the drought. It has driven people
into the depressing and destructive Newtown projects, in one
of which Jean individually experiences the rape-trauma
pattern.

Arthur, however, is not destined to be Jean's Galahad or her
green-world lover. He worships the wrong goddess, the beautiful body of his wife Lina Davis. To him she was "more perfect
than a human being could be, she was a goddess, a divinity."[42]
He doesn't even know the woman Lina, just the Bloduewedd
he has invented for himself: "His Lina was his alone forever
and ever; she did not even exist when he was gone" (JT:144).
"She knew that you didn't love her, not as she really was,"
Lina's father tells Arthur (JT:235). Tied to surfaces, Arthur
does not allow others their own reality and therefore finds
himself trapped in his narrow faith.

In Jean, Arthur looks for yet another goddess to save him,
recognizing in her the embodiment of the moon (which, her
last name suggests, might have some validity). The moon Arthur sees, however, is material, while for his and Jean's astro-
naut fathers it symbolized both their reality and their dreams.
Arthur recognizes his limitations, seeing himself as "another
part of that machine, symbiote, part technology, part metal,
part human drive" (JT:285).

Jean, however, has always been more open to myth as well
as history, and through her rebirth journey she will give cre-
dence to Arthur's insight about her. By returning to her personal and mythic past, to nature itself, and to the inner self
she has lost touch with, she completes a journey which prepares
her to become Galahad herself—an agent of change for her sick
society.

First, Jean must heal herself by the rebirth journey, which
she initiates by facing and surviving death. Returning to her
grandfather's house in the drought-stricken Northwest, she

walks into the desert to die. But the death by fire is not the
dead end we have seen in the snows of Demeter's withdrawal;
new life can flow from volcanoes, and the desert has hidden
resources for those who learn what to look for and at. "We've
changed, the plants haven't," her Indian friend Robert tells
her. "They're waiting the eternal wait; one year of no water,
they shrink a little, but they're out there, and below them, deep
in the ground, the water runs as always" (JT:154). With the
loving help of Robert and his wife, Serena, the medicine woman
of the tribe, Jean begins to heal. If Tanith Lee's reborn and
nameless fugitive from the volcano gains support from Darak
and Uasti, her Tammuz and Demeter, so too this fugitive from
the Newtowns will learn from Robert and Serena. "You can't
heal someone else," Serena tells her. "That night I told you to
heal yourself and you refused at first so I waited until you were
beside yourself again and then told that other self it had to
make your feet well, and it did so" (JT:162). Serena, the Wise
Woman, can talk directly to Jean's inner self; after a year in
the desert, Jean too can do so.

Jean learns to return to the "thinking place" her father had
told her about when she was a child. She also learns to communicate more completely through a growing knowledge of the
Indian language Wasco and by a developing trust in her own
intuitive understanding of things. These lessons enable her to
recapture the magic she had sought as a child. "You have the
magic," her father had told her then. "But you have to learn
how to use it. It is language. . . . You can change the world with
words" (JT:6). The magic Suzette Haden Elgin identifies in her
Ozark trilogy and *Native Tongue* will once more initiate
change.

But the magic of language is not on the surface, Jean knows.
She has always had a talent for reading through words, which
had earlier enabled her to be successful at a decoding project
she was working on. "Her interests," she tried to tell others,
"were in the hidden communications language made possible;
how people used words understood by both parties to say things
that had no connection with the spoken message" (JT:65). Jean
discovers that Wasco is a more flexible language for such communication than is English; as Serena complains, "Your words

mean such tight things, only this and no more, and there are matters that can't be described with such hard outlines" (JT:163).[43] Jean learns the value of storytelling, of mythmaking, with her Indian friends; later she will tell the story of her own experiences through a metaphorical confrontation with coyote and learn more about the experiences through the telling as well as the sharing (JT:246–48).

Using the magic she has gained, Jean too becomes a healer, finding ways to communicate to the inner self of her people to help them begin to heal themselves. She does this by offering hope to a hopeless world, by suggesting that a gold tube found in orbit is a message from aliens. While she doesn't lie, Jean leads others into affirming the existence of these aliens. She feels guilty for "using words to manipulate people, doing it deliberately, using the magic of words, the power" (JT:288); however, she must take the role of the coyote, of the Trickster, to initiate change.[44] Through her words, she is putting on the "accepting face" that Kadura recommends to Khira in Sydney Van Scyoc's *Darkchild* in hopes that "after a time it will no longer be just a face."[45]

Jean's gift of a golden grail of hope to a people without hope buys only time, but the time might be enough to let them heal themselves.[46] Already they could be seen moving toward unity as the concept of the alien brings them together, and toward hope as the promise of intervention from above seems to be the answer to their prayers. Jean, however, knows that the "alien message" is merely the magic of words, and she is ready to help along the healing process she has started in the people whenever and however she must. Yet how is magic conveyed but in words, in singing the songs and telling the tales, in formulas and riddles? Jean is back in contact with the ancient myth, the hidden message behind the words that she has always sought: "Nowhere along the line have I known what was coming, or what I should do, but it always seemed to be like something that I had known and simply had forgotten when it finally happened" (JT:292).

Through her personal and communal quest, Jean reaffirms both the individual and the community, finding in the wisdom of the Goddess and the magic of communication the new possibilities to offer a narrowing reality. Wilhelm speaks through her own words to a world caught itself in juniper time, in a time of drought and despair when only the natural junipers that know the desert can survive. The junipers are the "coyotes of the plant world. Tricksters," shifting their surfaces for survival (JT:290). Death in the desert is "simply a part of the eternal cycle," as Serena reminds Jean. "We rise, move about, learn, and grow, and in the end return."

"But we're more than that," Jean adds. "We can learn to change things" (JT:290). Change is already incorporated into the worldview of Jean's Indian friends, who return to their natural world but bring what is useful from the white man's world as well. Compatible technology—guns and fishing tackle, for instance—can be absorbed into their ever-new, always ongoing reality. In her world, Jean must initiate change for her stagnating society, must be the trickster to a people deceived by surfaces.

The timelessness of the archetypal patterns Pratt has consistently discovered in women's fiction unites the words of magic to reinstate the Goddess in these works of fantastic literature by women. Revealed again are the values of community, communication, and ecology as the individual agent of change learns the new expression for the communal need. Wilhelm has united the quests of rebirth and transformation for both the self and society to encourage us to heal ourselves. Lessing still holds out the promise of positive alien intervention; Canopus will instruct and heal if we will survive and serve the Necessity in this life and have faith that death will open new doors. Butler's archetypal frameworks allow us to see how seemingly insurmountable differences can be recognized as deceptive surfaces, shifting shapes. By combining her Afro-American and female visions, she has revealed a possible past, present, and future in which differences are seen as challenging and enriching rather than threatening and denigrating, and in which power is a responsibility. Russ's female hero grows from the isolated Alyx fighting for survival of self through the fragmented J's of *The Female Man*, seeking integration of self and society and finding at least the possibility of change: "We will all be changed. In a moment, in the twin-

kling of an eye, we will all be free. I swear it on my own head.
I swear it on my ten fingers. We will be ourselves" (FM:213).
Irene initiates such a change in *The Two of Them* by committing herself to Zubeydeh and those "other important and powerless people" who have the united power to create something
out of nothing. These extra(ordinary) people promise nothing
more—and nothing less—than Life for bodies and for souls.

On Bradley's Darkover, diverse women from different cultures help each other grow and see their world from new perspectives so that they can help their society grow. Beginning
from within the enclosure of the patriarchy that Darkover in-
herits from its Terran roots, they find personal power which
will enable them to transcend time, place, and gender to become
agents of change. For Lee's young women protagonists, surfaces
are again penetrated and masks are ripped away to reveal the
soul within the machinery of this world and the ongoing power
of the invisible world.

Love and the Goddess sustain us, and the power of individual
commitment to community, communication, and ecology can
promise new worlds in the recognition of old patterns. In fantastic literature by women, the archetypes again assume the
face of the Goddess, as these women join other women writers
who for three hundred years have sought a future in our past.
The circle is revealed as a spiral, never closing, always changing, shifting surfaces to reveal all the possible worlds within
each of us.

NOTES

1. Rosemary Jackson, *Fantasy: The Literature of Subversion* (London: Methuen, 1981): 178.

2. Eric Gould, *Mythical Intentions in Modern Literature* (Princeton,
N.J.: Princeton University Press, 1981): 137.

3. Annis Pratt, with Barbara White, Andrea Loewenstein, and
Mary Wyer, *Archetypal Patterns in Women's Fiction* (Bloomington:
Indiana University Press, 1981): 168.

4. Ibid.

5. Marta Weigle, *Spiders and Spinsters: Women and Mythology*
(Albuquerque: University of New Mexico Press, 1982): viii.

6. See the summary of Wolff's views in Nor Hall, *The Moon & the*

Virgin: Reflections on the Archetypal Feminine (New York: Harper & Row, 1980): 32–33.

7. Angelo S. Rappoport, *Myth and Legend of Ancient Israel*, Vol. 1 (New York: KTAV, 1966): 78–79.

8. Raphael Patai, *The Hebrew Goddess* (New York: KTAV, 1967): 208. Patai reveals Lilith as the prototype of the scarlet-clad prostitute when he refers to the scarlet dress she "was believed to wear when trying to seduce men" (320).

9. Ibid.: 235, 244–45.

10. Ibid.

11. Johann Wolfgang von Goethe, *Faust*, tr. Walter Arndt, ed. Cyrus Hamlin (New York: W. W. Norton, 1976): 102.

12. G. Scholem, *On the Kabbalah and Its Symbolism*, as quoted in Merlin Stone, *When God Was a Woman* (New York: Dial Press, 1976): 196.

13. Charlene Spretnak, *Lost Goddesses of Early Greece: A Collection of Pre-Hellenic Myths* (Boston: Beacon, 1978): 97.

14. Phyllis J. Day, "Earthmother/Witchmother: Feminism and Ecology Renewed," *Extrapolation* 23:1 (Spring 1982): 14.

15. Pratt, *Archetypal Patterns*: 29.

16. Marion Zimmer Bradley, Introduction to *The Birthgrave* by Tanith Lee (New York: Daw, 1975): 6. Subsequent references to *The Birthgrave* are to this edition and will be given in the text as B:page in parentheses.

17. Merlin Stone, *Ancient Mirrors of Womanhood: A Treasury of Goddess and Heroine Lore from around the World* (Boston: Beacon, 1979): 164.

18. Pratt, *Archetypal Patterns*: 21.

19. Ibid.: 178.

20. Tanith Lee, *The Silver Metal Lover* (New York: Daw, 1981): 17. Subsequent references are to this edition and will be given in the text as SM:page in parentheses.

21. Pratt, *Archetypal Patterns*: 39.

22. Ibid.: 70.

23. Marion Zimmer Bradley, *The Shattered Chain* (New York: Daw, 1976): 58. Subsequent references are to this edition and will be given in the text as SC: page in parentheses.

24. Nathaniel Hawthorne, *The Scarlet Letter*, 2d ed. (New York: W. W. Norton, 1978): chapter 13.

25. Ibid.

26. Marion Zimmer Bradley, *Thendara House* (New York: Daw, 1983): 219. Subsequent references are to this edition and will be given in the text as TH:page in parentheses.

27. Marion Zimmer Bradley, *City of Sorcery* (New York: Daw, 1984): 14. Subsequent references are to this edition and will be given in the text as CS:page in parentheses.

28. Pratt, *Archetypal Patterns*: 81.

29. Ibid.

30. Joanna Russ, *The Female Man* (New York: Bantam, 1975): 212.

31. Joanna Russ, *Picnic on Paradise* (New York: Ace, 1968): 156–57. Subsequent references are to this edition and will be given in the text as PP:page in parentheses.

32. Joanna Russ, *The Two of Them* (New York: Berkley, 1978): 141. Subsequent references are to this edition and will be given in the text as TT:page in parentheses.

33. Andre Norton, *Three Against the Witch World* (New York: Ace, 1965): 130.

34. Joanna Russ, *Extra (Ordinary) People* (New York: St. Martin's Press, 1984): 61, 93, 115, 145, 161. One exchange introduces the first story, preceding numbered pages. Subsequent references are to this edition and will be given in the text as EP:page in parentheses.

35. Pratt, *Archetypal Patterns*: 135–36.

36. Ibid.: 139–41.

37. Octavia E. Butler, *Survivor* (New York: NAL, 1978): 53. Subsequent references are to this edition and will be included in the text as SV:page in parentheses.

38. Discussed by Pratt in *Archetypal Patterns*: 173–74.

39. Ibid.: 170.

40. Octavia E. Butler, *Patternmaster* (New York: Avon, 1976): 117. Subsequent references are to this edition and will be given in the text as PM:page in parentheses.

41. Doris Lessing, *The Making of the Representative for Planet 8* (New York: Alfred A. Knopf, 1982): 117. Subsequent references are to this edition and will be given in the text as MR:page in parentheses.

42. Kate Wilhelm, *Juniper Time* (New York: Pocket Books, 1979): 27. Subsequent references are to this edition and will be given in the text as JT:page in parentheses.

43. Meridel Le Seur, quoted in Starhawk, *Dreaming the Dark: Magic, Sex & Politics* (Boston: Beacon, 1982): 24, says: "Nouns are patriarchal. They separate us from things, naming the thing and making it an object. The American Indian languages have no nouns, only relationships."

44. Paul Radin, *The Trickster: A Study in American Indian Mythology* (New York: Schocken, 1972): xxiv, says: "Only if we view it as ... an attempt by man to solve his problems inward and outward, does the figure of the Trickster become intelligible and meaningful."

45. Sydney J. Van Scyoc, *Darkchild* (New York: Berkley, 1982): 170.

46. Cf. Erzulia's self-healing methods in the future Mattapoisett that Marge Piercy projects in *Woman on the Edge of Time* (New York: Fawcett, 1976): 159.

5

Tales of the Future Past: The Promise

In *Juniper Time*, Kate Wilhelm gives Jean Brighton the ability to read through words, hear through stories, and see through surfaces. Similarly, Baird Searles has seen in Marion Zimmer Bradley's *The Mists of Avalon* a retelling of the Arthurian legends "mostly centered in the powers of the women and their ability to manipulate events and 'see' through time and space—what we would for the most part think of as psi talents."[1] Hans Christian Andersen reminds us in "The Snow Queen" what can happen when our ability to "see" in these ways is distorted, when the magic mirror is shattered and the pieces catch in our eyes and hearts. This same image has been used by Stephen C. Ausband in his discussion of contemporary attempts to "see" mythic truth beneath the surfaces of failing cultural myths:

If we have lost, for reasons having to do with our changed perspective on the world, an ability to make once-viable traditions seem anything more than dead collections of tales, that is not an indication that we are without myths. We are between myths—reaching sometimes backwards toward what we thought we knew, sometimes forwards into what we do not yet know—in an effort to find stories that will define us to ourselves. . . . We create order as we can, watching ourselves and our world sometimes in broken bits and pieces of tales, as we might study our reflections in the pieces of a shattered mirror.[2]

In the broken pieces of Tiamat and the Old Empire, Moon begins to find an order which joins science and myth, computer input and sybils, genetic engineering and mers into patterns that promise a new future in Joan D. Vinge's *The Snow Queen*. The "broken place" that is Doris Lessing's *Shikasta* is almost irreparable in her Canopean universe; and when the survivors of its violence look back, they can hardly believe that they couldn't "see" before what now seems obvious. In each story, surface distortions begin to dissolve when we regain the Goddess's gift of "sight."

A major distortion of the surface for women has been what Annis Pratt calls the "growing up grotesque" pattern. Women writers of fantastic literature challenge this denigration of "female values" by investing aliens with humanity and women and other discards of patriarchy with power. Lessing and Marge Piercy listen to the irrational insights of the "insane"; Piercy and Octavia E. Butler choose women of color as cultural heroes (or, for Butler, even men if their color is blue enough); Joanna Russ's superwomen sacrifice exceptional treatment to join with "unimportant and powerless people"; Sydney Van Scyoc finds humans "mutated" by their environment to be godlike; and Marion Zimmer Bradley may have found the Goddess herself with the outcasts of the forbidden tower and legendary city of sorcery on Darkover. Van Scyoc's young agents of change accept the humanity of such rejects as Rauthimages and winter children and such aliens as the redmanes and the stithi; Ursula K. LeGuin's "gentle man" Genly Ai learns to love the differences of Estravan; Tanith Lee's "ugly" and "plain" women learn to love themselves as they learn love from outlaws and androids; C. J. Cherryh's Sten Duncan strives to become more like The People he comes to know; Andre Norton's Jaelithe engenders a generation of change for her world by marrying Simon Tregarth; and Suzette Haden Elgin's Grannies share their minds with Mules.

Sometimes, however, it is not enough to offer power and humanity to those who have been powerless and dehumanized in a given society. Sometimes that society itself must be abandoned, attacked, or even destroyed—all of which are possible by the structural fabulation of fantastic literature. Lessing lets the survivors rebuild when the worst evils of Shikasta have done the destruction for her; she leads the Representative for Planet 8 away from a world destroyed by dis-aster, that fault in the stars. Suzy McKee Charnas, Sally Miller Gearhart, and Russ let women rebuild in the aftermath of violence; Susan Coon's living planets forcibly evict former, present, or potential residents who promise destruction. Bradley provides Isis for her malcontents; Julian May sends them to Pliocene Earth; Elgin offers them Ozark or, for the women confined to Earth, the privacy of Barren House.

Still, the new agents of change that overcome the social denigration which had limited their power are often willing to work for change from within the society rather than to go elsewhere. These potential Champions include Elgin's Drussa Silver; Butler's Anyanwu, Mary, and Amber and Teray; Pamela Sargent's Daiya; Lessing's Al Ith and Ben Ata; Vinge's Moon and Sparks; Van Scyoc's Khira and Darkchild, Keva and Danior, Reyna and Juaren, and her Sunwaifs; Norton's Kyllan, Kemoc, and Kaththea; the men of Bradley's Isis and the Kimassu Lady and her boys on Carr's Delyafam; Piercy's Connie; Russ's Jai Vedh, Irene Waskiewicz, and Abbess Radegunde; and Wilhelm's Jean Brighton. Clearly, most of these writers have not abandoned hope for their worlds.

Although the works we have examined are only a small portion of even what women alone have contributed to fantastic literature, they do begin to demonstrate its mythmaking capacities. Myth and mythmaking in this time of transition must be carried out by courageous individuals. Despite the argument that no one person can "invent myths," when the social vision is distorted the individual vision must initiate a new order. "Surely a myth is initially as much the work of an individual as a ballad is or an epic poem," K. K. Ruthven argues. "Someone has to supply the raw material which others may then add to or alter."[3]

Where better can material become part of that mythmaking process than in the popular genre of fantastic literature? While some believe a popular form could not be put to such serious use as mythmaking, actually these ephemeral publications which go out of print quickly and into imaginative retellings easily are as close to an oral tradition as can be found in the larger contemporary society. Writers like Elgin even manage to incorporate pure oral and folk tradition into the genre as well. Even in the works of an individual writer, such as Russ, this fiction can be read as a process; as Samuel R. Delany has demonstrated, each of her novels not only stands alone for its story but also comments on her earlier works.[4] Within the community of fantastic literature too, shared traditions become apparent, as can be heard in the names of Norton's Jaelithe, Bradley's Jaelle, and Russ's Jael—all of which might prove to be echoes of C. L. Moore's *Jirel of Joiry*.

What takes shape in each of these stories is an attempt at cultural myth, at the creation of a symbolic surface which speaks to contemporary experience while preserving the ancient myth within. The details can fall apart as the two sides of the "apple" fall away from the "stem" in Wilhelm's *Juniper Time* to translate the "alien message" as a pattern of the orbits of similar messages. The knowledge Jean Brighton offers her world with that apple is not in the deceptive surface but in the magic of her words and what one wants to read through them.

In that one work which occasionally even convinces critics of its value as myth, in Mary Shelley's *Frankenstein*, we find mythical figures that "are not usually recalled in their bookish context, but thought of as wholly traditional figures in the public domain of horror-movies and comic strips; before very long Frankenstein is no longer remembered as the name of Mary Shelley's 'modern Prometheus' but popularly confused with the monster he created."[5] Echoing earlier archetypes and ordering a pattern of its own, the Frankenstein myth tempts retelling, keeping alive its horror story of the perversion of the Goddess: of parental hate, communal rejection, failed communication, and a white, cold death in the ice and snow. Shelley saw well the world in which she lived; contemporary women, however, can balance the horror with hope if the alien is once more acknowledged as human and Persephone asks Demeter to return.

Furthering the mythic intent of their writing, many works of fantastic literature have followed Shelley's lead by retelling earlier cultural myths or acknowledging a mythmaking purpose in their works. Certainly the elaborate involvement of Celtic tradition in May's *Saga of Pliocene Exile* and Vinge's *The Snow Queen*, the compendious use of myth in Russ's *And Chaos Died*, and the echoes of Judaic and other sacred narratives in Lessing's *Shikasta* demand a metaphorical as well as a surface reading of the works. The very form of Lessing's *Marriages* concerns the development of "songs and tales"; similarly, David and Sais are taught such songs to preserve Canopean wisdom in *Shikasta*. The insertion of myths and folktales in LeGuin's creation of Gethen society, the oral traditions of the Grannies on Elgin's Ozark, the druidic lore behind Moyra Caldecott's Sacred Stones trilogy, and the echoes and perversions of the Triple Goddess on Norton's Witch World show the importance of mythical allusion and mythmaking to these works, even when their central purpose is not the retelling of such legends as it is in Evangeline Walton's *Mabinogion*-based novels or Bradley's version of Arthurian legend.

Other novels embody myth in the surface reality itself, imagining the Mother as a computer of the Old Empire with sybils receiving her "input" or the "Merging One" as buried computers beneath the mountains, for instance. As Vinge and Sargent give scientific concretization to the future face of the Goddess, Vinge's "Tales of the Future Past" and Sargent's arcadian surface introduce the past as well to dissolve temporal and spatial considerations, revealing the ancient myth forever finding new expressions as the surface reality of our lives changes.

Even the Goddess herself might reenter history to initiate change, as she rebels against the violence of the men in Gearhart's future and on Coon's living planets or adopts human form again as Drussa Silver for the ordinary people of Elgin's Freeway who need to learn to "see." Bradley involves alien intelligence as the Mother on Isis, suggesting that our gods must see through human eyes as well and must be asked the answerable questions. If we deny them their reality, as Avalon is denied reality in Christianized Britain, we limit only ourselves and our own perceptions. Equally, if we deny each other reality, as the women on Isis and Delyafam deny full human status to males, we divide the worlds and diminish all life.

On other worlds, myth lives in the way humanity can expand
and adapt rather than narrow and freeze itself; we must learn
to see with all six senses if we are to receive input from the
Goddess. Direct communication from the Mules on Ozark and
the redmanes on Brakrath could then offer us the horse sense,
the old wisdom, of those who live in tune with their worlds.
When humans learn this, they will be rewarded with the powers of nature, flooded with the communal support of SOWF,
given the guidance of the Providers to live in tune with the
Necessity, and taught the expansion of consciousness possible
to those who "know the spaces in things" which will offer fresh
perspectives on what is and what can be.

Uncovering the face of the Goddess and looking directly at
it will not turn us to stone, as the cultural myth of Medusa
threatens. Just the opposite is true, if these worlds within
women offer an accurate picture. The stones are simply protective surfaces; within their circle is the magic of communication for Caldecott, the library for Russ. Taking stone into
their hearts strengthens the barohnas of Brakrath and lets the
Goddess in the human emerge to offer life to their people. These
works rip away the grotesque Medusa mask person by person.
The nameless, faceless woman of Lee's *Birthgrave* discovers
her power and beauty at the end of her journey; Butler's wise
women from Anyanwu to Amber find within themselves and
others like them the source of unity, strength, communication,
and healing.

Within a plain Jane can be found a Jain, Lee also reminds
us, and the woman that emerges can change her world. A new
Mary can offer a new Pattern to live by; a young she'pan can
trust her Sight and revive a dying world. Women can be Responsible on Ozark and hopeful back on Earth, as Jean Brighton offers the magic of words, tells a new tale, to revive our
own dying world. Or women may advise and assist others who
are open to change, as Amber guides Teray, as Khira supports
Darkchild, and as Reyna seeks the starsilk of Birnam Rauth.
Nothing is alien to the Goddess, male, female, or other, when
differences build a bridge of love between us.

Where change may take us is not as important as how we
get there. The journey of life itself is central to this literature.

Perhaps the best of all possible worlds is only a whileaway, but before we reach it we have Life to live, as Russ reminds us. Any effective change will be gradual; it is the children of Destiny, of the Witch World, of Brakrath, of Doro and Anyanwu or hatched at Mattapoisett here on Earth, who will shape the future. Forcing changes, Norton reminds us, is the beginning of evil and leads to destructive power by distorting and misusing the power of nature rather than working with it. But if that change cannot be realized, it can be initiated, by us.

The journey, then, is central of importance in this literature, and true to the social purposes of fiction it needs to be seen as a shared journey. We gain knowledge of ourselves from knowing the other. The Breaking the Ice journey allows self and alien to face each other outside the social or even "natural" definitions already limiting the humanity of either in the eyes of the other. Genly Ai and Estravan fight their way across the Gobrin Ice together; Khira and Darkchild survive a winter alone, and their daughter Reyna and the winterchild Juaren confront an alien planet (alone except for the technological gifts of the Arnimi); Jane and Silver sing and paint a new world into existence on Tolerance Street.

The Goddess active within the human, providing "sight" and offering fresh perspectives on what is real and what is human, comes alive again in these SF myths. The living myth, not its deceptive stone image—its dead expression—concerns us on our human journey. The unanswerable questions still await us at the end of the journey; we learn for now "not to answer them" as we change with the process that is life. The Goddess threatens us as the devouring Mother when we deny our own humanity or that of Her other children; for those of us who learn from Her and consider what She has taught when we make our individual choices, however, she offers us Sisterhood, as Susan Griffin has recognized:

As I go into her, she pierces my heart. As I penetrate further, she unveils me. When I have reached her center, I am weeping openly. I have known her all my life, yet she reveals stories to me, and these stories are revelations and I am transformed. Each time I go to her I am born like this.... This earth is my sister.[6]

To retell the stories the earth has revealed to them is the common goal of these women writers of fantastic literature. SF myth is the proper vehicle for cultural myth, its own ephemeral nature and popular audience inviting transformation of the myth even as it is being expressed. The magic of language—using rather than rejecting the words we have and speaking through them as well as with them—can still offer the promise of change and transformations.

The timelessness of myth is achieved in this literature by the recognition of the simultaneity of different cultures; the repetition of archetypal patterns, symbols, and characters; the expanded possibilities of actual or imaginative time travel; the internal expansion of time through meditation or emotional perceptions; and recognition of the possibility that death is simply the door to more life or lives. Mythic freedom from place is achieved by reuniting the worlds that have drifted apart, stepping through Zones or doors or gates into parallel or simultaneous realities; by moving out from Earth to the scientifically feasible reality of other planets and galaxies, in a Hainish or Canopean or Tri-Galactic universe or through worlds discovered by Earthexodus pilgrims or future Earth explorers—and exploiters; and by moving through time to Earth past, present, future, or even post-Holocaust.

The values embodied in SF myth are unambiguous. The individual is responsible to and for the community—and vice versa. Good communication is essential to build a bridge between self and alien; song and story encompass more than is possible in "tight little words" and are essential to convey and keep current the history of myth. Finally, we must live within the Necessity of keeping balance between the natural world and humanity's use of and involvement with it. Science and technology are not necessarily inimical to this balanced world; they too can work with rather than against nature. In other words, community, communication and ecology undergird this form of contemporary mythmaking, as we continue to explore the answers to what it means to be human, the one question we have always acknowledged as open to our study. Even in Pope's sexist phrasing we can find, by reading through the words, that kernel of truth which makes his surface ironic: "the proper study of Mankind is Man."

It is to the women we turn in this study, because, as Pratt argues, it is in their fiction that we can still find the Goddess. Their perspective is essential in these trying times precisely because they are the "aliens within" patriarchal society. As such, they can offer new ways of thinking about self and society, power and powerlessness. As psychologist Carol Gilligan has argued,

If power is not used to take care of the world, it may well be destroyed. But if you are asking, how do you gain power if you care about other people, that is a complicated question in a competitive and hierarchical system. On the other hand, if you gain power by abandoning care and severing connections, what really is the point? If women have access to another way of thinking about relationships that is more cooperative and less hierarchical, then they know something that is very important for everybody. If they bring such knowledge into positions of social power, they may bring about important social change.[7]

Bringing about such change, incorporating their new knowledge into the system, is the aim of many women who seek social power today. A more subtle and gradual change is being initiated through the mythmaking of these women writers of fantastic literature, however, which may eventually change the system itself. When that change is realized, a new one will already have been initiated to encompass still newer knowledge. This is the power of myth, unceasing undercurrents which can either pull us under or keep us moving in the right direction. "Deep in the ground, the water runs as always," Robert reminds Jean Brighton in *Juniper Time*; the desert is only one more deceptive surface to those who can really "see."

Women have offered us magic in their words; they have offered us new ways of seeing our selves and our society; they have offered us care and connections. In fantastic literature by women, the Goddess once again guides and sustains us, here in "the middle of time."

NOTES

1. Baird Searles, Review of *The Mists of Avalon* in "On Books." *Isaac Asimov's Science Fiction Magazine* 7:4 (April 1983): 168.

2. Stephen C. Ausband, *Myth and Meaning, Myth and Order* (Macon, Ga.: Mercer University Press, 1983): 120.

3. K. K. Ruthven, *Myth* (London: Methuen, 1976): 70–71.

4. Samuel R. Delany, "The Order of Chaos," *Science-Fiction Studies* 6:3 (November 1979): 333–36 as well as additional information given at the *Women Worldwalkers* Conference, Lubbock, Texas, January 1983.

5. Ruthven, *Myth*: 71.

6. Susan Griffin, *Woman and Nature: The Roaring Inside Her* (New York: Harper & Row, 1978): 219.

7. Quoted by Martha Saxton in "Are Women More Moral Than Men? An Interview," in *Images of Women in American Popular Culture*, eds. Angela G. Dorenkamp et al. (New York: Harcourt Brace Jovanovich, 1985): 62.

Bibliography

PRIMARY SOURCES

Andersen, Hans Christian. "The Snow Queen" (1872).
Auel, Jean. *The Clan of the Cave Bear*. New York: Bantam, 1980.
————. *The Valley of Horses*. New York: Crown, 1982.
Bradley, Marion Zimmer. *City of Sorcery*. New York: Daw, 1984.
————. *The Forbidden Tower*. New York: Daw, 1977.
————. *The Mists of Avalon*. New York: Alfred A. Knopf, 1982.
————. *The Ruins of Isis*. New York: Pocket Books, 1978.
————. *The Shattered Chain*. New York: Daw, 1976.
————. *Thendara House*. New York: Daw, 1983.
Brontë, Charlotte. *Shirley* by Currer Bell. New York: Derby & Jackson, 1859.
Butler, Octavia E. *Mind of My Mind*. New York: Avon, 1977.
————. *Patternmaster*. New York: Avon, 1976.
————. *Survivor*. New York: NAL, 1978.
————. *Wild Seed*. New York: Pocket Books, 1981.
Caldecott, Moyra. *Shadow on the Stones*. New York: Fawcett, 1978.
————. *The Tall Stones*. New York: Popular Library, 1977.
————. *The Temple of the Sun*. New York: Popular Library, 1977.
Carr, Jayge. *Leviathan's Deep*. Garden City, N.Y.: Doubleday, 1979.
Charnas, Suzy McKee. *Walk to the End of the World*. New York: Ballantine, 1974.
————. *Motherlines*. New York: Berkley, 1978.

Cherryh, C. J. *The Faded Sun: Kesrith*. Garden City, N.Y.: Nelson Doubleday, 1978.

———. *The Faded Sun: Kutath*. Garden City, N.Y.: Nelson Doubleday, 1979.

———. *The Faded Sun: Shon'Jir*. Garden City, N.Y.: Nelson Doubleday, 1978.

Coon, Susan. *Cassilee*. New York: Avon, 1980.

———. *Chiy-une*. New York: Avon, 1982.

———. *Rahne*. New York: Avon, 1980.

———. *The Virgin*. New York: Avon, 1981.

Elgin, Suzette Haden. *The Communipaths*. New York: Ace, 1970.

———. *Furthest*. New York: Ace, 1971.

———. *Native Tongue*. New York: Daw, 1984.

———. *The Ozark Trilogy*. Garden City, N.Y.: Nelson Doubleday, 1981. Includes *Twelve Fair Kingdoms*, *The Grand Jubilee*, and *And Then There'll Be Fireworks*.

———. *Star-Anchored, Star-Angered*. New York: Daw, 1979.

Gearhart, Sally Miller. *The Wanderground: Stories of the Hill Women*. Watertown, Mass.: Persephone Press, 1978.

Goethe, Johann Wolfgang von. *Faust, Part I*. (1831). Tr. Walter Arndt. Ed. Cyrus Hamlin. New York: W. W. Norton, 1976.

Hawthorne, Nathaniel. *The Scarlet Letter* (1850). New York: W. W. Norton, 1978.

LeGuin, Ursula K. *The Left Hand of Darkness*. New York: Walker, 1969.

Lee, Tanith. *The Birthgrave*. New York: Daw, 1975.

———. *The Silver Metal Lover*. New York: Daw, 1981.

Lessing, Doris. *Documents Relating to the Sentimental Agents in the Volyen Empire*. New York: Alfred A. Knopf, 1983.

———. *The Making of the Representative for Planet 8*. New York: Alfred A. Knopf, 1982.

———. *The Marriages between Zones Three, Four, and Five*. New York: Vintage, 1980.

———. *Re: Colonized Planet 5, Shikasta*. New York: Vintage, 1979.

———. *The Sirian Experiments*. New York: Alfred A. Knopf, 1980.

May, Julian. *The Many-Colored Land & The Golden Torc*. Garden City, N.Y.: Nelson Doubleday, 1982.

———. *The Nonborn King & The Adversary*. Garden City, N.Y.: Nelson Doubleday, 1984.

Norton, Andre. *Horn Crown*. New Yesrk: Daw, 1981.

———. *Lore of the Witch World*. New York: Daw, 1980.

——— *Merlin's Mirror*. New York: Daw, 1975.

———. *Sorceress of the Witch World*. New York: Ace, 1968.

———. *Spell of the Witch World*. New York: Daw, 1972.

———. *Three Against the Witch World: Beyond the Mind Barrier*. New York: Ace, 1965.

———. *'Ware Hawk*. New York: Ballantine, 1983.

———. *Warlock of the Witch World*. New York: Ace, 1967.

———. *Web of the Witch World*. New York: Ace, 1964.

———. *Witch World*. New York: Ace, 1963.

Piercy, Marge. *Woman on the Edge of Time*. New York: Fawcett, 1976.

Russ, Joanna. *And Chaos Died*. New York: Ace, 1970.

———. *Extra (Ordinary) People*. New York: St. Martin's Press, 1984.

———. *The Female Man*. New York: Bantam, 1975.

———. *Picnic on Paradise*. New York: Ace, 1968.

———. *The Two of Them*. New York: Berkley, 1978.

Sargent, Pamela. *Watchstar*. New York: Pocket Books, 1980.

Shelley, Mary. *Frankenstein*. (1818). New York: Scholastic Book Service, 1967.

Silko, Leslie Marmon. *Ceremony*. New York: NAL, 1977.

Van Scyoc, Sydney J. *Bluesong*. New York: Berkley, 1983.

———. *Darkchild*. New York: Berkley, 1982.

———. *Daughters of the Sunstone*. Garden City, N.Y.: Nelson Doubleday, 1984. Edition used for *Starsilk*.

———. *Starmother*. New York: Berkley, 1976.

———. *Sunwaifs*. New York: Berkley, 1981.

Vinge, Joan D. *The Snow Queen*. New York: Dell, 1980.

Walton, Evangeline. *The Children of Llyr: The Second Branch of the Mabinogion*. New York: Ballantine, 1970.

———. *The Island of the Mighty: The Fourth Branch of the Mabinogion*. New York: Ballantine, 1970. Formerly published as *The Virgin and the Swine* (1936).

———. *Prince of Annwn: The First Branch of the Mabinogion*. New York: Ballantine, 1974.

———. *The Song of Rhiannon: The Third Branch of the Mabinogion*. New York: Ballantine, 1972.

———. *The Sword Is Forged*. New York: Pocket Books, 1983.

Wilhelm, Kate. *Juniper Time*. New York: Pocket Books, 1979.

SECONDARY SOURCES

Because this topic encompasses myth studies, women's studies, studies in American and English literature, and studies in science fiction and fantasy, nearly any secondary bibliography I could compile within length constraints would be incomplete. Therefore, I have merely listed the sources cited either in the text or in the notes.

Adler, Margot. *Drawing Down the Moon: Witches, Druids, Goddess-Worshippers, and Other Pagans in America Today.* Boston: Beacon, 1979.

Ausband, Stephen C. *Myth and Meaning, Myth and Order.* Macon, Ga.: Mercer University Press, 1983.

Barr, Marleen S. (ed.). *Future Females: A Critical Anthology.* Bowling Green, Ohio: Bowling Green State University Popular Press, 1981.

Baruch, Elaine Hoffman. Introductions in *Women in Search of Utopia.* Ed. Ruby Rohrlich and Elaine Hoffman Baruch. New York: Schocken Books, 1984.

Bernstein, Gene. "The Mediated Vision: Eliade, Levi-Strauss, and Romantic Mythopoesis." In *The Binding of Proteus.* Ed. Marjorie W. McCune, Tucker Orbison, and Philip M. Withim. London: Associated University Presses, 1980: 158–72.

Bradley, Marion Zimmer. Introduction to *The Birthgrave* by Tanith Lee. New York: Daw, 1975: 6–7.

Brigg, Peter. "The Archetype of the Journey in Ursula K. LeGuin's Fiction." In *Ursula K. LeGuin.* Ed. Joseph D. Olander and Martin Harry Greenberg. New York: Taplinger, 1979: 36–63.

Bulfinch, Thomas. *Bulfinch's Mythology.* Abridged by Edmund Fuller. New York: Dell, 1967.

Campbell, Joseph. *The Hero with a Thousand Faces.* Princeton, N.J.: Princeton University Press, 1968.

Cantor, Paul A. *Creature and Creator: Myth-making and English Romanticism.* Cambridge: Cambridge University Press, 1984.

Charnas, Suzy McKee. "A Woman Appeared." In *Future Females.* Ed. Marleen S. Barr. Bowling Green, Ohio: Bowling Green State University Popular Press, 1981: 103–108.

Cherryh, C. J. Introduction to *Lore of the Witch World* by Andre Norton. New York: Daw, 1980: 7–9.

Chesler, Phyllis. *Women and Madness.* New York: Avon, 1972.

Clareson, Thomas D. (ed.). *Many Futures, Many Worlds: Theme and Form in Science Fiction.* Kent, Ohio: Kent State University Press, 1977.

Collins, Bob. "Evangeline Walton: An Appreciation." *Fantasy Review* 8:3 (March 1984): 6.

Daly, Mary. *Beyond God the Father: Toward a Philosophy of Women's Liberation.* Boston: Beacon, 1973.

Day, Phyllis J. "Earthmother/Witchmother: Feminism and Ecology Renewed." *Extrapolation* 23:1 (Spring 1982): 12–21.

Delany, Samuel R. "The Order of 'Chaos'." *Science-Fiction Studies* 6:3 (November 1979): 333–36.

Dorenkamp, Angela G., John F. McClymer, Mary M. Moynihan and
    Arlene C. Vadum (eds.). *Images of Women in American Popular
    Culture.* New York: Harcourt Brace Jovanovich, 1985.
Doria, Charles and Harris Lenowitz (eds. and trs.). *Origins: Creation
    Texts from the Ancient Mediterranean.* Garden City, N.Y.: An-
    chor/Doubleday, 1976.
Douglas, Wallace W. "The Meanings of 'Myth' in Modern Criticism."
    In *Myth and Literature: Contemporary Theory and Practice.* Ed.
    John B. Vickery. Lincoln: University of Nebraska Press, 1966:
    119–28.
Dundes, Alan (ed.). *Sacred Narrative: Readings in the Theory of Myth.*
    Berkeley: University of California Press, 1984.
Eliade, Mircea. *Myths, Dreams and Mysteries: The Encounter between
    Contemporary Faiths and Archaic Realities.* Tr. Philip Mairet.
    New York: Harper & Row, 1957.
———. *Myths, Rites, Symbols.* Vol. 1. Ed. Wendell C. Beane and Wil-
    liam G. Doty. New York: Harper & Row, 1975.
Foster, Frances Smith. "Octavia Butler's Black Female Future Fic-
    tion." *Extrapolation* 23:1 (Spring 1982): 37–49.
Frazer, Sir James George. *The New Golden Bough.* A new abridgment.
    Ed. Theodor H. Gaster. New York: Criterion Books, 1959.
Fredericks, Casey. *The Future of Eternity: Mythologies of Science Fic-
    tion and Fantasy.* Bloomington: Indiana University Press, 1982.
Friend, Beverly. "Virgin Territory: The Bonds and Boundaries of
    Women in Science Fiction." In *Many Futures, Many Worlds.* Ed.
    Thomas D. Clareson. Kent, Ohio: Kent State University Press,
    1977: 140–63.
Frye, Northrop. *Anatomy of Criticism.* Princeton, N.J.: Princeton Uni-
    versity Press, 1957.
———. "New Directions From Old." In *Myth and Mythmaking.* Ed.
    Henry A. Murray. Boston: Beacon, 1960: 115–31.
Gayley, Charles Mills. *The Classic Myths in English Literature and
    in Art.* New Edition. Lexington, Mass.: Xerox College Publish-
    ing, 1939.
Gearhart, Sally Miller. "Future Visions: Today's Politics: Feminist
    Utopias in Review." In *Women in Search of Utopia.* Eds. Ruby
    Rohrlich and Elaine Hoffman Baruch. New York: Schocken
    Books, 1984: 296–309.
Gershuny, H. Lee. "The Linguistic Transformation of Womanhood."
    In *Women in Search of Utopia.* Eds. Ruby Rohrlich and Elaine
    Hoffman Baruch. New York: Schocken Books, 1984: 189–202.
Gould, Eric. *Mythical Intentions in Modern Literature.* Princeton, N.J.:
    Princeton University Press, 1981.

Graves, Robert. *The Greek Myths*. Vol. 1. New York: Penguin, 1960.
———. *The White Goddess*. Amended and enlarged edition. New York: Farrar, Straus & Giroux, 1948.

Griffin, Susan. *Woman and Nature: The Roaring Inside Her*. New York: Harper & Row, 1978.

Hall, Nor. *The Moon & The Virgin: Reflections on the Archetypal Feminine*. New York: Harper & Row, 1980.

Hamilton, Edith. *Mythology*. New York: NAL, 1969.

Harding, Lee (ed.). *The Altered I*. New York: Berkley, 1978.

Hartman, Geoffrey. *The Unmediated Vision*. New York: Harcourt, Brace & World, 1966.

Hassler, Donald M. *Comic Tones in Science Fiction: The Art of Compromise with Nature*. Westport, Conn.: Greenwood Press, 1982.

Hawthorne, Nathaniel. "The Custom House," Introduction to *The Scarlet Letter*. 2nd. ed. New York: W. W. Norton, 1978.
———. Preface to *The House of the Seven Gables*. New York: Scholastic Book Services, 1965.

Honko, Lauri. "The Problem of Defining Myth." In *Sacred Narrative: Readings in the Theory of Myth*. Ed. Alan Dundes. Berkeley: University of California Press, 1984: 41.

Jackson, Rosemary. *Fantasy: The Literature of Subversion*. London: Methuen, 1981.

Jobes, Gertrude and James. *Outer Space: Myths, Name Meanings, Calendars from the Emergence of History to the Present Day*. New York: Scarecrow Press, 1964.

Khanna, Lee Cullen. "Change and Art in Women's Worlds: Doris Lessing's *Canopus in Argos: Archives*." In *Women in Search of Utopia*. Eds. Ruby Rohrlich and Elaine Hoffman Baruch. New York: Schocken Books, 1984: 269–79.

Kramer, Samuel Noah (ed.). *Mythologies of the Ancient World*. Garden City, N.Y.: Doubleday, 1961.

Lauter, Estella. *Women as Mythmakers: Poetry and Visual Art by Twentieth-Century Women*. Bloomington: Indiana University Press, 1984.

LeGuin, Ursula K. "American SF and the Other." In *The Language of the Night*. Ed. Susan Wood. New York: G. P. Putnam's Sons, 1979: 97–100.
———. Introduction to *The Altered I*. Ed. Lee Harding. New York: Berkley, 1978: 5–14.
———. Introduction to "Vaster Than Empires and More Slow." In *The Wind's Twelve Quarters: Short Stories by Ursula K. LeGuin*. New York: Harper & Row, 1975: 148.
———. *The Language of the Night: Essays on Fantasy and Science Fiction*. Ed. Susan Wood. New York: G. P. Putnam's Sons, 1979.

Leon-Portilla, Miguel. "Mythology of Ancient Mexico." In *Mythologies of the Ancient World*. Ed. Samuel Noah Kramer. Garden City, N.Y.: Doubleday, 1961: 443–69.

Lessing, Doris. Preface to *The Sirian Experiments*. New York: Alfred A. Knopf, 1980.

———. *A Small Personal Voice: Essays, Reviews, Interviews*. Ed. Paul Schlueter. New York: Alfred A. Knopf, 1974.

Lundwall, Sam J. *Science Fiction: What It's All About*. New York: Ace, 1971.

McCune, Marjorie W., Tucker Orbison and Philip M. Withim (eds.). *The Binding of Proteus: Perspectives on Myth and the Literary Process*. London: Associated University Presses, 1980.

Miller, David L. *The New Polytheism: Rebirth of the Gods and Goddesses*. New York: Harper & Row, 1974.

Mixon, Veronica. "Futurist Woman: Octavia Butler." *Essence* 15 (April 1979): 12–13.

Moers, Ellen. *Literary Women*. New York: Oxford University Press, 1977.

Monaghan, Patricia. *The Book of Goddesses and Heroines*. New York: E. P. Dutton, 1981.

Murray, Henry A. (ed.). *Myth and Mythmaking*. Boston: Beacon, 1960.

Myers, Robert E. (ed.). *The Intersection of Science Fiction and Philosophy: Critical Studies*. Westport, Conn.: Greenwood Press, 1983.

Nin, Anaïs. *The Novel of the Future*. New York: Collier, 1968.

Olander, Joseph D. and Martin Harry Greenberg (eds.). *Ursula K. LeGuin*. New York: Taplinger, 1979.

Patai, Raphael. *The Hebrew Goddess*. New York: KTAV, 1967.

Pearson, Carol S. "Of Time and Revolution: Theories of Social Change in Contemporary Feminist Science Fiction." In *Women in Search of Utopia*. Eds. Ruby Rohrlich and Elaine Hoffman Baruch. New York: Schocken Books, 1984: 260–68.

———. "Women's Fantasies and Feminist Utopias." *Frontiers* 2:3 (1977): 50–61.

Pratt, Annis, with Barbara White, Andrea Loewenstein and Mary Wyer. *Archetypal Patterns in Women's Fiction*. Bloomington: Indiana University Press, 1981.

Preston, James J. (ed.). *Mother Worship: Themes and Variations*. Chapel Hill: University of North Carolina Press, 1982.

Radin, Paul. *The Trickster: A Study in American Indian Mythology*. New York: Schocken Books, 1972.

Randolph, Vance. *Pissing in the Snow and Other Ozark Folktales*. New York: Avon, 1976.

Rank, Otto. *The Myth of the Birth of the Hero and Other Writings.* Ed. Philip Freund. New York: Vintage, 1964.

Rappoport, Angelo S. *Myth and Legend of Ancient Israel.* Vol. 1. New York: KTAV, 1966.

Righter, William. *Myth and Literature.* London: Routledge & Kegan Paul, 1975.

Rigney, Barbara Hill. *Lilith's Daughters: Women and Religion in Contemporary Fiction.* Madison: University of Wisconsin Press, 1982.

Roberts, Robin. "The Paradigm of *Frankenstein*: Reading *Canopus in Argos* in the Context of Science Fiction by Women." *Extrapolation* 26:1 (Spring 1985): 16–23.

Rohrlich, Ruby. Introduction II to *Women in Search of Utopia.* Eds. Ruby Rohrlich and Elaine Hoffman Baruch. New York: Schocken Books, 1984.

———— and Elaine Hoffman Baruch (eds.). *Women in Search of Utopia.* New York: Schocken Books, 1984.

Rosinsky, Natalie M. *Feminist Futures: Contemporary Women's Speculative Fiction.* Ann Arbor: University of Michigan Research Press, 1984.

Russ, Joanna. "Recent Feminist Utopias." In *Future Females: A Critical Anthology.* Ed. Marleen S. Barr. Bowling Green, Ohio: Bowling Green State University Popular Press, 1981: 71–85.

Ruthven, K. K. *Myth.* London: Methuen, 1976.

Sanders, Scott. "Women as Nature in Science Fiction." In *Future Females: A Critical Anthology.* Ed. Marleen S. Barr. Bowling Green, Ohio: Bowling Green State University Popular Press, 1981: 46–62.

Saxton, Martha, with Carol Gilligan. "Are Women More Moral Than Men? An Interview." In *Images of Women in American Popular Culture.* Eds. Angela G. Dorenkamp, John F. McClymer, Mary M. Moynihan, and Arlene C. Vadum. New York: Harcourt Brace Jovanovich, 1985: 58–63.

Schlobin, Roger. "Andre Norton: Humanity Amid the Hardware." In *The Feminine Eye.* Ed. Tom Staicar. New York: Frederick Ungar, 1982: 25–31.

Searles, Baird. Review of *The Mists of Avalon* in "On Books." *Isaac Asimov's Science Fiction Magazine* 7:4(April 1983): 166–69.

————. Review of *The Nonborn King* in "On Books." *Isaac Asimov's Science Fiction Magazine* 7:5(May 10, 1983): 168–69.

Shinn, Thelma J. *Radiant Daughters: Fictional American Women.* Westport, Conn.: Greenwood Press, June 1986.

Smith, Curtis C. (ed.). *Twentieth Century Science Fiction Writers.* New York: St. Martin's Press, 1981.

Spencer, Paul. "An Interview with Evangeline Walton." *Fantasy Review* 8:3 (March 1984): 7–10.

Spencer, Sharon. *Space, Time and Structure in the Modern Novel.* Chicago: Swallow Press, 1971.

Spretnak, Charlene. *Lost Goddesses of Early Greece: A Collection of Pre-Hellenic Myths.* Boston: Beacon, 1978.

Squire, Charles. *Celtic Myth and Legend, Poetry and Romance.* New York: Bell, 1979.

Staicar, Tom (ed.). *The Feminine Eye: Science Fiction and the Women Who Write It.* New York: Frederick Ungar, 1982.

Starhawk. *Dreaming the Dark: Magic, Sex & Politics.* Boston: Beacon, 1982.

Stone, Merlin. *Ancient Mirrors of Womanhood: A Treasury of Goddess and Heroine Lore from around the World.* Boston: Beacon, 1979.

———. *When God Was a Woman.* New York: Dial Press, 1976.

Suvin, Darko. *Metamorphoses of Science Fiction.* New Haven: Yale University Press, 1979.

Van der Bogert, Franz. "Nature through Science Fiction." In *The Intersection of Science Fiction and Philosophy: Critical Studies.* Ed. Robert E. Myers. Westport, Conn: Greenwood Press, 1983: 57–70.

Vickery, John B. (ed.). *Myth and Literature: Contemporary Theory and Practice.* Lincoln: University of Nebraska Press, 1966.

———. *Myths and Texts: Strategies of Incorporation and Displacement.* Baton Rouge: Louisiana State University Press, 1966.

Walker, Barbara G. *The Woman's Encyclopedia of Myths and Secrets.* San Francisco: Harper & Row, 1983.

Warrick, Patricia. "Science Fiction Myths and Their Ambiguity." In *Science Fiction: Contemporary Mythology.* Ed. Warrick et al. New York: Harper & Row, 1978: 1–8.

Warrick, Patricia, Martin Harry Greenberg and Joseph Olander (eds.). *Science Fiction: Contemporary Mythology.* The SFWA-SFRA Anthology. New York: Harper & Row, 1978.

Weigle, Marta. *Spiders and Spinsters: Women and Mythology.* Albuquerque: University of New Mexico Press, 1982.

Wendland, Albert. *Science, Myth, and the Fictional Creation of Alien Worlds.* Ann Arbor: University of Michigan Research Press, 1985.

Women in Science Fiction: Special Issue. *Extrapolation* 23:1 (Spring 1982).

Yoke, Carl. "From Alienation to Personal Triumph: The Science Fiction of Joan D. Vinge." In *The Feminine Eye: Science Fiction and the Women Who Write It.* Ed. Tom Staicar. New York: Frederick Ungar, 1982: 103–130.

Zimmerman, Jan. "Utopia in Question: Programming Women's Needs into the Technology of Tomorrow." In *Women in Search of Utopia*. Eds. Ruby Rohrlich and Elaine Hoffman Baruch. New York: Schocken Books, 1984: 168–76.

Index

About the Author

THELMA J. SHINN, Professor of English and Women's Studies, Arizona State University, is the author of *Radiant Daughters: Fictional American Women* (Greenwood Press, 1986). She has contributed to *American Women Writers* and *Contemporary Literary Criticism* and such journals as *Modern Drama, Literature and Psychology, Critique, Contemporary Literature, The Nathaniel Hawthorne Journal*, and *Colby Library Quarterly*.